"Alexander Chapman and K[...] field."

—Marsha M. Lineh[...]

Manual for Treating Borderline Personality Disorder

"Finally, adolescents and adults who self-harm have a clear and comprehensive guide that explains in layperson's terms the etiology and maintenance of these challenging behaviors. This guide is useful for individuals struggling with how to reduce their self-harm as well as family members who need help learning how to respond effectively."

—Alec L. Miller, Psy.D., professor of clinical psychiatry and behavioral sciences at Albert Einstein College of Medicine

"Gratz and Chapman have written an organized, plain-spoken, and compassionate educational workbook for individuals who engage in nonsuicidal, intentional self-harm. Their practical, evidence-based information and comments address the confusions and inaccuracies surrounding the functions of this behavior. This book will help readers replace the anger, fear, and judgment that so often arises in response to this destructive and addictive behavior."

—Elizabeth T. Murphy. Ph.D., director of the Dialectical Behavior Therapy Skills Program at the McLean Hospital Outpatient Clinic, clinical instructor in psychology at Harvard Medical School

"Gratz and Chapman again show their expertise, as well as their compassion for those struggling with serious difficulties. In this book, the authors provide readers with an in-depth, nonjudgmental discussion of self-injury, from the basics to its causes and treatments to helpful coping skills. Targeting not only the sufferers, but also their loved ones, the book serves a wide audience."

—Perry Hoffman, Ph.D., president of the National Education Alliance for Borderline Personality Disorder

freedom
from self-harm

**Overcoming Self-Injury with Skills
from DBT and Other Treatments**

KIM L. GRATZ, PH.D.
ALEXANDER L. CHAPMAN, PH.D.

NEW HARBINGER PUBLICATIONS, INC.

Publisher's Note

Distributed in Canada by Raincoast Books

Copyright © 2009 by Kim L. Gratz & Alexander L. Chapman
New Harbinger Publications, Inc.
5674 Shattuck Avenue
Oakland, CA 94609
www.newharbinger.com

Acquired by Catharine Sutker; Cover design by Amy Shoup
Edited by Nelda Street; Text design by Tracy Marie Carlson

Library of Congress Cataloging-in-Publication Data

Gratz, Kim L.
 Freedom from self-harm : overcoming self-injury with skills from dbt and other treatments / Kim L. Gratz and Alexander L. Chapman ; foreword by Barent Walsh.
    p. cm.
 Includes bibliographical references.
 ISBN-13: 978-1-57224-616-4 (pbk. : alk. paper)
 ISBN-10: 1-57224-616-2 (pbk. : alk. paper)
 1. Self-mutilation--Popular works. 2. Cutting (Self-mutilation)--Popular works. I. Chapman, Alexander L. (Alexander Lawrence) II. Title.
 RC552.S4G73 2009
 616.85'82--dc22

                                    2009007498

11 10 09

10 9 8 7 6 5 4 3 2 1   First printing

To all of my clients who have struggled with self-harm. Your courage and strength are an inspiration.

—Kim L. Gratz

To all of those who have struggled with self-harm. I wish you freedom and fulfillment.

—Alexander L. Chapman

Contents

PART I
UNDERSTANDING SELF-HARM

Chapter 6

PART II
HOW DO I GET HELP FOR SELF-HARM?

Chapter 7

Chapter 8

Chapter 9

PART III
COPING STRATEGIES FOR MANAGING SELF-HARM

Chapter 10

Chapter 11

Chapter 12

Chapter 13

Foreword

For over thirty years, I have been treating people who hurt themselves by cutting, burning, picking, and hitting. These behaviors are generally not about suicide, but they do often provide effective relief from painful emotions such as anxiety, sadness, anger, guilt, and shame. During this thirty-year period, hundreds of research studies and scores of books have been published on the troubling topic of deliberate self-harm. Ultimately, what people really want to know about self-harm—especially if they have a problem with the behavior—is *What can I do about it?* One important answer to this fundamental question is *Read this book!*

Freedom from Self-Harm by Kim Gratz and Alexander Chapman is the best book yet written for people who want to understand and stop self-harming. It is not primarily for professionals; rather, it speaks directly to those who are immersed in the problem and seeking a way out.

What is particularly impressive about this volume is the way it transforms the most current research findings into a readable text offering a host of practical suggestions. Drs. Gratz and Chapman are noted researchers well trained in the rigors of empirical methodology, but in this book they speak in commonsense, accessible language. Read just a few pages of this book and you will see immediately that it conveys compassion and respect.

Accessible language and a nonjudgmental tone is important, but the real value in this book is in the insights and solutions it offers. The authors define self-harm, discuss what causes the behavior, and review its functions. Their discussion of the biological elements of self-harm is notable for its clarity to the nonscientific reader. If you've ever been confused and frustrated about why you self-harm over and over again, this book offers explanations that are reassuring, normalizing, and above all optimistic.

One of my favorite chapters is "Myths About Self-Harm." Our popular culture tends to disseminate misinformation about self-harm and, even worse, impose a wide range of negative judgments. This chapter dismantles the most common misunderstandings, substituting facts based on research. For example, isn't it reassuring to read that self-harm is generally *not* about suicide, is much more complicated than "attention-seeking" and "manipulative," and does not mean one is "crazy" or "mentally ill." Such pejorative ideas need to be put to rest for good.

This book also explains that self-harm has changed markedly since 2000. The behavior has moved beyond clinical populations such as people in psychiatric hospitals, group homes, and special education schools; self-harm is now commonplace in middle and high schools and universities. The exceptionally widespread nature of the problem indicates that large numbers of people are in emotional distress and need help in coping.

This volume emphasizes that there is a way out. The authors start in a place that most others skip. They do not assume that everyone wants to stop. In the chapter "So, What's Wrong with Self-Harm?" they provide a series of well-reasoned arguments about the disadvantages of self-harm: it may be addictive, may result in greater damage than expected, and may involve tolerance and withdrawal. They also refer to the negative social consequences. I particularly like their point that "self-harm can make your 'coping muscles' atrophy." That is to say, the longer you rely on self-harm, the harder it is to give up, and the less developed your healthier coping skills may be. Although the authors make compelling arguments against self-harm, they empower the reader to consider the pros and cons and make up his or her own mind.

For those who have decided *Enough already with hurting myself,* this book provides practical techniques for assessing what triggers the behavior and how to avoid or manage these triggers. Especially helpful is the review of evidence-based treatments as a guide to where and how to seek help. Some readers may be surprised to learn that the best way to cope with negative emotions is not to flee them but to fully encounter and accept them. This advice is based on proven treatments such as Marsha Linehan's dialectical behavior therapy, Stephen Hayes's acceptance and commitment therapy, and Kim Gratz's own emotion regulation group therapy. This book provides a detailed roadmap for identifying, befriending, and achieving greater acceptance of disturbing emotions.

The "Coping with Self-Harm Urges" chapter is the most detailed discussion of urges that I have read. It breaks down urges into specific components and teaches the reader how to understand, track, accept, and manage urges to self-harm. Gratz and Chapman's discussion is actually applicable to many other kinds of urges, such as using substances, eating, gambling, or even shopping.

The book also provides many substantial suggestions about healthy coping skills. Particularly useful examples include changing thoughts that support self-harm, altering cues that lead to self-harm, using guided imagery, breathing mindfully, expressing emotions, and communicating effectively with others. These techniques are not just mentioned but described in such detail that the reader can employ them immediately and successfully.

Not surprisingly, this book concludes with a positive message about life after self-harm. The authors have worked with many people who have overcome the behavior, and their experiences with success inform the content of the entire book.

If you or someone close to you has a problem with self-harm, do yourself a favor: don't just *read* this book; *use* it. You'll find it like talking deeply with a trusted friend, feeling you're understood, listening to wise counsel, and emerging refreshed, ready to move on to a better day.

Barent W. Walsh, Ph.D.
Executive director, The Bridge of Central Massachusetts
Author of *Treating Self-Injury: A Practical Guide*

Acknowledgments

This book would not have been possible without the love and patience of my husband, courage and strength of my clients, encouragement and support of my mentors, and wisdom and friendship of my coauthor. First and foremost, I would like to gratefully acknowledge the clients whose strength, courage, passion, and struggles with self-harm prompted me to pursue research in this area. Working with them for the past twelve years has been an honor and a blessing. They have been (and continue to be) the inspiration behind my research and treatment development, and have taught me more about self-harm and how to recover from this behavior than anything or anyone else. They truly are survivors in every sense of the word, and I thank them for sharing their lives with me. I am also tremendously grateful to my mentors in graduate school, first Sheree Conrad and then Liz Roemer. They encouraged me to pursue my own interests and gave me the space, freedom, and support to do so. Their encouragement and wisdom are the cornerstones of my career, and Liz's continual mentoring and friendship helps sustain and ground me. Likewise, I will always be grateful to Elizabeth Murphy for her brilliance, wisdom, humor, and friendship. Her passion for her work and respect for mine sustained me for years. My career and life are infinitely better for knowing her.

I have no doubt that this book would not have been written without the contributions of my friend, colleague, and coauthor, Alex Chapman. He is an amazing writer and brilliant researcher and clinician, and I am honored to have had the opportunity to collaborate with him for the past few years. Thanks also to the incredible editorial staff at New Harbinger, especially Catharine Sutker, Jess Beebe, and Nelda Street. Their support throughout this process is much appreciated.

Finally, I am eternally grateful to my parents, Linda and Dave, for their unwavering support and love throughout my life, to Daisy, for her unconditional love, and to my husband and partner (in every sense of the word), Matt Tull. On a very practical level, this book would not have been possible without Matt's support, patience, wisdom, and willingness to cook for me many late nights. I cannot begin to express how much I appreciate him and how blessed I am to have him in my life.

—Kim L. Gratz

As Kim and I finished up our last book (*The Borderline Personality Disorder Survival Guide*, New Harbinger Publications, 2007), a new book was the last thing on my mind. But our work together was such a positive experience that I was excited when we started to talk about writing a book that could help people who self-harm. I feel very fortunate to have Kim as a friend and colleague, and I am grateful that Dr. Amy Wagner (back in 2002) suggested that I e-mail one of her colleague's students (Kim), who had research interests similar to my own. Earlier in graduate school, one of my very first clients struggled with self-harm. Through learning about her struggles and navigating my way with the supportive encouragement and guidance of Dr. Richard Farmer, I realized that I wanted to devote my research and clinical work toward helping people who can't see any other way out of their emotional pain. Inspired to continue with this work, I went on internship at Duke to learn more about dialectical behavior therapy (DBT), and I am grateful for all I learned from Drs. Tom Lynch and Clive Robins. Dr. Marsha Linehan, whom I was fortunate to work with as a postdoctoral fellow, has been a wonderful model as a compassionate and brilliant scientist and therapist. I am forever grateful to my clients for allowing me to enter their lives and for teaching me volumes about how to help others who struggle with self-harm. I would like to thank the editorial team at New Harbinger (including Catharine Sutker, Jess Beebe, and Nelda Street) for their invaluable feedback as this book came together. Finally, I feel grateful for the love, support and encouragement of my wonderful wife Katherine, and for my family and my two beautiful sons, Max and Quinn.

—Alex Chapman

Introduction

Marlene was fifteen years old when she first burned herself. It had started out innocently enough: she was dared to do it by a group of friends to prove how tough she was. Her friend John especially egged her on until she finally gave in and burned herself. Although she felt a small rush and sense of power when she finally did it, she didn't think much about it at the time. Then, about six months later, she had a particularly awful day. She had felt really sick for a week or so, and when she finally went to the doctor, she found out she was pregnant. Not only that, but when she told her boyfriend about it, he panicked and took off. She felt lost, empty, and angry with herself for letting this happen. She was completely overwhelmed and couldn't think of anything she could do to make herself feel better. And that's when she saw the lighter and candle sitting on her bookcase. Without even thinking, she knew what she wanted to do.

If you self-harm, you might feel completely alone a lot of the time. You might feel as if you're the only one who struggles with such intense urges, emotional turmoil, or feelings of being out of control. You may even think that you're the only person you know who self-harms. At times, you might be frustrated with yourself because it's so hard to stop, or you might feel sad about the way our society views people who harm themselves. Many people who self-harm feel quite isolated in their personal struggles with this behavior. But you are definitely not alone.

YOU ARE NOT ALONE

In fact, self-harm is quite common—shockingly common. As many as 4 percent of young adults in the United States have engaged in self-harm (Briere and Gil 1998; Klonsky, Oltmanns, and Turkheimer 2003). That's around twelve million people in the United States alone. And, studies have found that self-harm may be even more common in high schools and colleges. In fact, some studies have found that approximately 20 percent of high-school students and up to 40 percent of college students have self-harmed (Gratz, Conrad, and Roemer 2002; Paivio and McCulloch 2004; Zoroglu et al. 2003).

If this surprises you, you're not alone. It surprises most researchers too. In fact, self-harm seems to be more common now than it ever was before. Self-harm is actually more common than many mental disorders, such as schizophrenia, bipolar disorder, eating disorders, and, in some cases (especially among college students), even depression. Finally, as we discuss in chapter 1, although some people view self-harm as a "female" problem, it's actually just as common among males as it is among females.

So, what exactly is self-harm? Why do people harm themselves? What causes self-harm? Who self-harms? What can people do to help themselves? What treatments are out there? How can you cope with your emotions and desires to self-harm? In this book, we answer these and other questions about self-harm.

We have primarily devoted this book to people who harm themselves. We sincerely hope it helps you take an important step toward freedom from self-harm and onto a path that leads you where you want to be in your life. If you care for someone who self-harms or if you're a professional who treats people who self-harm, we hope this book will give you some of the tools and information you need to make a difference.

WHAT EXACTLY IS SELF-HARM?

Deliberate self-harm is when one intentionally damages one's own bodily tissue without intending to die. Because the purpose of self-harm is to intentionally cause injury to one's own body, it doesn't include things like smoking, drug use, drinking, bingeing, purging, or other behaviors that may be harmful. And the reason for this is that, for the most part, people don't do these types of things to *intentionally cause injury* in the moment. Instead, this book focuses on things people do to inflict tissue damage on purpose, such as cutting, burning, self-hitting, skin picking, biting, and banging one's head. Often, people do these types of things to hurt themselves without trying to kill themselves. And, that's the type of self-harm we're talking about in this book—the type where you try to hurt yourself but not to kill yourself.

Not only does self-harm affect the lives of the individuals who suffer from it, it also influences the lives of their loved ones. It can be frightening when someone you love shows up with scars or serious burns, bruises, or cuts on her or his body. Family members and friends often have no idea how to respond to self-harm, and in some cases, the way they react can make the problem even worse. One of the best ways to overcome fear and get on the right track is to find out exactly what you're dealing with.

So, why are we writing a book about self-harm? Well, the short answer is that there's a lot of information out there on self-harm, some of which is inaccurate or even harmful. So, we wanted to pull together the best information to help you get on the road to recovery.

Self-harm has been getting a lot of attention these days from researchers and treatment providers, as well as the media and popular press. For example, researchers are spending a lot more time studying the characteristics of people who self-harm and the possible causes of self-harm. They're even developing new treatments for self-harm. In fact, there's so much interest in this behavior these days that a group of researchers in 2006 formed an international association devoted just to self-harm (the International Society for the Study of Self-Injury, or ISSS). In addition, popular television shows and movies such as *Beverly Hills 90210*, *7th Heaven*, *Thirteen*, and *Girl, Interrupted* have shown characters who self-harm.

Now, on the one hand, this surge of attention is a good thing: Self-harm is a serious behavior, and the more people are aware of it, the better. The problem is that not all of the information out there is accurate, and sometimes self-harm is portrayed in ways that are confusing and even hurtful.

In fact, finding accurate information on self-harm can be like wandering in a desert looking for water. For example, the Internet is full of information that, at a distance, looks helpful and accurate but, upon closer inspection, turns out to be just a mirage. Some Internet sites even promote self-harm and can be dangerous for people who are trying to stop this behavior. What's more, despite all the exciting research on self-harm in the past few years, this research is usually described in treatment manuals and research papers. And, without professional training, it can be really hard to make sense of the information presented in these professional sources.

We research self-harm as well as treat people who self-harm, and we have seen what this behavior does to peoples' lives. It disrupts relationships, makes it hard to cope with stress, and creates shame and emotional turmoil. Therefore, we believe it's critical for people to have as much up-to-date, helpful, and accurate information as possible to help them understand and overcome self-harm. If you struggle with self-harm or care for someone who does, it's essential for you to have information that you can actually understand and use. That's what this book is all about. You can think of it as a guidebook to help people understand and overcome self-harm.

HOW TO USE THIS BOOK

If you and the people who care about you are armed with accurate information, self-harm may seem less confusing and frightening. Our first chapter (chapter 1) paints a clear picture of exactly what self-harm is, who self-harms, when and why people start harming themselves, and when people normally stop this behavior.

In chapter 2, we discuss a variety of myths about self-harm and give you accurate information to combat these harmful myths. As you probably know, mental health problems carry a huge social stigma in our society. *Social stigma* is disapproval for behavior that doesn't fit society's norms and is particularly strong for mental health problems. Some people think that mental health issues are caused by "bad character" or "weak willpower." Others feel nervous around and may try to avoid people who have mental health problems.

Self-harm is certainly no exception to this rule. This is probably because it's so hard for some people to understand why others would want to harm themselves. One reason for this is that self-harm goes directly against our evolutionary drive to protect ourselves and our bodies. Another reason is that self-harm is kind of like serious drug use: it goes against what society thinks of as "normal." And, let's face it, visible bodily injuries make some people really nervous.

Although it's understandable why people sometimes react negatively to those who self-harm, it's certainly not helpful. In fact, social stigma about self-harm can make your problems worse. For instance, you might feel ashamed about self-harm and be afraid to tell people about it. You might also think that you're "sick" or that there's something wrong with you. We believe that it's very important to combat the harmful stigma about self-harm, and we've devoted chapter 2 to arming you with information that you can use against this stigma. There's nothing "sick," "weird," or "pathological" about self-harm. It's simply a behavior that people learn to rely on, in many cases to cope with overwhelming emotions that seem intolerable.

Other chapters (chapters 3 and 4) give you information about what causes self-harm and the types of problems that often go along with self-harm, such as depression, anxiety disorders, and borderline personality disorder. In chapter 5, we talk about people's reasons or motivations for harming themselves, what self-harm seems to do for people, and why it's so hard to stop this behavior. In addition, in chapter 6, we discuss some of the problems with self-harm and the havoc it can wreak on your life.

Overall, the information in chapters 1 through 6 will give you a clear sense of what you are struggling with. People who self-harm often judge themselves for this behavior, and may think that they're "bad" or "defective" for self-harming. If you struggle with self-harm and have ever felt ashamed of yourself as a result, we hope that the information in these chapters will help you understand your experiences and show you that you're not alone in your struggles.

YOU NEED TO KNOW HOW TO GET HELP

If you want to stop harming yourself, it's very important to find help. And yet, it can be very difficult to figure out how to get help for self-harm. In our experience, some people don't get help until they end up in the emergency room with serious injuries. Even therapists and people who are there to help sometimes don't know what to do. If you self-harm, you might've had bad experiences in therapy. Your therapist might have freaked out or judged you when you harmed yourself. Or, you might have tried to get treatment, only to find out that the therapist or treatment program didn't accept people who self-harmed.

The good news is that there are effective treatments for self-harm and there are people (like us) who specialize in the treatment of this behavior. There are also many other therapists who don't specialize in self-harm but are great therapists and can help you anyway. You just have to find them. And, we'll tell you how to do that in chapter 7. We also include a couple of chapters on different treatments for self-harm, including psychological treatments (chapter 8) and medication treatments (chapter 9). Knowing more about these treatments will help you find the treatment that's best for you.

SELF-HARM IS OFTEN A COPING STRATEGY

We all learn different behaviors to help us cope with emotions, life stress, or other difficulties. Some people drink, use drugs, talk with friends, go to therapy, or do breathing exercises or yoga to help themselves feel calmer or to reduce stress. In general, we all tend to rely on what works best for us. And, you might have learned that self-harm works well for you.

The problem is that self-harm is very addictive. If you self-harm, at times you might feel as if you're in prison, locked up and unable to escape or stop hurting yourself. In fact, self-harm often takes on a life of its own. This is because self-harm, like drugs, can really hook people, and it can be very difficult to break free.

Because self-harm is so powerful, many people who self-harm go back and forth between wanting to quit and not wanting to quit. You might have noticed this in yourself. You might also have noticed that, even though your motivation to stop self-harm may sometimes waiver, when you're in a clear state of mind, you really do want to quit. Working to change self-harm can take a lot of hard work and energy, and it sometimes seems impossible. To help with this, we've included a chapter devoted to helping you increase your motivation to stop self-harm and your chances of succeeding (chapter 10).

People who self-harm often struggle with strong, seemingly uncontrollable urges to harm themselves. They might spend a lot of time thinking about self-harm, planning self-harm, or trying to figure out when they can harm themselves. Simply seeing a knife, razor, or candle can trigger overwhelming urges to engage in self-harm. Although resisting these urges is often a big struggle, there are things you can do to manage your urges to self-harm. We teach you a variety of skills for resisting urges to harm yourself in chapter 11.

People often say that self-harm is one of the quickest, easiest ways to feel better when they're emotionally upset. Because of this, self-harm can trap people like quicksand. It can be tremendously difficult to struggle your way to the surface and free yourself from the allure of quick, easy emotional relief or the powerful rush you might feel when you harm yourself. Because emotions are so wrapped up in self-harm and because most people say that they self-harm to escape their emotions, we've included a chapter devoted to effective skills you can use to cope with your emotions (chapter 12). Some of these skills come from Dr. Marsha Linehan's (1993b) work on DBT, and others come from other treatments (such as Dr. Kim Gratz's emotion regulation group treatment for self-harm [Gratz and Gunderson 2006] and Dr. Steve Hayes and colleagues' [1999] acceptance and commitment therapy). All in all, we hope these skills will provide you with other ways of managing your emotions, so that you don't feel as if you need to resort to self-harm to cope.

WHO IS THIS BOOK FOR?

As we mentioned earlier, this book is primarily for people who harm themselves. But, we believe that people who care for those who harm them selves, including treatment providers, friends, family members, and students who are learning to treat self-harm, will find this book useful as well. This book will be especially helpful if any of the following statements fits you:

- You harm yourself and want to know more about self-harm.

- You want to find out how to get help for self-harm.

- You experience intense emotional turmoil, and want to learn helpful coping skills.

- You're in treatment and want to learn more about self-harm, its causes, and the things you can do to help yourself.

- You care about or treat people who harm themselves, and you want an easily accessible source of information that tells you exactly what self-harm is all about.

You may notice that starting at the beginning and reading through to the end is the most helpful way to use this book. That way, you'll clearly understand what self-harm is before you move on to the chapters that describe how to seek help and how to cope with self-harm. But you could also use this book as a "user's manual" by checking out certain sections for information as needed. Either way, we hope this book provides you with the information you need to tackle self-harm and move forward in your life in the directions that are most important to you.

PART I

UNDERSTANDING
SELF-HARM

Chapter 1

What Is Self-Harm?

Rebecca sat in her room in the dark wondering what was wrong with her. Why did she keep hurting herself? Why couldn't she stop? She had told herself so many times, "This is the last time. I will never do this again." And yet, when things felt out of control and she didn't think she could cope with the pain for a moment longer, she was drawn back in like a moth to a flame. The problem was, in the end, she always felt the same way: ashamed, guilty, and so very alone. Tonight, like so many other nights, she found herself wondering if anyone else struggled with this, or if she really was as crazy and alone as she felt.

DEFINING SELF-HARM

So, what exactly is self-harm? Well, as we mentioned in the introduction, self-harm is something people do purposely to harm themselves physically in the moment, without intending to kill themselves. To give you a better sense of exactly what we're talking about, though, we'll go through each part of this definition in detail below.

The Damage Is Physical

The first part of this definition has to do with injuring yourself physically. There are many things we can do to hurt ourselves psychologically or emotionally, such as saying mean things to ourselves or hanging out with people who don't treat us well. But, these actions don't usually cause physical damage. Self-harm, on the other hand, involves inflicting damage to your body, for example, by causing lacerations, bruises, burns, or scrapes. When someone has self-harmed, you can see the damage. And, in fact, this is one of the reasons people sometimes prefer self-harm to other harmful behaviors that don't leave a mark. We'll tell you more about this in chapter 5.

The Damage Is Immediate

The next part of this definition has to do with the fact that self-harm involves inflicting physical damage *right at that moment*. Some things people do to themselves harm their bodies gradually, over time. For example, drinking alcohol excessively for many years can damage your internal organs and harm your physical health. Similarly, the cycle of bingeing and purging seen in *bulimia*, an eating disorder, can eventually damage the body. In both of these cases, though, the damage usually comes only after many months or years of doing the behavior. With self-harm, on the other hand, the damage happens right away. This is a critical point, because the very purpose of self-harm is to cause physical damage right at that moment.

The Harm Is Intentional

Another part of this definition of self-harm is that the physical damage caused by self-harm is intentional, or done on purpose. Imagine if someone who'd been drinking all night tried to drive home. This kind of reckless behavior could definitely result in physical injury. But, unless causing physical injury was the entire reason the person decided to drive under the influence, this would not be considered a form of self-harm. To be regarded as self-harm, the purpose of the behavior has to be to inflict bodily injury to oneself. Now don't get us wrong—reckless behaviors like this may very well result in serious harm, and we certainly don't recommend them. But, they're not considered to be a form of self-harm, because the harm that occurs is an accident.

This also brings us to another important point: to call a behavior "self-harm," not only does inflicting bodily injury have to be the purpose of the behavior, it also has to be something that's guaranteed to work every time. So, self-harm differs from risky behaviors such as driving too fast or riding a motorcycle without a helmet, which don't necessarily result in physical injury each and every time you do them. With self-harm behaviors like cutting or burning, you're pretty much guaranteed to cause immediate physical damage every time.

The Intention Is Not to Commit Suicide

Now, the final part of the definition that we really want to emphasize is that people who self-harm are not trying to kill themselves. Many people confuse self-harm with suicide attempts, and assume that anyone who self-harms must be attempting to end her or his life. This is simply not true. In fact, most people who self-harm are trying to cope with their lives, not end them. Some researchers even consider self-harm to be the opposite of suicide attempts, because some people use self-harm to prevent killing themselves (Favazza 1998; Pattison and Kahan 1983).

Now, one reason why people seem to confuse self-harm with suicidal behaviors is that they often look similar. For example, as we mentioned earlier, one of the most common forms of self-harm is cutting. But this is also something some people do to end their lives. So, when people see someone who has cut herself or himself, they sometimes assume that the person must have attempted suicide. And, it becomes even more confusing when you consider that sometimes people who self-harm hurt themselves more severely than they'd intended. In these cases, if a treatment provider or loved one doesn't take the time to ask about the purpose of the behavior, it can be easy to mistake self-harm for a suicide attempt. Of course, the problem with this is that self-harm and suicide attempts require somewhat different treatments. Therefore, confusing self-harm with a suicide attempt can result in a treatment that's not as helpful as it could be.

So, let's recap: When we talk about self-harm in this book, we're talking about anything people do on purpose to cause physical damage to their bodies right away, without the intention of killing themselves.

Some of the most common forms of self-harm include cutting, burning, or biting oneself; punching or hitting oneself; and even scratching or picking at the skin to the point of causing scrapes or cuts. Now, if these last two examples surprise you, you're not alone. We've both treated people struggling with self-harm who didn't think of it as self-harm because it differed from the kind of self-harm they'd seen in movies and on TV (where self-cutting is commonly shown). Basically, because they picked their skin or scratched themselves instead of cutting themselves, they weren't sure their behavior was a form of self-harm. In fact, they didn't know what to think about it. But picking, scraping, and scratching can definitely be forms of self-harm.

Here's the bottom line: if the behavior you struggle with is something you do on purpose to cause damage to your body, something that results in immediate physical damage, and something that's not an attempt to kill yourself, then it's a form of self-harm. If you're wondering whether you may be struggling with self-harm, it might be useful to ask yourself the following questions:

- Do you do things to harm yourself immediately, in the moment?

- Do the things you do cause visible tissue damage?

- Do you intend to harm yourself? Is that the reason you do these things?

- Are you doing this behavior *without* intending to kill yourself?

If you answered yes to all of these questions, keep reading to learn more about the behavior you're struggling with.

HOW COMMON IS SELF-HARM?

So, just how common is self-harm? Well, as we mentioned in the introduction, a couple of studies in the United States have found that about 4 percent of adults have harmed themselves at least once in their lifetimes (Briere and Gil 1998; Klonsky, Oltmanns, and Turkheimer 2003). And, even though 4 percent may not seem like a lot, this makes self-harm more common than many psychiatric disorders that people struggle with, such as borderline personality disorder (Skodol et al. 2002) and some anxiety disorders (Kessler et al. 2005).

What's more, it seems as if self-harm is becoming very common in high schools and colleges. Now, we don't know exactly how common it is in these school settings, but some studies of specific high schools and colleges have found that as many as 20 percent of high-school students and 40 percent of college students say that they've harmed themselves at least once, and as many as 15 to 17 percent of college students say they've harmed themselves frequently (Gratz 2001, 2006; Gratz, Conrad, and Roemer 2002; Paivio and McCullough 2004; Zoroglu et al. 2003)! If this surprises you, you're not alone. Most people are shocked to learn just how common self-harm is in high schools and colleges. And yet, studies in different schools across the United States, Canada, and Europe are finding similar rates of self-harm again and again.

So, why is self-harm so much more common than people once thought? Well, some clinicians and researchers think that self-harm has become more common in the past few years than it was a decade ago. Although we don't know exactly why this may be the case, some people think it has to do with *social contagion*. Basically, the idea here is that people learn self-harm from their friends or siblings, or from seeing it featured in movies or on TV. Now, this doesn't mean that you'll start to self-harm just because you know someone who self-harms. But, we do think that people who are struggling with their emotions and aren't sure how to cope may be more likely to try self-harm if they know people who've used self-harm to feel better. In fact, some high-school and college guidance counselors have told us that self-harm is so much more common in their schools these days that it seems to be spreading like a cold or flu.

Altogether the most important point to keep in mind is that self-harm is not uncommon, and if you struggle with self-harm you're definitely not alone.

WHO SELF-HARMS?

If "Who self-harms?" seems like a fairly straightforward question, it might surprise you to learn that researchers have only recently begun to answer it. In fact, it wasn't too long ago when many people would have answered this question incorrectly. How so? Well, for a long time, people thought that self-harm was something that only people with *borderline personality disorder* (*BPD*) did. BPD is a disorder characterized by instability in emotions, thinking, relationships, identity, and behavior. And, one of the most common symptoms of BPD is self-harm (Gunderson 2001; Linehan 1993a). In fact, self-harm is so common among people with BPD that it was once referred to as the "behavioral specialty" of people with this disorder (Mack 1975). And for a long time, treatment providers and researchers alike thought that self-harm only occurred among people who had BPD.

As it turns out, though, that's not true. Now, don't get us wrong—self-harm is still found the most among people with BPD, probably because of all the emotional turmoil and life problems that go along with BPD. In fact, as many as three quarters of people with BPD engage in self-harm (Gunderson 2001; Linehan 1993a). But, we now know that people who don't have BPD also harm themselves. In fact, self-harm can be seen among people with a variety of different disorders, including depression, post-traumatic stress disorder, dissociative disorders, eating disorders, and anxiety disorders. We'll tell you more about the disorders that tend to go along with self-harm in chapter 4. For now, all you need to know is that self-harm occurs among a variety of people who struggle with different problems. So, if you self-harm, it doesn't necessarily mean you have BPD or any other psychiatric disorder. Instead, it really only means that you're probably struggling with some difficult emotions and trying to cope with them in the way that seems to work best for you.

Now, you might also have wondered whether self-harm is more common among people of certain ethnicities or socioeconomic classes, and whether it's more common among females or males. Well, for a long time, researchers and treatment providers thought that self-harm was something that only girls and women did. People just assumed that boys and men didn't harm themselves in these kinds of ways. This is probably because there's a general assumption that males express anger and aggression outwardly (for example, by yelling or fighting), whereas females tend to express anger and aggression inwardly (for example, by harming themselves). Now, although there is some research evidence to back up this idea, the assumption that boys and men don't harm themselves is completely false. In fact, several studies have found that men self-harm just as much as women, and in many of the same ways (Gratz 2001; Gratz and Chapman 2007). Therefore, we really want to emphasize that self-harm is not just a problem that girls and women struggle with; boys and men struggle with it too.

As for the other characteristics we mentioned, self-harm is an equal opportunity behavior. Not only do both females and males do it, but people of all races, ethnicities, and social classes do it as well. This is a behavior that doesn't discriminate: it seems to be something that anyone could do, if she or he were in enough pain and had no idea how to cope with it.

On the other hand, self-harm does appear to be a little more common among gay, lesbian, and bisexual people. So, why might this be the case? Well, one explanation is that society in general doesn't completely accept people who aren't heterosexual. In fact, many people who are gay, lesbian, or bisexual talk about feeling alienated, alone, and different from other people around them as they're growing up. They may even feel bad, weird, or abnormal. And for some people, feeling abnormal, alienated, different, or ashamed is exactly the kind of experience that can lead to self-harm. Of course, most gay and lesbian people don't harm themselves, and many heterosexual people do harm themselves. But in our society, being different in any way isn't easy, and can sometimes lead to emotional turmoil and feelings of distress. And, as we mentioned before, although self-harm has a lot of downsides, it can provide some relief from emotional pain in the moment—which, for many people, can be very enticing.

Self-harm also seems to be most common among adolescents and young adults. In fact, this is one way in which self-harm is just like other self-destructive and impulsive behaviors, such as excessive drinking, drug use, and eating-disordered behaviors. All of these behaviors tend to occur more often among young people than older people, and self-harm is no exception. Studies have found that self-harm is most common among those aged fifteen to thirty-five and that it seems to become less common after that (O'Loughlin and Sherwood 2005; Skegg 2005; Welch 2001). Now, this doesn't mean that people younger than fifteen or older than thirty-five don't harm themselves. We've both worked with people who started self-harming well into their thirties or forties, or well before the age of ten. Self-harm is just a lot less common at these younger and older ages. In fact, self-harm is rarely seen in people older than fifty.

Although we aren't exactly sure why this is, most researchers think it has to do with changes in hormones as people get older. Basically, due to hormonal changes as people age, most people become less impulsive and more even-keeled as they get older.

THE SELF-HARM TIMELINE: WHEN IT STARTS AND HOW LONG IT LASTS

Most people who harm themselves begin this behavior at the age of thirteen or fourteen. It's probably not a coincidence that this is the age when people also start to have stronger and more intense emotions. In fact, because of the emotional turmoil that so often occurs in early adolescence, many people find that the ways they previously managed their emotions and coped with life's problems stop working as well. And, when old ways of coping fail, people can become desperate enough to consider something like self-harm, just to get some relief.

Of course, you might be wondering what causes people to try self-harm the first time or to choose self-harm over other ways of coping with emotions, like talking with friends, or using drugs or alcohol. Well, there are two main reasons why someone might try self-harm. The first has to do with social contagion. As we mentioned earlier, people who are struggling with their emotions and unsure how to cope may be more likely to try self-harm if they see their friends, loved ones, or media figures engaging in self-harm. Seeing people they know or respect harm themselves might make self-harm seem like a viable option.

The second reason is that some people actually stumble upon self-harm accidentally the first time. We've both worked with clients who remember hurting themselves accidentally and suddenly realizing that it distracted them from something they were upset about. In that moment, all of their attention was focused on their physical pain instead of their emotional distress. For some people, this is a powerful lesson that harming themselves physically may take their attention away from unwanted emotional pain, distress, and worries.

Now, different people seem to go in different directions after they've tried self-harm once. Some people try self-harm a few times, over the course of a year or two, and then "grow out of it" or decide that it isn't for them. These are the people who experiment with self-harm, just as some people experiment with drugs during adolescence and young adulthood. And, for these people, self-harm might be something they can recover from on their own or with some support from a therapist or loved ones.

Other people, however, come to rely on self-harm in order to cope. For them, self-harm can continue over many years, even decades. In fact, for some people, self-harm can take on a life of its own and get completely out of control. In these cases, the self-harm itself can actually start to feel more out of control than the person's emotions. It just works so well and so quickly that some people find it harder and harder to resist using it—even to cope with smaller problems that they might once have coped with in another way. And, when this happens, people get "hooked" on self-harm, and use it more and more frequently over time.

A third group of people who try self-harm probably fall somewhere between these first two groups. These are people who might self-harm occasionally over many years, just when things get particularly difficult. They don't always harm themselves, and they may even go for years without doing this. But, when things get extremely stressful, they might go back to this behavior for a while and then try to stop again when the stress has passed.

Now, it's definitely the case that some people start to self-harm before they reach adolescence. In fact, some people start harming themselves as early as five or six years old. Starting self-harm at a very young age is usually a sign that you're dealing with a lot of intense problems, like abuse, neglect, or other really stressful experiences. So, it probably isn't that surprising that beginning self-harm in childhood often means that the self-harm will last longer and be more severe than for people who start to self-harm later in their lives.

Finally, as we mentioned before, most people stop harming themselves as they get older. We rarely see people over fifty-five or so who harm themselves (although some surely do), and even people over forty don't tend to self-harm as much as younger adults. That said, though, some people can struggle with self-harm for as many as thirty or forty years.

WHAT TO DO IF YOU STRUGGLE WITH SELF-HARM

Although some people can recover from self-harm on their own, many find it easier to stop this behavior if they have the support of a mental health professional. As we discussed above, the more you come to rely on self-harm, the harder it can be to stop on your own. Not only can a mental health professional support you in trying to stop self-harm, this person can also teach you alternative ways of coping with your emotions and life stressors, so that you don't feel as if you have to give up your only coping strategy and have nothing to replace it with.

We recommend that you seek a professional with training and experience in the treatment of self-harm. As we will discuss in chapter 7, many different types of mental health professionals can treat someone who self-harms, including clinical psychologists, psychiatrists, social workers, people with master's degrees in psychology, and people with Ph.D.s or master's degrees in counseling psychology. Any of these professionals may be able to help you or someone you love recover from self-harm. More important than the professional's particular training or degree is her or his level of experience with and knowledge about self-harm. In particular, you should make sure that this professional (1) knows that self-harm is different from suicidal behaviors; (2) has knowledge, training, and experience with alternative coping strategies; (3) is nonjudgmental toward people who self-harm; (4) knows how to treat self-harm; and (5) is willing to work with you to stop this behavior. In chapter 7, we tell you more about how to seek treatment for self-harm, and the things to consider as you attempt to find the right treatment provider for you.

SUMMARY

Below is a brief summary of what we covered in this chapter. We hope you find this information helpful as you explore this book and learn more about self-harm.

- ⚜ Self-harm is something you do on purpose to harm yourself physically, without the intention of killing yourself.

- Self-harm is different from other types of self-destructive behaviors that don't result in immediate physical injury, like drug use, reckless driving, and bingeing and purging.

- Self-harm is different from suicidal behaviors. When people self-harm, they're usually trying to cope with their lives, not end them.

- Self-harm is an equal opportunity behavior. People of all races, ethnicities, and social classes engage in self-harm, as do both females and males.

- Self-harm is more common than people once thought. Not only do people with psychiatric disorders (such as BPD) engage in self-harm, so do many high-school and college students. In fact, some people think that self-harm has become more common in the past few years, especially among adolescents and young adults.

- Like many impulsive behaviors, self-harm becomes less common as people get older. In fact, some people think self-harm "burns out" with age.

- Seek help from a trained professional if you struggle with self-harm.

Now that you know a little more about what self-harm is, the next chapter focuses on explaining what self-harm is not. In particular, the next chapter is devoted to clearing up some common myths about self-harm.

Chapter 2

Myths About Self-Harm

Everywhere Peter turned, he felt bombarded by misconceptions about self-harm. Why couldn't anyone understand what he was going through? It was as if he had awakened to find himself on a different planet, where everyone spoke another language. It's not that he didn't understand that self-harm can be scary and confusing to people who don't harm themselves. He did. But the thing he couldn't understand was why they couldn't get beyond their misconceptions and hear what he was saying. Just last week, he got into an argument with an ER nurse about why he'd cut himself. No matter how much he insisted that he had had no intention of killing himself, she kept telling the other staff that he'd attempted suicide, and paged the psychiatrist on call to get him hospitalized. Then, to make matters worse, the next day his father accused him of cutting himself to get attention, even though he'd tried to hide it from everyone. Why couldn't anyone understand that he was just trying to relieve some of his pain and cope with his depression?

As we mentioned earlier, self-harm can be really difficult to overcome. If you're struggling with intense emotional pain, anything that works as well and as quickly as self-harm to escape that pain—even if only for a moment—can be really difficult to give up. Therefore, we want to provide you with all the tools we can to assist you on your journey to recovery. And one of the most important tools on the road to recovery is knowledge. Think of accurate information as your compass: knowing the facts about self-harm will help point you in the right direction, toward recovery. If you can understand what you're struggling with, you'll be in a much better position to overcome it and move forward.

In fact, this is true for most things in life. You wouldn't try to take a math test without knowing something about math, would you? And if you did, you probably wouldn't do so well on it, because you wouldn't have the information you'd need to pass it. Of course, the good thing about math tests is that you only have to take them after you've taken a math class and learned some math. And, even if you hate math, there's a lot of information available about it, and entire classes devoted to helping you learn this information from childhood on.

Unfortunately, the same thing cannot be said for mental health problems. Unlike with math, there isn't a class in school devoted to helping people deal with mental health problems, or a textbook that contains all of the information you need to know to "pass" this part of life. Most people who are struggling with mental health problems have to seek out the information they need on their own. And, unlike with math, there aren't always clear-cut answers readily available. Instead, most people find that they need to sift through a pile of inaccurate and unhelpful information to find the facts they're looking for and the help they need. It can be like trying to find a needle in a haystack without knowing exactly what a needle looks like.

So, what does this have to do with self-harm in particular? Well, self-harm is a problem especially prone to misinformation. One reason for the abundance of misinformation about self-harm may be that self-harm is such a shocking, confusing, and frightening behavior to most people who aren't struggling with it (and even to some of those who are!). When people don't understand a behavior, and especially when that behavior scares them, it's often easier to simply judge the person who's engaging in that behavior than it is to make an effort to really understand what's going on with that person. And that's exactly the kind of thing that can lead to inaccurate information and harmful myths. To really understand something that another person is going through, you have to be willing to listen to that person and try to understand where that person is coming from. And if the problem that person is struggling with scares you or makes you very uncomfortable, it can be really hard to listen with an open mind. The problem, though, is that myths about self-harm only lead to further confusion and more misunderstandings about this behavior, which makes people who harm themselves feel even worse.

So, although we understand that self-harm can be a scary behavior (especially when someone you love is struggling with it), we believe that understanding this behavior and being able to separate the facts about it from the myths will help to make it a little less scary and easier to manage. Therefore, we wanted to clear up some of the myths about self-harm that we believe are the most common and most damaging.

EIGHT COMMON MYTHS ABOUT SELF-HARM

Below we describe and debunk eight of the myths about self-harm, in the hope of helping you understand what self-harm is and isn't.

Myth 1: Self-Harm Is the Same as a Suicide Attempt

As we mentioned earlier, one of the biggest misconceptions about self-harm is that it's the same thing as a suicide attempt. For many people who don't struggle with self-harm, certain forms of self-harm (like severe cutting) just look so much like a suicide attempt on the surface that it can be difficult to interpret those behaviors in any other way. People just assume that those actions must be suicide attempts. If self-harm were widely recognized and understood, people might not confuse it with suicide attempts, no matter how similar these behaviors look on the surface. Unfortunately, though, self-harm remains a mystery to many people. The general public has been aware of suicide attempts for much longer than self-harm, and many people still haven't had much exposure to self-harm and what it is. What's more, for someone who hasn't struggled with this behavior, the idea that people would harm themselves physically in order to help themselves cope can be almost incomprehensible. Therefore, it can be easy to jump to the conclusion that all people who harm themselves physically must be trying to commit suicide.

In fact, experiences like Peter's, at the beginning of this chapter, can be quite common for people who harm themselves. We've both worked with many clients who have described going to a hospital to get their wounds cared for, only to find the hospital staff assuming that they had tried to kill themselves. What's more, this misperception can persist even after they've tried to explain that they never had any intention of killing themselves. Now, one reason for this may be that health care providers— like everyone else—are not immune to myths about self-harm, and some of them may sometimes fall into the trap of assuming that self-harm must be a suicide attempt. However, another reason why health care providers may sometimes seem to ignore people's explanations for their self-harm probably has to do with the fact that some people who attempt suicide feel so ashamed and scared afterward that they deny that they tried to kill themselves. Instead, they may say that it was an accident or a mistake. So, it's a good bet that quite a few health care providers working in emergency rooms have treated people who tried to kill themselves but were too ashamed or scared to say so, or only admitted this after being in the ER for some time. And, as a result, these health care providers may have learned that it's safest to assume that anything that looks like a suicide attempt probably *is* a suicide attempt—even if the person says otherwise.

In fact, as much as this myth doesn't help you if you're struggling with self-harm, it's somewhat understandable when you think about how scary suicide is for people. If you believed that someone you love had just tried to commit suicide, you'd probably try to intervene and get help for that person as quickly as possible. And, that might be the only thing on your mind until you felt that your loved one was safe. So, it makes sense that someone might be inclined to jump to conclusions about the intention of self-harm. In a way, people might just feel safest assuming the worst-case scenario and starting from there, especially when the consequences for making a mistake seem so extreme and dire.

Of course, the problem is, this is just not helpful. If you struggle with self-harm and have had people misinterpret your behavior, you're probably well aware of how frustrating it can be to be misunderstood. Feeling as if no one understands what you're going through or the reasons you self-harm can be very isolating, and may sometimes make you feel as if you're losing your mind! Besides, when people don't understand why you do the things you do, or the problems you're trying to solve with your self-harm, it can be very difficult for them to give you the help you need.

So, please remember that self-harm and suicide attempts aren't at all the same. In fact, these behaviors are very different. People who try to end their own lives are generally in a state of extreme hopelessness, and may have pretty much given up on themselves and the world. People who self-harm, on the other hand, are trying to cope with their problems in the way that seems best to them at the time. Although they might be experiencing incredible emotional pain, they're not trying to escape all of life's problems forever. They're attempting to cope. And, we believe that this is very different from a suicide attempt.

Myth 2: Self-Harm Is "Superficial" and Not Dangerous

This may seem to be almost the opposite myth from the previous one. The myth here is that self-harm is basically no big deal, or that it's not serious or dangerous. Some people think that if you cut yourself a bit from time to time, you're really not in any danger physically. Now, it's certainly true that some people don't harm themselves very seriously. They might never need medical attention for their self-harm, their scars might go away quickly, or they might not even scar at all. In fact, in some ways, people might say that self-harm is even less dangerous than smoking. So, it's understandable that people might think self-harm is not that dangerous.

The problem, as we discuss in chapter 6, is that a few key things make self-harm more dangerous than it seems. First, some people need more and more serious self-harm to get the same effect (usually, emotional relief of some kind) over time. This is called *tolerance* (and we discuss it more in chapter 6). So, what might start as relatively superficial cutting might end up being life threatening. Other people find that they have to get closer and closer to lethal self-harm in order to get the same thrill or rush they used to get.

Second, some people self-harm when they're in a dissociated state. *Dissociation* basically means to be "checked out," spaced out, or unaware of your surroundings or your body. If you self-harm when you're dissociating, you might not even be aware of how seriously you're harming yourself.

Third, repeated self-harm is one of the best predictors of eventual death by suicide (van Egmond and Diekstra 1989). This is partly because people who hurt themselves are at risk of accidentally taking it too far and killing themselves. Also, many people struggle with both self-harm and suicidal behaviors. In the long run, harming yourself can increase your feelings of shame and self-hatred, and these emotions might make you more likely to try to kill yourself.

Myths 1 and 2 are like two sides of the same coin. On the one hand, it's critical that people not assume that self-harm is a "suicide attempt" and freak out, treating self-harming individuals as if they're lying. On the other hand, people must take self-harm seriously and not dismiss it simply because the bodily damage, at times, isn't great.

Myth 3: Self-Harm Is Manipulative

This is another common myth about self-harm that's simply not true. And, just like the last myth we discussed, this myth probably came about as a result of a misguided attempt to explain self-harm. The problem is, this myth can be very damaging to people who harm themselves and can interfere with their getting the help they need.

So, how exactly do we think this myth came to be? Well, one reason, ironically, may have to do with the desire to help people who are struggling with self-harm. Basically, because self-harm is so serious, many people find that they want to intervene quickly to help or support a loved one or client who self-harms. However, when they find themselves rushing to provide help, support, and reassurance to that person again and again, they can feel as if they're being "manipulated" into providing that help and support. It's as if they respond so quickly that they start to feel that they can't control their own behaviors and that they're being forced to provide support and reassurance. This then makes them conclude that the person engaging in self-harm is using this behavior to "manipulate" them into providing attention and help.

Now, the problem with this way of thinking is that you can't infer people's intentions based on the effects of their behavior. For example, let's say that as you were walking through the mall one day, you saw a man and woman talking to one another. The woman sort of loomed over the man, and he was looking down and crying. If you decided to infer the woman's intentions based on the man's behavior, you might guess that she was trying to hurt his feelings or be mean to him in some way. Based on his tears, you'd probably think she had said something to try to make him cry. And, in some cases, you could be right. It's possible that she could have been angry at him, or in a really bad mood, and so said something to hurt his feelings. The problem is, you could also be wrong. Maybe the man's tears had nothing to do with the woman or what she'd said. For example, he might have been in the middle of an allergy attack, or his contact lenses might have been bothering him. Or, maybe the man was crying because of something the woman had said unintentionally. Perhaps she had said something that made him think of someone who'd passed away recently, or opened up to him about her feelings in a way that made him feel sad. Or, maybe she really did hurt his feelings but without meaning to. Saying that people use self-harm to manipulate others into providing support is like saying that the woman in our example purposefully said something to the man to get him to cry. The problem is, there's really no way of knowing what her intentions were, and making assumptions about why he was crying could lead to very wrong conclusions. In the same way, knowing that self-harm may lead others to provide attention or help doesn't actually tell us *why* someone engages in those behaviors. In fact, as we discuss in chapter 5, research clearly indicates that influencing others isn't the primary reason people hurt themselves.

What's more, even if people have learned that the only way to get any kind of attention from someone else is to engage in a behavior as extreme as self-harm, the fact that they resort to this behavior doesn't mean that they're manipulative. It may simply mean that they desperately need some kind of attention from another human being, and haven't yet learned any other way of getting that need met. In fact, attention and regard from others is a basic human need. Of course, we'd all rather get positive attention than negative attention; however, in some cases, that positive attention isn't available. In these cases, people are generally willing to accept negative attention rather than no attention at all. So, the assumption that someone who engages in self-harm to get some needed care or attention is "manipulative" overlooks the basic human need involved in this situation.

The bottom line is that self-harm is not an attempt to manipulate others. The mistaken assumption that people who self-harm are manipulative only reinforces the stigma surrounding this behavior, making it even more difficult for people to recover from self-harm.

Myth 4: If You Self-Harm, You Have BPD

One of the biggest myths about self-harm that many treatment providers even believe is that all people who self-harm have borderline personality disorder (BPD). Some treatment providers just assume that self-harm is a sign of BPD, and a reason to diagnose someone with this disorder. And, in fact, some people who harm themselves do meet criteria for BPD. As we mentioned in chapter 1, self-harm is one of the most common symptoms of BPD, and as many as 75 percent of people with BPD harm themselves (Gunderson 2001; Linehan 1993a). So, it's pretty clear that self-harm is something that a lot of folks with BPD struggle with.

The problem is that the opposite isn't necessarily true. Even if most people with BPD engage in self-harm, this doesn't mean that most people who self-harm have BPD. That is faulty logic, like saying that just because all dogs have four legs, everything with four legs is a dog. It just doesn't work that way. And, in fact, we know that many people who struggle with self-harm don't have BPD. In fact, one study of forty-seven college students who harmed themselves found that none of them met criteria for a diagnosis of BPD (Andover et al. 2005).

So, what does this mean if you struggle with self-harm? Well, one thing it means is that you shouldn't assume you have BPD. You *might* have BPD, and it's probably a good idea to get a formal diagnostic assessment when you begin looking into treatment options. But, it seems as if there's probably a bigger chance that you won't meet criteria for BPD, even if you struggle with some of the same symptoms, like overwhelming emotions and relationship problems. In fact, you might not have any psychiatric disorder! Although most people who harm themselves struggle with other problems and are in a great amount of emotional pain, this doesn't mean that you definitely have a psychiatric disorder like BPD if you harm yourself. And, the only way to know is to meet with a professional for a formal diagnostic assessment. We'll tell you more about the steps you'll need to take to get a good diagnostic assessment in chapter 7, as well as some of the things to keep in mind as you begin that process.

Myth 5: Self-Harm Is a Female Problem

Just like the belief that only people with BPD harm themselves, the belief that only girls and women harm themselves is just plain wrong. In fact, this myth couldn't be farther from the truth. More and more research is finding that boys and men harm themselves just as much as girls and women do (Gratz 2001; Gratz and Chapman 2007; Klonsky, Oltmanns, and Turkheimer 2003). And, they seem to do so for many of the same reasons. In fact, the reasons males and females harm themselves are much more similar than different, and usually have to do with trying to feel better or cope in some way (Gratz and Chapman 2007; Nock and Prinstein 2005).

Now, one reason for this myth may be that there was a time when most people who sought help for their self-harm or ended up in treatment were female. As we mentioned in chapter 1, many people struggle with self-harm in secrecy, out of fear, shame, or simply because they aren't yet ready to consider giving up this behavior. And, it makes a lot of sense to us that males might be even more hesitant to tell people about their self-harm, for fear of what others would think of them. Now, don't get us wrong; we don't think that there's any reason why males need to feel ashamed of this behavior. As we've said before, it works in the moment and serves very important purposes for people who use it. But, it makes sense to us that, if it's a common misperception that only females engage in self-harm, males who do this might feel particularly weird, crazy, or alone. If you thought that you were one of the only males on the planet who harms himself, you probably wouldn't jump at the chance to tell someone about your struggles.

So, even though you may not hear as much about males struggling with self-harm, this is not because they don't. As we said before, self-harm is an equal opportunity behavior that's just as common among boys and men as it is among girls and women.

Myth 6: Self-Harm Is Crazy, Sick, and Irrational

This myth couldn't be farther from the truth. Even though self-harm may seem incomprehensible to people who haven't struggled with it, this behavior always serves an important purpose in the moment. In fact, as we'll talk about more in chapter 5, people often harm themselves in order to meet some basic human needs, such as to feel better or to release emotional pain. And, anything that works as well as self-harm does to meet these needs couldn't possibly be crazy. Think about it this way: if you immediately felt much worse or really sick or upset every time you harmed yourself, chances are that you wouldn't do it much longer. We humans don't tend to do things that don't have some benefit for us. On the contrary, we tend to do things that make us feel better in some way. And, for some people, self-harm is one of these behaviors.

Now, the fact is that self-harm is more dangerous than many other things people do to make themselves feel better, and it definitely has a lot of downsides in the long run. But, it meets some important needs in the short term, and can be a very quick-acting and powerful way to get some relief from overwhelming emotions. So, even though we hope people will work to replace self-harm with other ways of coping with distress that don't have the same downsides or long-term problems, we definitely can see the ways self-harm works in the moment. And, as we said before, any behavior that meets someone's needs is not irrational.

Myth 7: You Must Resolve Your Underlying Issues Before You Can Stop Self-Harm

Both this myth and the next are a bit different from the ones we mentioned previously. They are less about self-harm itself and more about the ways to overcome this behavior. The gist of this myth is that the only way people can recover from self-harm is to overcome all of their pain, resolve their issues, and solve all of their emotional and interpersonal problems first. The problem with this myth is that there's absolutely no reason to think that you need to wait until you've overcome all of your past negative experiences before you can stop self-harming. In fact, we believe that stopping self-harm will put you in a better place to be able to start working through your problems and resolving them. If you self-harm, a lot of your time, energy, and mental resources probably goes into planning self-harm, resisting urges to self-harm, and hiding your self-harm. And, after the positive effects have worn off, many people start to feel guilty and ashamed for having harmed themselves again.

So, all of this focus on self-harm actually makes it harder to focus your energy on other problems; it can basically distract you from these other problems and make it harder to resolve them. So, in the end, we believe that one of the most important things in treatment is to try to stop self-harm immediately, so that you'll have more energy to focus on solving your other problems and building the life you want.

Myth 8: If You Resolve All Your Underlying Issues, Your Self-Harm Will Go Away

This myth probably sounds like the opposite of myth 7, and in some ways it is. Basically, this myth says that if you focus your attention on your unresolved feelings toward your parents or the problems you had growing up, your self-harm will pretty much stop on its own. In other words, once you've come to terms with and resolved the pain and problems from your past, your self-harm will naturally go away. One of the problems with this myth, though, is that recovery from self-harm is just not this simple. Of course, we agree that it's important not to focus only on self-harm. As we mentioned before, people who self-harm struggle with many different problems and are often in intense emotional pain. Therefore, we are all for people coming to terms with the problems and pain from their pasts, and working to overcome the negative experiences they've had. However, even if you do this, you'll probably still need to make a direct effort to stop your self-harm.

As we mentioned before, self-harm can be a very powerful and addictive behavior that, over time, can start to take on a life of its own. This means that even if you fix the problems that made you start harming yourself to begin with, it might still be hard to stop. For example, let's say you started harming yourself in order to cope with the stress of an abusive relationship. But, over time, you began to use self-harm to cope with other sources of stress as well. In fact, you soon started turning to self-harm whenever you felt upset. Now, let's say you decided to leave that abusive relationship. Do you think your self-harm would just automatically stop as a result? Of course not! Once self-harm has become your "go-to" coping strategy, fixing the problem that caused you to start harming yourself won't take away all of your urges to self-harm. In fact, as we mention in chapter 6, the more you rely on self-harm to cope with the problems and stress in your life, the more your other coping skills weaken and waste away, until eventually you feel as if self-harm is the only thing you can do to cope with any situation.

SUMMARY

In this chapter, we debunked some common myths and misperceptions about self-harm. Of course, this wasn't an exhaustive list, and there are many more myths out there; however, the ones we presented seem to be some of the most common and important myths currently surrounding this behavior. The research on self-harm is growing every day, and we have a much better understanding of this behavior today than we did even ten years ago. Unfortunately, though, despite this better understanding, many of these myths continue to persist. So, as you read the rest of this book and start your journey down the road to recovery, here are a few things to keep in mind:

- Self-harm is not the same thing as a suicide attempt. It's not about trying to end your life.

- Even though self-harm is not the same as a suicide attempt, it can be serious and shouldn't be dismissed as "superficial."

- Instead, self-harm is something people use to cope, and in the moment, it serves an important purpose and can help people meet some basic human needs. Therefore, self-harm is in no way crazy or irrational.

- Self-harm is something that many different people struggle with. It's not found just among people with BPD. In fact, there are probably more people struggling with self-harm who don't meet criteria for BPD than who do.

- Self-harm is not something that only females do. Boys and men harm themselves just as much as girls and women do.

- To recover from self-harm, you don't need to resolve all of your problems or work through all of the negative experiences you had in the past. Instead, we think it's a good idea to find a treatment that focuses on helping you learn how to stop your self-harm and cope in other ways. In fact, stopping your self-harm may be just what you need to find the energy and emotional resources to work on some of the problems in your life!

Now that you know a bit more about what self-harm is and isn't, we think it's a good idea to let you know the types of things that cause self-harm.

Chapter 3

What Causes Self-Harm?

Ron began harming himself in his midtwenties. He had just been diagnosed with two separate chronic illnesses, he was having marital problems, and his parents had just divorced. Moreover, his father disowned him after he had to speak in court during the divorce proceedings. Sad and overwhelmed, he was lighting a candle when he had the sudden impulse to burn himself. Unfortunately, this made him feel so much better that he became hooked on self-harm.

In this chapter, we give you some ideas about what might cause self-harm. Although researchers haven't pinpointed the definitive causes of self-harm, there has been an explosion of research on this behavior, and some answers are emerging. You can think of the causes of self-harm in different ways. For instance, there's your biology, such as the way your brain works, your brain chemistry, and your genes. Your biology might set you up from an early age to be vulnerable to developing self-harm. Or, things that happen to you (such as trauma) might change your biology or brain activity, increasing your risk of self-harm. Other types of causes are events that happen in your environment, such as having upsetting childhood experiences, knowing other people who self-harm, or experiencing stress. Finally, factors that keep self-harm going could include feelings of emotional relief, beliefs or expectations about self-harm, or reactions of other people to your self-harm.

As you read this chapter, keep in mind that none of these causes operates completely alone. Just as you can't have a choir with only a soloist, you probably can't have a behavior like self-harm with only one cause. Instead, your biology, the environment, what self-harm does for you, and how you think about self-harm all work together to cause self-harm.

YOUR BIOLOGY AND BRAIN CAN MAKE YOU VULNERABLE TO SELF-HARM

Over the past decade or two, researchers have really begun to search for biological factors that might make people vulnerable to self-harm. You can think of your biology as being like the type of wood or other materials that make up a house. One of the authors lives in a place where it rains a lot from November through early March. Unfortunately, some condominiums in the area were built with the wrong materials for this climate, leading to a problem called the "leaky condo crisis." Basically, the wetness from the rain would seep into the new condos, leading to rot and mold. The materials used to build these condos made them vulnerable to wet weather, much like how your biology might make you more vulnerable to certain types of life stressors. Now, if these condos had been built in the desert, there wouldn't have been any problem. The problem came because of the poor fit between the condo materials and the climate. Similarly, for some people who self-harm, there's a poor fit between their biology and the environments in which they find themselves. As a result, they're vulnerable to developing self-harm.

Chemicals in Your Brain

You probably won't be too surprised to learn that your brain may play a role in your self-harm. You might even have wondered whether you harm yourself because your brain works differently from other people's brains. Well, in some ways this might actually be true. What's very interesting is that the areas of the brain that seem to be involved in self-harm are the same areas that are directly related to pain and emotional distress. Of course, you might have guessed that, given that self-harm involves tissue damage and, at least sometimes, results in pain, and that many people self-harm when they're emotionally upset. To be more specific, it seems that the chemical messengers in your brain (called *neurotransmitters*) involved in your natural pain-relieving system (the *opioid system*) and emotional system (the *serotonin system*) may play a role in self-harm.

We'll tell you more about how neurotransmitters work in chapter 9. For now, we just want you to know the particular neurotransmitters that seem to be most involved in self-harm.

THE SEROTONIN SYSTEM

One neurotransmitter that seems to play a role in self-harm is called *serotonin*. Serotonin is a neurotransmitter that regulates mood, hunger, temperature, sexual activity, sleep, and aggression, among other things. Low levels of serotonin are related to depression, emotional distress, and aggression. Some research on serotonin has suggested that people who self-harm might actually have less serotonin activity in their brains' synapses than people who don't self-harm. The *synapses* in the brain are basically the spaces between two neurons. Neutrotransmitters travel from one neuron to the other, like ships traveling from dock to dock. It seems that people who self-harm basically have fewer ships leaving the dock: less serotonin traveling out of one neuron and over to another (Herpertz et al. 1995; Simeon et al. 1992). And, this suggests that people who don't have enough serotonin activity might be at-risk for self-harm.

There's a fair amount of solid research on the relationship between serotonin and self-harm. Researcher Dr. Emil Coccaro and his colleagues believe that one of the major effects of serotonin problems is irritability, and the lower people's serotonin activity, the more likely they are to act on this irritability by doing something impulsive or aggressive (Coccaro et al. 1997). One such impulsive, aggressive behavior is self-harm.

So, why would biological factors that set you up to experience more emotional distress be involved in self-harm? Well, the simple answer is that most people who self-harm do so when they're upset. People almost never say that they harm themselves when they feel happy or calm (Chapman and Dixon-Gordon 2007; Kleindienst et al. 2008). In fact, anger and other negative emotions seem to be very common triggers for self-harm. And, most people say that they harm themselves in order to feel better emotionally (Brown, Comtois, and Linehan 2002). So, if you have low activity in your serotonin system, you might experience a lot of emotional distress. And, as a result, you might be vulnerable to harming yourself in order to relieve this distress.

THE OPIOID SYSTEM

Another set of neurotransmitters that might play a role in self-harm is called *endogenous opioids*. *Opioids* are neurotransmitters that operate primarily in areas of the brain related to pleasure, euphoria, and pain relief. They work like drugs such as heroin, morphine, or oxycodone. You've probably heard of the term *endorphin*. Well, opioids are the same thing as endorphins—your brain's natural form of morphine. Opioids are released when you experience pain—sort of like a natural, built-in, painkilling drug. When people talk about the "runner's high," they're talking about the endorphin rush they get when they exercise.

One idea about the role of opioids in self-harm is that people who harm themselves have overly active opioid systems. Some researchers think that people who self-harm are predisposed to experience a large burst of opioid activity *primarily when they get hurt* (Coid, Allolio, and Rees 1983; Russ 1992). If this is true, then people who self-harm might experience a flood of opioid activity when they get hurt (including from self-harm), a stronger flood than in people who don't self-harm.

So, this is how it might work: Self-harm causes physical injury to the body and sometimes results in pain as well. Therefore, acts of self-harm trigger opioid activity. Because opioid activity is related to pleasure, calmness, pain relief, and even mild euphoria, self-harm can lead to these types of feelings, possibly because it triggers opioid activity. The problem is that people who self-harm might be prone to a very strong opioid response. If you have a very strong opioid response, you'll probably get a lot more pleasure or relief from self-harming than other people might. It's much easier to get addicted to something that gives you a strong rush, euphoria, or strong emotional relief than it is to get addicted to something that only gives you a small amount of relief or pleasure. So, some people might be especially prone to get addicted to self-harm because of their strong opioid activity. Once they harm themselves, they get a large amount of pleasure and relief, and are likely to get hooked on self-harm.

As we mentioned, opioid activity also relieves pain. So, strong opioid activity might explain why some people who self-harm don't experience pain. In fact, some people who self-harm have told us that they don't experience much pain when they get hurt accidentally, such as when they accidentally get cut or bump their shins. This could be because they have extra-strong opioid systems.

Some evidence for this explanation for self-harm comes from studies on medications for self-harm behavior. For instance, some studies have found that people reduce their self-harm when they regularly take a medication that blocks their opioid receptors (Roth, Ostroff, and Hoffman 1996). The idea is that if your opioid receptors are blocked, the opioids in your brain can't bind to the neurons and, as a result, can't cause feelings of calmness, pleasure, or relief. The fact that blocking this pleasurable opioid response can help stop self-harm suggests that calmness or relief plays a role in self-harm.

Of course, the problem is that not all studies have found the same good effects of these types of medications, and studies have yet to show that people who self-harm have a large increase in opioid activity when they harm themselves. Although it makes some sense that your brain's natural pain-relief system might play a role in self-harm, there's less evidence for the role of opioids in self-harm than there is for the role of serotonin (Winchel and Stanley 1991).

YOUR PERSONALITY AND SELF-HARM

Your personality may also play a role in self-harm. You can think of personality as what makes each of us unique, or different from other people. Personality traits are characteristics we have that stay pretty much the same across different situations and throughout our lives. Most researchers agree that personality is partly innate (or something we're born with) and also partly shaped by our life experiences. In this way, personality is a lot like a rock. There are some basic things that make up a rock, like its chemical composition, color, minerals, and so on. But, the rock might take on a different shape or become smaller depending on where it is. A rock at the bottom of a stream will eventually wear down into smaller rocks, whereas a rock sitting on a hillside might change shape over time because of the wind and rain. Certain elements might leach out of the rock, leaving it with a different ratio of minerals than it started with. But, it's awfully hard to change the fact that it's a rock, just as it's hard to change your basic personality. Some researchers have suggested that certain personality traits might set people up to self-harm.

Impulsivity and Negative Emotions

One personality trait that might make people more likely to self-harm is impulsivity. *Impulsivity* is the tendency to act quickly without thinking about whether that action is actually a good idea (Schalling 1978). Some studies have found that people who self-harm are more impulsive than people who don't self-harm (Favazza and Conterio 1989; Herpertz, Sass, and Favazza 1997; Herpertz et al. 1995). Remember how we mentioned that people who self-harm have lower levels of serotonin than people who don't self-harm? Well, researchers have also found that low levels of serotonin are related to higher impulsivity (Coccaro et al. 1997). So, it makes sense that self-harm and impulsivity might go hand in hand.

Impulsive people often seek thrills, do things on the spur of the moment without thinking, and crave excitement. Sometimes, impulsive people have a hard time delaying gratification. If you're really impulsive, you might find that you have a hard time waiting for things you want. For example, if you saw some shoes you really liked, you might have a hard time waiting a couple of weeks while you save up the money, so you might just buy them on credit instead. In a similar way, you might have a hard time waiting for relief when you feel bad, so you might turn to self-harm instead of using healthier coping strategies that take longer to work.

Impulsive people often have a hard time stopping themselves from doing things. Very impulsive people are a lot like cars with no brakes. When the engine revs and the wheels start turning, it's incredibly hard to stop. If you're impulsive, once you set your mind on harming yourself, you might have a very hard time putting the brakes on, even if you know that self-harm isn't a good idea. You might also harm yourself on the spur of the moment without really thinking about the negative consequences of self-harm (such as scarring, disapproval, or shame).

Another personality trait related to self-harm is *neuroticism*: the tendency to experience strong negative emotions. It's probably not surprising that the more negative emotions you have, the more likely you are to self-harm. What's more, the dynamite combination of impulsivity and negative emotions can make it even harder to resist self-harm. When people are very upset, they often do whatever they can to try to make themselves feel better in the moment. And, at these times, they have a hard time stopping themselves from doing things that have negative long-term consequences, such as eating fattening snacks (Tice, Bratslavsky, and Baumeister 2001). Just as impulsive people are like cars with no brakes, people who are impulsive and neurotic are like powerful race cars with no brakes (and with strong emotional "engines"). So, if you feel more emotional distress than other people do and also are more impulsive, it might be especially hard to avoid harming yourself.

PAINFUL CHILDHOOD EXPERIENCES AND SELF-HARM

Another possible cause of self-harm is painful or traumatic childhood experiences. For quite some time, many researchers thought that painful childhood experiences were one of the most important causes of self-harm. In fact, researchers used to think that most people who self-harm were abused as children. Nowadays, however, we know that things aren't this simple.

Now, on the one hand, studies have found that many people who harm themselves have experienced physical, sexual, or emotional abuse (Boudewyn and Liem 1995; Briere and Gil 1998). And having these experiences does seem to make people more likely to self-harm. On the other hand, not all people who self-harm have been abused. In fact, it's safe to say that less than half the people who self-harm were abused in the past (Gratz, Conrad, and Roemer 2002; Gratz and Chapman 2007; Zoroglu et al. 2003). And, of course, not everyone who is abused goes on to self-harm. So, the relationship between abuse and self-harm is not nearly as strong as people once thought.

We also know now that childhood experiences other than abuse can make you vulnerable to self-harm. For example, some studies have found that having your feelings or emotional needs neglected, ignored, or minimized may be even more important than actual physical or sexual abuse (Dubo et al. 1997; Paivio and McCulloch 2004). The reason for this is unclear, but people who are emotionally neglected are often not taught how to manage or deal with their emotions. And, if you don't know any other way to cope with emotions, you might resort to self-harm.

Another important childhood experience is having a poor emotional connection or bond with caregivers. Developing an emotional bond with your parents or caregivers is one of the first milestones in life, and can protect you from many stressful experiences. Having a weak bond, on the other hand, can make it hard to learn how to deal with relationships and emotions. In fact, some studies have shown that people who remembered not being particularly close to their parents as they were growing up were more likely to self-harm as adults (Gratz, Conrad, and Roemer 2002).

Another type of childhood experience that can make you more likely to harm yourself is harsh punishment. As we'll discuss in chapter 5, some people say that they self-harm in order to punish themselves (Brown, Comtois, and Linehan 2002), and in fact, self-punishment does seem to help relieve feelings of intense guilt and shame. But, how do people learn to punish themselves in the first place? Not all people punish themselves. For instance, when some people do something wrong or fail to live up to their own (or others') expectations, they're disappointed but they're not hard on themselves. Other people are hard on themselves, and may actually feel like punishing themselves when this happens. So, what's the difference between these two types of people?

Well, one possibility is that some people learn to punish themselves by enduring harsh punishment as a child. It's as if you learn that punishment is somehow necessary when you make a mistake or do something "wrong" (even if what you did was just a simple, human mistake). Basically, if people are punished severely for any mistake they make, they're probably going to learn to punish themselves as well. In fact, if you were punished a lot as a child, you might even have learned that if you punish yourself first (by self-harming), other people won't punish you.

Sally vividly recalled a time when she scratched her father's boat as she was driving it into the dock. Her father was extremely angry. Sally felt afraid of what her father might do and angry with herself for scratching the boat. In her anger with herself, she hit herself in the face. When her father noticed the bruises on her face, he stopped yelling at her and asked her what was wrong. Over time, Sally learned that she could avoid punishment if she harmed herself first.

WHAT PUTS YOU AT RISK FOR SELF-HARM?

Answer the questions in each category with a yes or no. Note that we haven't included some of the biological factors (such as serotonin and the opioid system) because there's really no good way to figure out whether you have some of those risk factors just by filling out a questionnaire. Often, the things that put people at risk for self-harm are different for different people. Answering these questions will help you figure out what might have placed you at risk. You can think of the items that you answer with a yes as your risk factors. Although many of these risk factors have happened already (and you can't go back in time and change them), it can be helpful for you to understand what made you vulnerable to self-harm in the first place. Once you do this, give yourself a break (if you're hard on yourself for self-harming). It's not your fault that you started self-harming. It is, however, up to you to help yourself stop.

IMPULSIVITY

- ꧂ Do you have a hard time delaying gratification (waiting for things you want)?

- ꧂ Do you have a hard time stopping yourself from doing things that you know will get you in trouble?

- ꧂ Do you seek out thrills or new activities?

- ꧂ Do you feel the need for a lot of stimulation and activity?

- ꧂ Do you often act on the spur of the moment without really thinking things through?

NEUROTICISM OR NEGATIVE EMOTIONS

- ꧂ Do you often feel that you're in a negative mood?

- ꧂ Are your negative moods really strong or intense?

- ꧂ Do you often feel depressed or sad?

- ꧂ Do you often feel irritated, angry, or agitated?

- ꧂ Do you feel stressed out a lot of the time?

- ꧂ Do you sometimes feel so stressed and tense that you don't know what to do?

- ꧂ Do you get stressed out about "little" things that other people don't get stressed about?

- ꧂ Do you often feel worn down by all the stresses in life?

CHILDHOOD EXPERIENCES

- ☘ Were you mistreated or abused when you were a child?

- ☘ Was your relationship with your parents distant or detached?

- ☘ Do you feel as if you never got the emotional support you needed as a child?

- ☘ When you were growing up, did you often experience harsh punishment?

WHY DO YOU KEEP HARMING YOURSELF?

We've gone through some of the things that can make you more likely to harm yourself in the first place, like your brain, biology, personality, and childhood experiences. But, what might keep you self-harming once you've started? We have some ideas about that as well.

Self-Harm Has Benefits

Probably, the most important reason that you keep harming yourself is that you get something out of it. Generally, people don't keep doing something unless they get something out of it. It's the same with self-harm. As it turns out, self-harm has certain benefits, or consequences, that make you more likely to keep harming yourself once you've tried it.

One of these benefits is *negative reinforcement*. Psychologists use the term *reinforcement* to describe anything that increases the chances that you'll behave the same way again in a similar situation. For example, let's say that you felt ashamed and rejected after your friend told you that she didn't want to have dinner with you, and you cut yourself and felt better. Well, because you felt better after cutting, you'll be more likely to do it again the next time your friend turns you down. That emotional relief (feeling better) *reinforced* the cutting behavior. When your self-harm helps you get rid of something unpleasant, *negative reinforcement* is at play.

We believe that negative reinforcement is the most important benefit that keeps self-harm going. In fact, it seems that people self-harm mainly because it provides relief from unwanted emotions, thoughts, situations, or sensations (Chapman, Gratz, and Brown 2006). As we discuss in chapter 5, by far, the most common reason people give for harming themselves is to get some relief from their emotions (Brown, Comtois, and Linehan 2002) or from unpleasant states of mind (Rodham, Hawton, and Evans 2004). People also often say that they self-harm in order to relax, control their racing thoughts, or feel relief from depression (Favazza and Conterio 1989).

And it's often true that, in the moment, self-harm makes you feel better (Chapman and Dixon-Gordon 2007; Laye-Gindhu and Schonert-Reichl 2005)! If you never felt any better after harming yourself, you probably wouldn't keep doing it. The problem is that, later on, the effects of self-harm aren't nearly as positive. When it comes to reinforcement, however, what happens right away (not later on) makes the most difference. Even though you might not like the long-term effects of self-harm (scarring, shame, and so on), the instant gratification keeps you hooked.

Although negative reinforcement plays an important role in self-harm, another reason that people might keep self-harming is *positive reinforcement*. With positive reinforcement, self-harm is more likely to happen again because it gets you something you want. And, some of the clients we work with have said that they feel excited, euphoric, or relaxed after harming themselves.

Other people's reactions to your self-harm can also positively or negatively reinforce self-harm. For instance, you might get positive reinforcement when people are kind, warm, or supportive, or if they pay attention to you after you harm yourself. People's reactions to you might also negatively reinforce your self-harm. If someone stops being mean or demanding after you harm yourself, this person might be negatively reinforcing your self-harm. Remember, negative reinforcement is when something is taken away or stopped (such as mean behavior or demands), whereas positive reinforcement is when something is added (such as warmth and support).

As an example, let's say you had a big fight with your partner, and afterward you felt ashamed, angry, or desperate. You also felt as if your partner really didn't understand how upset you were. And, to cope with these feelings, you harmed yourself. If you felt better afterward, that would be negative reinforcement. Another thing that might reinforce your self-harm is your partner's reaction. For example, if your partner rushed to your side and apologized, told you how much she or he cared about you, and was really warm, that could be positive reinforcement. So, even though you harmed yourself to get rid of your emotions, your partner's reaction can reinforce your self-harm as well—meaning that several different things can reinforce your self-harm all at once. No wonder self-harm is so hard to give up!

Of course, because self-harm can be so scary to others, many people will be alarmed and upset when you self-harm. Now, you might be thinking that if people get really upset with you, this might make you want to stop self-harming. Unfortunately, however, it doesn't always work that way. For example, one of us was working with a client, whom we'll call "Stacey," who felt emotionally neglected by her mother. Stacey's mother gave her plenty of money and "went through the motions" with her by being polite and respectful, but she never made much effort to spend time with her or ask her how she felt. After Stacey started self-harming, however, her mother was very upset and concerned. Even though Stacey found her mother's reactions annoying sometimes (like when she would yell or tell her to quit self-harming), these were signs that her mother cared about her. Also, her mother started to visit and call more often than she used to, and paid a lot more attention to how Stacey was doing. Therefore, simply by giving her the attention and caring she always craved, her mother's response once again *positively reinforced* Stacey's self-harm.

Self-Harm Loves Itself

As it turns out, the more you self-harm, the more likely you are to keep self-harming. One reason for this is that the longer you keep hurting yourself, the more you'll notice the benefits and ignore or minimize the downsides of self-harm. We'll talk about this more in chapter 6, but for now, suffice it to say that the longer you self-harm, the less concerned you become about the negative effects of self-harm. So, over time, you may become less concerned about scars, social disapproval, or how severely you harm yourself. What's more, the more you self-harm, the more you might notice or pay attention to the positive effects of self-harm. So, if you self-harm to feel better emotionally, the whole idea of feeling better emotionally becomes bigger and bigger, overshadowing any concern you might have about seriously harming yourself.

Thoughts Can Fuel Self-Harm

Beyond the actual effects of self-harm, certain types of thinking can drive self-harm as well. One important type of thinking is called *self-efficacy*. Self-efficacy has to do with your confidence in your own ability to do the things you need to do, cope with stress, or solve problems. If you have strong self-efficacy beliefs, then you believe that you can manage stress and solve your problems when they come up. If, however, you have weak self-efficacy beliefs, you might believe that you can't cope with or manage stress. Although there hasn't been much research on self-efficacy and self-harm, we've seen people who often self-harmed because they didn't believe that they could cope with some stressful event that was on the horizon.

> *Janice often felt like hurting herself before she had to do something stressful at work. Even though she was an excellent employee, whenever she knew her supervisor was going to shadow her and evaluate her performance, she felt terribly anxious. She was sure that she would mess up and fail, or be nervous and jittery. The fact that this never actually happened didn't change those fears one bit. Whenever those worrisome thoughts came up, Janice experienced strong urges to hurt herself, because she didn't believe that she could cope with the review. She also thought that harming herself would make it easier for her to be less nervous and anxious about her performance.*

A second thinking pattern is your confidence in your ability to actually harm yourself. When you believe that you can do something, you're much more likely to do it. If you believe that you can lift a hundred pounds, you're more likely to try it than if you believe you can't. Now, many people probably don't believe that they could actually take a knife and intentionally cut themselves. But, if you do believe that you can harm yourself, you may be more likely to try it.

Now, the more you harm yourself, the more confident you'll be in your ability to harm yourself (Joiner 2002). In this way, self-harm is just like any behavior. The more confident you are that you can step off that platform and high-dive, the more likely you'll be to do so. And, the more you get used to high-diving (or self-harming), the more confident you'll be that you can do it again.

A third important thinking pattern that can influence self-harm is what you expect will happen if you harm yourself. If you have positive expectations, you're more likely to harm yourself than if you have negative expectations. This makes sense, right? If you expect that you'll feel better, be better able to cope with stress, or feel excited after you harm yourself, you're probably more likely to do it. If, on the other hand, you believe that you'll feel humiliated or ashamed, or that you'll have unsightly scars, you might be less likely to harm yourself. The problem is that when people are upset, they pay more attention to the idea of feeling better than to all of the negative effects of self-harm.

Finally, some people think that another thinking pattern, involving negative thoughts about your body, increases the risk of self-harm (Shaw 2002; Walsh 2006). If you think negatively about your body, for example, by evaluating yourself as "fat," "ugly," or "disgusting," you might stop caring about what happens to your body, and you might be at greater risk of harming yourself (Muehlenkamp, Swanson, and Brausch 2005). Basically, if you don't care what happens to your body, it becomes a lot easier to harm yourself.

When you really think about this, it makes sense. Let's say you have an old car. It's not perfect, but it gets you around, has good power, and is cute. When you look at it, however, you think, "What an ugly car! I wish I had a better car." You're probably not going to care too much if you get rear-ended, the bumper falls off, or you accidentally scratch the door. On the other hand, if you really treasure your car, notice how cute it is, and feel thankful that it gets you around town, you might care more about what happens to it.

WHAT KEEPS YOU SELF-HARMING?

Answer the questions in each category with a yes or no. The things that keep self-harm going are different for different people. Answering these questions will help you figure out what might be perpetuating your self-harm. Pick the category with the most yes answers as a starting point in your efforts to stop your self-harm.

SELF-HARM HAS BENEFITS

- Do you feel better emotionally after you self-harm?

- Do other people give you attention or support after you self-harm?

- Do other people stop being demanding or doing things you don't like after you self-harm?

- Do you feel excited or happy after you self-harm?

- Do you feel calmer after you self-harm?

- Do you feel more capable of coping with stress after you self-harm?

SELF-HARM LOVES ITSELF

- Have you self-harmed for a long time?

- Are you less nervous about hurting yourself than you used to be?

- Do you notice the positive effects of self-harm more than you used to?

- Do you notice the positive effects of self-harm more than the negative effects?

- Do you care less about the scars than you used to?

- Do you care less about what other people think than you used to?

- Do you take more risks and hurt yourself more seriously than you used to?

WHAT CAN YOU DO ABOUT ALL OF THIS?

So far, we've explained some possible causes of self-harm. Of course, it's important to remember that there may be different causes for different people, and not everyone who self-harms is at risk for the same reasons. However, now that you know some of the most common causes of self-harm for a lot of people, the next question is what do you do about this?

Dealing with Your Biology

Well, when it comes to the biological factors, there are a few options. One option is medication (see chapter 9). The problem, however, is that there isn't a lot of good evidence for medication as a treatment for self-harm. A second option (if you get an endorphin rush when you self-harm) is to do some really intense exercise whenever you feel the urge to hurt yourself. Run, bike, or swim; or do push-ups, jumping jacks, or some other activity that might give you the endorphin rush that you get when you harm yourself.

A third option is to overcome your biology by learning how to manage your emotions, stop yourself from acting impulsively, or deal with stress. These are all things that you can learn in psychological therapy, and we discuss these different treatment options in chapter 8. We'll also give you a head start on coping with these biological factors in chapters 11 and 12, where we teach some effective ways of coping with stress and managing negative emotions.

The important thing to remember is that you can change your biology by changing your behavior. If you learn how to manage stress, your body won't react so strongly to difficulties in life. Learning how to deal with negative emotions and depression can also affect the chemical activity in your brain. So, just because some causes of self-harm might be biological doesn't mean that you can't change them.

Dealing with Childhood Experiences

When it comes to childhood experiences, the bad news is that you can't change those. Unfortunately, the world is simply not fair to some people, and (as much as you might want to) you can't just erase your history. The good news, though, is that you can learn to overcome the effects of your history. If childhood experiences made it hard to develop stable relationships, you can learn new skills for navigating relationships in the here and now. If nobody ever taught you how to manage your emotions, you can learn those skills now in therapy or by reading this book.

Another thing you can do is work with a therapist to come to terms with the painful experiences from your past. Some therapists are very good at helping people understand what happened to them in the past, make sense of their emotional reactions to these experiences, and move forward in new directions in the here and now. If you experienced trauma in your childhood and are still haunted by the memories of this experience, you might also want to try something called *exposure therapy*. In exposure therapy, your therapist helps you reexperience memories of your trauma in a safe environment. Over time, these memories become less and less threatening, until eventually they become more like other bad memories you have—painful and upsetting, but not disruptive to your life or traumatic to remember. Now, as much as exposure therapy can be incredibly helpful for people with past traumas, we strongly advise that you work on stopping your self-harm and learning new coping strategies before doing therapy focused on childhood trauma (particularly childhood sexual abuse). If you haven't learned other ways to cope with overwhelming emotions (besides self-harm), it could be very hard to avoid using self-harm to cope with all of the emotions that are bound to come up during this therapy.

Finally, if you learned to punish yourself, perhaps the first step you can take is to stop judging yourself when you think you've done something wrong. The next time you feel like calling yourself "bad" or "worthless," or find yourself saying things like you "should" be better in some way, catch yourself. Stop right there. Then, instead, describe specifically what it is you want to change, making sure to stick to the facts and be objective. Turn your judgments into preferences or goals. For example, if you say to yourself, "I am such a screwup with friends. I keep messing things up by being so sensitive about everything!" you could change this to, "I would like to be less sensitive to what my friends say [this would be your preference, or what you want]. If I work on that, things will go better [this would be the goal—to make things go better with friends]."

Of course, changing the way you talk to yourself takes a lot of hard work, and it's probably best to have a therapist to help you along the way. Here's an example of how this might work:

Mark had always had problems controlling his anger, but lately things had gotten worse. Not only was he fighting with his partner, but he also kept blowing up at his son for no reason at all. The last time, he felt so bad afterward that he couldn't stop thinking, "I'm such a terrible father!" That thought just kept swirling around and around in his head until he finally punished himself by cutting his hand. After working on this problem in therapy, though, Mark began to "catch" himself whenever he started to judge himself, and found a way to turn it around. For instance, instead of saying to himself, "I'm such a terrible father," he'd say, "I feel guilty for yelling at my son." When he thought, "I shouldn't be so screwed up and angry all the time," he'd say, "I want to learn how to manage my anger." When he changed these judgmental statements, Mark felt a lot less shame, was less interested in punishing himself, and actually began to work on managing his anger in healthy ways.

Winning the Tug-of-War with Emotional Relief

If emotional relief drives your self-harm, then one way around this is to learn how to manage your emotions effectively. As we've mentioned, many people harm themselves in order to cope with overwhelming emotional pain. If you harm yourself to get relief from your emotions or to feel better in some way, one way to stop self-harm is to learn other strategies for managing your emotions. We'll tell you more about some of these strategies in chapter 12.

Dealing with Other People's Reactions to Your Self-Harm

On the other hand, if other people's reactions reinforce your self-harm, one way to deal with this is to talk to those people and explain what might be happening. Now, it may sound weird to do this, but if the people around you are especially kind to you when you self-harm, you could ask them to cut it out—to stop being so nice when you hurt yourself. Now, this doesn't mean that you should ask them to be mean instead or to treat you poorly. That would cause even more problems for you. But, it might help if you told them not to be quite as warm or supportive, and not to pay quite as much attention to you after you hurt yourself. It would probably also help to explain why you're asking this of them, and to tell them that their kindness (although appreciated) could be inadvertently reinforcing your self-harm and making it harder to stop. In fact, we would encourage you to have them read this chapter (also, see chapter 10 for some guidance on how to talk with others about your self-harm).

Yet another way to deal with others' reactions is to learn how to get what you want from people in a way that doesn't involve hurting yourself. We've seen a lot of people get on the road to stopping self-harm after learning some interpersonal skills. If this is a problem for you, it's possible that you never had a chance to learn how to manage conflicts with other people or to ask for what you really want from others. Remember that your needs are perfectly valid; you may just have to get better at getting what you need. If you learn new skills in this area, they can make all the difference and might make it easier to begin giving up your self-harm.

Dealing with Thinking Patterns That Fuel Self-Harm

Finally, to change your thinking patterns, you'll need to practice new ways of thinking. For example, if you have many positive expectations about self-harm (such as, it'll make you feel better, excited, or relieved), one helpful strategy is to think of all the things you hate about self-harm and then put together a list (see chapter 10 for more instructions on how to do this, and for a work sheet you can use). The list might include things like ugly scars, shame, rejection by other people, humiliation, having to hide scars, and so on (see chapter 6 for more downsides of self-harm). Carry this list around with you, and take it out whenever you really want to harm yourself. Go through all of the downsides of harming yourself over and over in your mind. Over time, these downsides of self-harm will come to mind much more automatically, and being aware of them might help you resist your urges to harm yourself and do something else instead.

SUMMARY

- ❦ Your biology and personality can put you at risk for self-harm.

- ❦ Childhood experiences such as sexual or physical abuse, emotional or physical neglect, poor bonding with caregivers, or severe punishment can increase the risk for self-harm.

- ❦ Positive consequences, such as emotional relief or reactions from other people, can reinforce and maintain self-harm.

- ❦ The more you harm yourself, the easier it is to harm yourself, and the more you'll pay attention to the benefits of self-harm (and ignore the negative consequences).

🌺 Beliefs about your ability to cope, your ability to self-harm, the things that will happen if you harm yourself (such as positive consequences), and your body can all influence the chance of self-harm.

🌺 You can take action and overcome self-harm.

Now that you know more about some of the causes of self-harm, we will move on in the next chapter to talk about some of the problems that go along with self-harm. As you may know, self-harm often goes hand in hand with problems such as depression, anxiety, and drug and alcohol use. On the road to recovery, it's important to know about what else you might be dealing with along the way.

Chapter 4

Psychiatric Disorders That Often Accompany Self-Harm

Jen was struggling to stop her self-harm, but her sadness and depression just kept knocking her down. She'd dealt with depression since the age of sixteen, when her father had died, and she'd started harming herself at age seventeen. Back then, she found that self-harm distracted her from all of the negative thoughts about herself that came along with her depression. And, in the end, she was always at the greatest risk of harming herself when she was depressed. Even when she eventually got a handle on her self-harm and was able to go for weeks without hurting herself, she found it difficult not to resort to self-harm when overcome with depression.

As we mentioned, self-harm usually starts as a solution to other problems that people are struggling with, such as overwhelming emotions or relationship problems. Over time, though, self-harm can take on a life of its own, causing even more problems and exacerbating the very problems it was supposed to solve! It's almost as if you're walking around carrying a hundred-pound weight, and someone drops another hundred-pound weight on you (that's the self-harm). It becomes harder and harder to keep going with the weight of self-harm and your other problems sitting on top of you.

What kind of problem do people with self-harm often have? Well, as you'll read about below, people who self-harm often have other psychiatric problems that make life difficult for them. In this chapter, we'll tell you about some of the most common mental health problems that people with self-harm often struggle with, as well as the treatments for these problems.

PSYCHIATRIC DISORDERS AND SYMPTOMS THAT GO ALONG WITH SELF-HARM

Many (although certainly not all) people who self-harm have a psychiatric disorder of some kind. For example, you may have noticed that, in addition to self-harm, you also struggle with symptoms of depression or anxiety, post-traumatic stress, or BPD. If so, you've probably noticed that coping with the symptoms of psychiatric disorders on top of self-harm can be very overwhelming. The stress that comes along with depression or other disorders can make it even harder to resist urges to self-harm. In fact, if you struggle with symptoms of other psychiatric disorders, you might find that you sometimes harm yourself to relieve these symptoms (for example, to cope with anxiety or tension, calm your worried mind, or distract yourself from sadness or depression). Therefore, it's important to understand the disorders that often go along with self-harm. Below, we discuss the most common disorders among people who self-harm, possible reasons why people who self-harm sometimes have these disorders, and treatment options to consider.

Borderline Personality Disorder

By far, the disorder that most people think of when they hear "self-harm" is borderline personality disorder (BPD). And, there's good reason for this: as many as 75 percent of individuals with BPD harm themselves (Gunderson 2001; Linehan 1993a). Probably the best estimate is that about 25 percent of people who self-harm are diagnosable with BPD (Andover et al. 2005; Herpertz et al. 1995). So, why would there be such a strong relationship between self-harm and BPD?

SELF-HARM IS ONE OF THE CRITERIA FOR BPD

Well, one of the biggest reasons may be that self-harm is one of the criteria for BPD. Technically, there are nine criteria for BPD, and you have to have at least five of them in order to get the diagnosis. These criteria include:

- Frantic efforts to avoid abandonment

- Unstable relationships with other people

- Unstable or unclear identity

- Impulsive (spur of the moment) behavior that can be self-destructive

- Suicidal and self-harm behaviors

- Unstable emotions

- Chronic feelings of emptiness

- Very intense anger or difficulty controlling anger

- Dissociation (feeling spaced out or disconnected from your body or surroundings) or suspicious thoughts when you're under a lot of stress

Taken together, the criteria for BPD include instability in several areas of life. People with BPD struggle with their emotions, and often have chaotic and upsetting relationships with other people. They also sometimes struggle with their identities, not knowing exactly who they are or what they're like. Finally, people with BPD often struggle with their behavior, finding it difficult to control impulsive or self-destructive behaviors.

Because one of the criteria for BPD is repeated self-harm or suicidal behavior, it's not surprising that there's so much overlap between BPD and self-harm. Making self-harm one of the symptoms of BPD basically guarantees that many people with BPD will engage in self-harm. And, if you self-harm regularly, you already meet one of the criteria for BPD. Because BPD has nine criteria and it only takes five to get the diagnosis, you only need four more. Therefore, people who self-harm are one step closer to being diagnosed with BPD than people who don't.

PROBLEMS WITH EMOTION REGULATION

Of course, another reason for the link between BPD and self-harm has to do with how people manage their emotions. Much like people who self-harm, people with BPD have difficulty managing their emotions. When they're upset, they often have no idea how to make themselves feel better. And, people with BPD seem to be more emotional than the average person to begin with (Levine, Marziali, and Hood 1997). Therefore, people with BPD often experience intensely painful emotions that feel scary, uncontrollable, and threatening.

This combination of being a really emotional person and not knowing how to manage emotions is a lot like being behind the wheel of a powerful car with no brakes. And, for some people, self-harm becomes an emergency brake that they can pull whenever they start hurtling out of control. Because self-harm can work so well to relieve emotional pain, people may come to rely on it whenever they feel overwhelmed or out of control.

So, what does this have to do with the link between BPD and self-harm? Well, people with BPD and people who self-harm seem to have these problems managing their emotions in common. Both groups of people struggle with their emotions and have a hard time finding healthy ways to manage emotional pain. In fact, we believe that one of the things that people with BPD and those who self-harm have in common is the tendency to want to avoid or escape their emotions (Chapman, Gratz, and Brown 2006).

Now, even though self-harm and BPD often go hand in hand, many people still make the mistaken assumption that everyone who self-harms must have BPD. The knee-jerk diagnosis of BPD for anyone who self-harms is illogical and potentially harmful. It's like saying, "*Some* animals with four legs are dogs, so I'm going to assume that *every* animal with four legs is a dog." As you can imagine, this could be a very dangerous assumption if it caused someone to adopt a polar bear as a pet! And, as we mentioned, this assumption is simply not accurate. In fact, most studies find that fewer than 50 percent of people who self-harm meet criteria for BPD. So, therapists who assume that anyone who self-harms must have BPD will be wrong more often than not. And, this assumption can lead to misdiagnosis and inappropriate treatment. Whether or not you meet criteria for BPD, knowing one way or another will help you find the right treatment for your self-harm.

EFFECTIVE TREATMENTS FOR BPD

As we describe in our book, *The Borderline Personality Disorder Survival Guide: Everything You Need to Know About Living with BPD* (New Harbinger Publications, 2007), there are effective treatments for people with BPD, and just having BPD doesn't mean that you'll struggle with this disorder for life.

So far, the treatment with the best evidence for BPD is *dialectical behavior therapy* (DBT; Linehan 1993a). We'll tell you more about DBT in chapter 8. For now, you just need to know that DBT involves a combination of individual and group therapy, and teaches you skills to regulate your emotions, tolerate distress, deal with other people, and be aware of the present moment. Because DBT is based on the idea that BPD and self-harm are related to difficulties in managing emotions, clients are taught a variety of skills for managing their emotions.

In addition to DBT, other treatments for BPD have also shown good effects. In particular, *mentalization-based treatment* (MBT; Bateman and Fonagy 1999, 2001, and 2008) has been found to be effective in treating BPD and in helping people with BPD stop self-harm. We'll tell you more about MBT in chapter 8. Other treatments, such as schema-focused therapy (Young 1994) and transference-focused psychotherapy (Clarkin et al. 2007), have also been found to help people with BPD. Although these treatments are newer and have less research to back them up, the great news is that now there's a variety of different approaches that can help people with BPD.

Post-Traumatic Stress Disorder

When Jen was younger, her father had struggled with alcohol problems, and physically and sexually abused her. She was burdened for many years with nightmares, flashbacks, and the pervasive sense that she was somehow to blame for what her father had done to her. In addition to helping with her depression, Jen found that self-harm sometimes made it easier to cope with her symptoms related to

*childhood trauma. For instance, when she blamed herself for
what happened, she often felt as if self-harm were a good punishment,
giving her what she "deserved." She also found that self-harm
quickly cut off intrusive thoughts and memories of the abuse.
Because self-harm helped her to cope with depression and
post-traumatic stress, it was very hard for her to stop.*

Another psychiatric disorder that's quite common among people who self-harm is *post-traumatic stress disorder* (*PTSD*). About 50 percent of individuals who have PTSD report that they've harmed themselves at some point in their lives (Cloitre et al. 2002). PTSD is a disorder that occurs after a person experiences a *traumatic event.* Although many people use the term "trauma" to refer to any distressing or upsetting event, the *DSM-IV* (the manual used by psychiatrists and psychologists to diagnose mental health problems) has a specific definition of the term "traumatic event" that's somewhat different from how most people think about it. According to the *DSM-IV*, a traumatic event occurs when someone experiences a serious threat to her or his own safety or well-being (or witnesses another person experiencing such a threat or serious harm) and, as a result, experiences feelings of fear, helplessness, or horror (American Psychiatric Association 1994).

Now, many people who experience a traumatic event find a way to cope and move forward with their lives without developing PTSD. Some people, however, experience lasting symptoms for months or even years after a traumatic event. Some of these symptoms include:

- Avoiding all thoughts and memories of the trauma

- Avoiding places or people that remind you of the traumatic event

- Having intrusive memories that keep coming back over and over again

- Feeling emotionally numb

- Having a difficult time falling or staying asleep

- Feeling constantly "on guard," or as if danger is lurking around every corner

- Being "jumpy," or easily startled

🌿 Having nightmares or *flashbacks* (feeling as if the experience is happening all over again) about the traumatic event

🌿 Dissociating

As we mentioned in chapter 3, many people who harm themselves have experienced physical, sexual, or emotional abuse in childhood. And, these types of experiences can be very traumatic and may sometimes result in PTSD (especially if the abuse was prolonged, repeated, or perpetrated by a caregiver). Therefore, it's not surprising that there's some overlap between PTSD and self-harm.

For people who have PTSD, self-harm can be a way to relieve unwanted or overwhelming emotions and experiences related to the traumatic event. For instance, if you have PTSD, you might find that self-harm stops intrusive thoughts about the traumatic events that you've experienced, relieves painful trauma-related emotions, or soothes you when you have nightmares or flashbacks. Remember when we mentioned that some people harm themselves to snap out of a dissociative state? Well, dissociation is common among people with PTSD, and self-harm might help stop those symptoms as well.

Because self-harm and PTSD have some of the same risk factors and causes (for example, childhood abuse) and because self-harm can be so helpful (in the short term) in coping with PTSD symptoms, it's not surprising that many people with PTSD turn to self-harm to cope.

SELF-HARM CAN MAKE IT HARDER TO RECOVER FROM PTSD

Now, although self-harm might provide temporary relief from the painful symptoms of PTSD in the short run, it can actually make things worse in the long run. You can think of it in this way. People with PTSD are basically afraid of three things:

1. Memories of the traumatic event, which they experience as frightening and disturbing

2. Certain people, places, and situations that remind them of the traumatic event

3. Painful emotions that are associated with the traumatic event

Now, if these memories, feelings, or people and places aren't actually dangerous (that is, if you're not likely to be harmed by them right now), your fear is what we might call a "false alarm." This means that you feel afraid, but there's no real threat to you in the moment.

Well, as it turns out, the best way to overcome this type of fear is to expose yourself to the thing you're afraid of over and over again until you realize that nothing bad is happening to you. What you'll notice is that the longer you stay in contact with something that scares you (or keep yourself in touch with your disturbing memories or feelings) without anything terrible happening to you, the more your fear will lessen. This lessening of your fear is called *habituation*, which means that your body is getting used to the frightening situation or object.

The problem is that keeping yourself in the frightening situation is probably the last thing in the world you want to do. You'd probably rather avoid your thoughts and memories, stay away from people or places that frighten you, or otherwise escape your feelings of terror, agitation, and pain. And, self-harm is another way to escape your feelings. If you self-harm to get rid of your fear (or if you avoid places, people, and memories), you interfere with the habituation process, basically keeping the fear alive, so that you feel just as afraid the next time you're in that situation. The memories, painful feelings, people, and places will remain just as scary and powerful. In this way, self-harm can actually interfere with recovery from PTSD.

EFFECTIVE TREATMENTS FOR PTSD

If you have PTSD, the good news is that some very good treatments are available. Generally, the research shows that the best treatment for PTSD is a type of *cognitive behavioral therapy* (*CBT*) called *prolonged exposure*. Prolonged exposure has the client repeatedly reexperience the memories of the trauma in a safe environment (like a therapist's office). After this type of treatment, people often feel less afraid, have fewer nightmares and flashbacks, and stop avoiding people and places (Foa, Keene, and Friedman 2004).

Usually, CBT also includes *cognitive therapy*. In cognitive therapy, you and the therapist spend time figuring out what types of thinking patterns might be contributing to your PTSD symptoms. Some of these thinking patterns include constant mistrust of other people, negative thoughts about yourself, fears that you're in danger or that you'll be victimized, among other types of thoughts. In cognitive therapy, you first work to become aware of your thoughts, and then you work on changing your ways of thinking about things that don't seem to be working so well for you. The research on cognitive therapy, however, says that if you only do cognitive therapy (without exposure therapy), you might not get as many benefits as you would if you also did exposure therapy (see Resick and Calhoun 2001).

You also may have heard of other types of treatment for PTSD. One of these treatments is called *eye movement desensitization and reprocessing* (*EMDR*; Shapiro and Forrest 1997). In EMDR, you basically go through prolonged exposure to memories of trauma while watching the therapist's fingers as she or he moves them laterally back and forth. The idea is that certain types of eye movements can make exposure therapy work better. In several studies, however, researchers found that EMDR actually works no better than prolonged exposure therapy itself (Bradley et al. 2005; Taylor et al. 2003). And, these findings have led many researchers to believe that the eye movements in EMDR may not actually be necessary.

If you're looking for treatment for PTSD, keep in mind that it's generally a good idea to work on stopping your self-harm before you begin to dive into memories of your trauma. This is because getting into these memories can be very emotionally overwhelming. And, if you haven't yet learned the skills to deal with overwhelming emotions, what do you think you'll feel like doing when you're emotionally overwhelmed? Exactly, you'll probably feel like harming yourself, because you've found that it works so well to make you feel better.

Now, that's not to say that you can't start treatment for PTSD until you've completely given up self-harm, but it's best to be cautious about this. In particular, Dr. Marsha Linehan (who developed DBT) has said that it's best to avoid addressing childhood sexual abuse until you've stopped harming yourself (or stopped attempting suicide, if that's something you do as well) and learned other ways of managing your emotions (Linehan 1993a). Our book can give you a jump start on learning skills to manage your emotions when you read chapter 12.

Depression

Self-harm is also related to depression and its symptoms (Klonsky, Oltmanns, and Turkheimer 2003). *Major depressive disorder* (*MDD*) involves having the following symptoms for two weeks or longer:

- Sadness and emptiness

- Changes in appetite, weight, or both

- Sleep problems

- Concentration difficulties

- Feelings of worthlessness and hopeless thoughts about the future

- Loss of pleasure in activities

- Low motivation and energy

- Thoughts about death or dying

- Suicidal thoughts

One reason we think depression is related to self-harm is simply that people who are depressed struggle with emotional distress and upsetting thoughts. And, self-harm can be one coping strategy for dealing with these experiences. Self-harm might distract you from your worries or negative thinking, or temporarily alleviate your sadness or emptiness.

Also, people who are depressed often think that they're deeply flawed or worthless, and this type of thinking can sometimes trigger self-harm. Remember when we mentioned in chapter 3 that people sometimes self-harm to punish themselves? Well, sometimes depression comes with an overwhelming feeling of self-loathing. As a result, if you're depressed and have these feelings, you might feel the desire to punish yourself by harming yourself.

There's also some evidence that the biological factors involved in depression may play a role in self-harm as well. As we mentioned in chapter 3, there's evidence for problems in the brain's serotonin system among depressed people and people who self-harm. You may remember that serotonin is a neurotransmitter that regulates mood, hunger, temperature, sexual activity, sleep, and aggression, among other things. Well, low levels of serotonin activity are related to depression and emotional distress. Therefore, it's possible that another common link between self-harm and depression is a problem in the serotonin system.

EFFECTIVE TREATMENTS FOR DEPRESSION

Unlike with PTSD, there's no reason to wait until you've stopped self-harming to get treatment for your depression. We still suggest that you make stopping self-harm your highest priority. But, there's nothing dangerous about getting treatment for depression if you're still harming yourself at times, and in fact, if your depression improves, you might find it easier to stop your self-harm.

Fortunately, there are several very effective treatments for depression. The treatment that's been studied the most is cognitive therapy (Beck et al. 1979), or cognitive behavioral therapy (CBT). As mentioned previously, cognitive therapy involves modifying thoughts that are causing you problems in life. So, in cognitive therapy for depression, you and your therapist work on changing negative thoughts about yourself, the world, and other people. You might also tackle feelings of worthlessness, which might be related to the thought that you're flawed, unlovable, or incapable as a person.

Another big part of CBT for depression is *behavioral activation*. Behavioral activation involves getting active to overcome depression. Basically, the goal is to get yourself more and more involved in activities that you enjoy and that make you feel capable.

In fact, since the early nineties, researchers have found that the behavioral activation part of CBT works so well that many people don't even have to focus on changing their thoughts (Dimidjian et al. 2006; Jacobson et al. 1996). Instead, just changing your behavior can change both your mood and your thoughts, and reduce your depression. A recent study actually showed that behavioral activation alone is just as good as antidepressant medication and better than cognitive therapy for people who are severely depressed (Dimidjian et al. 2006).

Another effective treatment for depression is *interpersonal therapy* (*IPT*; Weissman, Markowitz, and Klerman 2000). Unlike cognitive therapy or behavioral activation, IPT doesn't focus on helping you change your thoughts or behaviors. Instead, it focuses on helping you change your relationships. IPT is based on the idea that depression is caused by problems in your relationships, such as a lack of relationships, conflict with others, a lack of social support, grief over the loss of someone who has died, or difficulty managing changes in roles (for example, becoming a spouse or a parent, or dealing with life after divorce). In IPT, you and your therapist work on addressing these relationship problems in order to improve your life and reduce your depression. So far, the studies have shown that IPT is probably just as effective as cognitive therapy, especially for people who have severe depression (Parker et al. 2006).

Eating Disorders

Another set of disorders that's common among people who harm themselves is eating disorders. In one study, around 44 percent of people who self-harmed also had an eating disorder of some sort (Zlotnick, Mattia, and Zimmerman 1999). As you may already know, there are several different types of eating disorders: anorexia nervosa, bulimia nervosa, and eating disorders not otherwise specified. People who have anorexia nervosa restrict food intake to prevent weight gain. Folks with bulimia nervosa binge-eat (eat an extraordinarily large amount of food at one time) and then attempt to get rid of the calories by vomiting, using laxatives, or exercising to the extreme.

Now, you might be wondering why eating disorders might sometimes go hand in hand with self-harm. Well, there are several probable reasons for this.

DIFFICULTY MANAGING EMOTIONS

The first reason is that people who self-harm and those with eating disorders both have difficulty managing their emotions. Indeed, bingeing and purging are often ways to cope with overwhelming emotions. Eating is, in fact, one of the most common things that people do to soothe themselves. People who self-harm and people who have bulimia nervosa seem to have a very hard time managing their emotions when they're upset. As a result, they resort to coping strategies that feel soothing in the moment but have major downsides in the long run.

BODY DISSATISFACTION

A second reason for the overlap between self-harm and eating disorders is that people who self-harm and people with eating disorders often are dissatisfied with their bodies. As we mentioned in chapter 3, one problem that can contribute to self-harm is negative thinking about your body shape or weight. If you don't care about your body or if you hate your body, it can be a lot easier to harm yourself. And, not surprisingly, negative thoughts about body shape and weight play a major role in eating disorders as well, contributing to restricting and purging behaviors. People who are dissatisfied with their bodies or think that they're fat are much more likely to starve themselves to lose weight. And, people who binge-eat to soothe themselves are much more likely to purge if they're dissatisfied with their bodies or afraid of gaining weight.

SENSE OF CONTROL

A third thing that people who self-harm have in common with those with eating disorders is the desire for a sense of control. One fundamental need that all of us humans have is the need to feel in control of at least some aspects of our lives. Because feeling as if you have absolutely no control can be so scary and distressing, many people will go to great lengths to try to gain some sense of control. And, engaging in self-harm and restricting food intake are two ways to do just that.

Indeed, people often say that when they self-harm, they feel a sense of control. For instance, maybe one of the only things you feel that you can control in your life is when, how, and how much you hurt yourself. If your emotions, relationships, and life in general feel as if they're spinning out of control, doing something that feels completely under your control (like self-harm) might be one way of giving yourself a small sense of power and capability.

We've had clients tell us that even though they may not be able to control their feelings or the way other people treat them, at least they can control how they harm themselves. One of the primary reasons why self-harm may work so well to provide a sense of control is that many people would find it incredibly hard to intentionally inflict physical damage on themselves. As a result, self-harm can feel like something that most people would never be able to do. And, feeling as if you have the strength and determination to do something that most people would be terrified to do could definitely make you feel powerful and in control.

It can be quite similar with food restriction. People who restrict their food intake often say that they feel a sense of control from doing this. When they feel as if everything else in their lives is out of control, they can at least control when and how much they eat. And, because refusing to eat is usually a very hard thing to do (especially since we all need food in order to live), restricting food intake can make people feel very powerful and in control.

Of course, the problem is that this sense of control over self-harm and food restriction is actually an illusion. Over time, both restricting and self-harm behaviors can take on a life of their own, and if you engage in these behaviors, the desire to restrict your eating or to hurt yourself may very well start to control you (rather than the other way around).

In summary, there are three characteristics that people who self-harm and people with an eating disorder often have in common, which might explain why self-harm and eating disorders often go hand in hand. These include:

- Difficulties regulating emotions

- Body dissatisfaction

- Desire for a sense of control

TREATMENTS FOR EATING DISORDERS

Different treatments have been found to be helpful for different types of eating disorders. For bulimia nervosa, the most common treatment is CBT. There have been over fifty studies of CBT for bulimia nervosa, and the findings have been quite encouraging. For instance, people generally experience about an 80 percent reduction in bingeing and purging throughout treatment, and by the end of treatment, about 40 to 50 percent of people stop bingeing and purging entirely (Wilson, Grilo, and Vitousek 2007).

In CBT for bulimia nervosa, your therapist helps you do several things:

- Change thoughts about your body that set you up to purge

- Establish regular eating patterns and eliminate dieting

- Become less afraid of certain foods (such as desserts or high-fat foods)

- Manage emotions and solve problems in life more effectively

- Prevent relapses, or times when you resort back to old patterns of bingeing or purging

Another promising treatment for bulimia nervosa and binge-eating disorder is DBT. Because DBT aims to help people manage their emotions effectively, researchers thought that it might be a good fit for people who binge-eat. Studies of a group-based DBT (involving the skills group but no individual therapy) found very good results for people with binge-eating or bulimia nervosa, with up to 89 percent of the clients stopping binge-eating by the end of treatment (Safer, Telch, and Agras 2001; Telch, Agras, and Linehan 2001). Now, the good news about this is that DBT is also one of the best treatments for self-harm, so if you struggle with bulimia nervosa or binge-eating disorder and self-harm, you might be able to tackle both of these problems at once by entering DBT.

CBT is also one of the most common treatments for anorexia nervosa (Bulik et al. 2007). In addition, there's good evidence that family-based treatments work well for adolescents with anorexia nervosa (Eisler et al. 2000; Geist et al. 2000; Robin et al. 1994; Robin, Siegel, and Moye 1995). Usually, the main focus of treatments for anorexia nervosa is on normalizing weight, improving self-esteem, dealing with thoughts about one's body, and helping with interpersonal or family problems. Although the treatments for anorexia nervosa aren't quite as promising as those for bulimia nervosa, studies have found that as many as 40 to 60 percent of clients return to a normal weight following treatment.

Substance-Use Disorders

Finally, substance-use disorders are also common among people who self-harm, with about 52 percent of people who self-harm meeting criteria for a substance-use disorder (Zlotnick, Mattia, and Zimmerman 1999). There are two basic types of substance-use disorders: substance abuse and substance dependence. If you have *substance abuse*, this means that your use of a particular substance (like alcohol or drugs) causes problems in your life. For instance, drinking might lead to fights with people you're close to, or drug use might make it hard to keep a job.

Substance dependence is more like what we think of as "addiction." Substance dependence basically means that you're hooked on a substance and that you have at least some of the following experiences:

- ❧ You have a hard time stopping yourself from using drugs or alcohol.

- ❧ You think a lot about using or put a lot of effort into planning to use drugs or alcohol.

- ❧ You have uncomfortable symptoms when you stop using (withdrawal symptoms).

- ❧ You develop a stronger tolerance for the substance over time so that it takes more and more of the drug or alcohol to get you high.

Now, why would so many people who self-harm also have problems with drugs and alcohol? Well, much like eating disorders and BPD, people with substance-use disorders and people who self-harm all seem to have problems managing their emotions. And, just like self-harm, drugs and alcohol are powerful ways to feel better emotionally in the moment. So, if you don't know any other way to relieve your emotional pain, you might resort to drugs, alcohol, or self-harm. The desire to get away from emotional pain is perfectly normal. It's just that people who self-harm or use drugs often haven't learned any other ways to feel better.

TREATMENTS FOR SUBSTANCE-USE PROBLEMS

If you struggle with substance-use problems, the good news is that there are several helpful treatments. The treatment that may be best for you depends a bit on what kind of drug or alcohol problems you have. For instance, if you're hooked on heroin or other opiate drugs (such as morphine or oxycodone), it might be very helpful for you to take what's called an "opiate replacement medication," like methadone. This is because the withdrawal symptoms that accompany opiate use are especially severe, and people often go back to using drugs just to get rid of these symptoms. Opiate replacement medications help you get rid of withdrawal symptoms, but don't give you the same kind of high that the real drugs give you.

Generally, researchers recommend that if you're dependent on drugs or alcohol, it's best to get psychological treatment in addition to medication treatment. There are many different psychological treatments, but the ones with the best evidence are the following:

Cognitive Behavioral Therapy (CBT): (1) Helps you change the thinking patterns that set you up to use drugs; (2) teaches you skills to manage your emotions, deal with other people, refuse alcohol and drugs, and solve problems in your life; and (3) teaches you to identify and manage factors that might set you up to relapse.

Motivational Enhancement: (1) Helps you get motivated to stop using drugs, and (2) helps you develop an action plan for quitting.

Relapse Prevention: Helps you avoid relapses by (1) teaching you coping skills to manage high-risk situations (situations where you're in danger of using drugs or drinking) and urges to use, (2) teaching you how to think differently about relapse (by not seeing it as a failure but, rather, a slipup), and (3) helping you avoid high-risk situations.

Other treatments can help too. For instance, people often find 12-step programs like Alcoholics Anonymous quite helpful. In addition, there's evidence that DBT is helpful for substance-use disorders. So, if you have BPD, this might be a very good option for you.

SUMMARY

- Several different psychiatric disorders often go along with self-harm, sometimes making it even harder to stop harming yourself.

- Some of the most common disorders that accompany self-harm are borderline personality disorder, post-traumatic stress disorder, depression, eating disorders, and substance-use disorders.

🌿 There are effective treatments for each of these disorders.

🌿 Be cautious about actively addressing past trauma before you have a handle on your self-harm and have learned other coping skills for dealing with your emotions.

In this chapter, we reviewed some of the psychiatric disorders that most commonly accompany self-harm. We hope that this information will help you get the help you need. In the next chapter, we talk a lot more about exactly why people seem to harm themselves, focusing mainly on what needs or purposes self-harm seems to serve.

Chapter 5

The Many Purposes of Self-Harm: Why People Harm Themselves

Susan knew she needed to stop cutting herself. Every time she did it, she told herself it would never happen again. And yet, each time, within only a few days she found herself being drawn to her razor like a moth to a flame. Even though she knew she'd regret it and feel even worse about herself afterward, this didn't seem to matter in the moment. When she was really stressed out or lonely, all she could think about was how much better she'd feel if she cut herself. And for some reason, that promise of relief, albeit short lived, was all she could see.

So far, we've given you a lot of the facts about self-harm. We've explained what self-harm is and isn't, the kinds of problems that tend to go along with self-harm, and some of the things that may cause people to start harming themselves. In this chapter, we discuss why people harm themselves. In particular, we tell you about some of the most common reasons people give for harming themselves, and explain what exactly it is that people seem to get out of self-harm.

If you don't harm yourself (or even if you do), why people harm themselves might be one of the biggest mysteries of all. In some ways, self-harm seems to go against one of the most basic human drives: self-preservation. Human beings spend a lot of time and energy trying to feel safe, protected, and comfortable. And, on the surface, self-harm seems to be the opposite of this, in that it involves intentionally causing tissue damage. In fact, we think this is one reason self-harm can be so confusing and alarming to others.

Yet, even though it may appear as though self-harm goes against the drive for self-preservation, things aren't always as they seem. As we discussed in chapter 2, self-harm can actually help people meet some basic human needs—including the need to feel comfortable and protected. In fact, as we discuss below, people often say that self-harm makes them feel better, calmer, and more at peace with themselves (at least in the moment).

COMMON FUNCTIONS OF SELF-HARM

So, what purposes does self-harm serve? What needs does it help people meet? Below, we discuss some of the most common reasons people give for harming themselves.

To Feel Better

Since the late 1990s, a lot of studies have asked people why they harm themselves, and the single most common reason they give is to feel better in some way. For many people, one of the main things that makes stopping self-harm so difficult is that they feel so much better right after they harm themselves. In fact, feeling better emotionally is one of those basic human needs we mentioned before. All people need some way to help themselves feel better, and no one wants emotional pain to persist forever. And, despite its downsides in the long run, self-harm is very good at relieving emotional distress in the short run. For people in tremendous amounts of emotional pain, this quick-acting and virtually guaranteed relief can be a powerful force that keeps them harming themselves.

Now, the reasons why self-harm makes people feel better aren't completely clear. However, we do have some ideas about why self-harm may work in this way.

DISTRACTION

One reason is that self-harm may distract you from emotional pain. In particular, it seems to be the physical pain or damage to the body that results from self-harm that's most distracting. It's as if the sudden pain, or the sight of tissue damage or blood, grabs your attention and takes it away from what was upsetting you. As an example, let's say you were feeling really upset and couldn't stop thinking about a fight you just had with your parents. All of a sudden, you trip over a shoe on the floor and bang your shin on the coffee table. In that moment, the pain in your leg probably captures all of your attention and distracts you from your thoughts and feelings about the fight. For that moment, all you can focus on is the pain in your leg. Well, for some people, self-harm works just like this. And, even for people who don't experience pain when they harm themselves, the sight of blood or other aspects of their self-harm may still capture their attention. And, no matter what it is about self-harm that may distract you, when your attention is focused on something other than what upset you, you'll feel much less upset.

EXPRESS FEELINGS

Self-harm can also help people feel better by helping them to express feelings that they can't otherwise express. Many clients we've worked with have described experiencing such intense emotional distress that they just can't put it into words. It's as if their pain is so intense that words just don't seem to do it justice. In fact, some clients have told us that trying to put their pain into words just seems to minimize it, which makes them feel even worse. So, what does this have to do with self-harm? Well, for some people, an extreme action like self-harm seems to be the best way to express an intense emotional experience. It's as if the visible damage to their skin portrays their pain more completely and vividly than words ever could. In this way, some people believe that harming themselves allows them to express their emotions more fully than they ever could through words alone. For this reason, self-harm can be a way of expressing pain. And one thing we know about coping in general is that expressing and communicating emotional pain can help alleviate or lessen that pain.

RELEASE NEGATIVE EMOTIONS AND TENSION

Another way self-harm can make you feel better is by providing a release valve for overwhelming tension and negative emotions. When people who experience intense emotions don't have a way of expressing those emotions, they can start to feel like a pressure cooker with a defective regulator on top. It's as if all of the energy that goes along with their feelings stays bottled up inside until they feel as if they're going to burst. For some people, this can create such an unbearable feeling of tension that they'd do just about anything to escape it. And self-harm can be one way of releasing that tension. It's like opening the relief valve on the pressure cooker; the steam is released and your tension floats away.

In fact, in some ways, self-harm is similar to some medical treatments for infections. When you get a bug bite, the site of that bite can become inflamed as your body tries to fight the infection. This can result in a buildup of fluid under the skin. Eventually, that fluid needs to be released, and some treatments involve *lancing* the bite area, or cutting or puncturing the wound so that the fluid has a way of getting out. The idea behind this type of treatment is that the buildup of fluid isn't healthy, and therefore needs to be released from the body.

In the same way, some people experience the buildup of their emotions as so unpleasant and intense that they desperately try to find some way to release that tension. And, in the moment, self-harm can be a very powerful and effective way of doing just that.

To Make Emotional Pain Clearer and More Tangible

Many people who self-harm describe experiencing such overwhelming emotional pain that they have no idea exactly what they're feeling. It's as if all of their emotions have jumbled together to form a big ball, and there's no way to disentangle them and figure out what they are. The problem is that not knowing what you're feeling can actually make your emotions more overwhelming and distressing. Having *emotional clarity*, or knowing exactly what emotions you're feeling, can actually make your emotions seem more manageable. In fact, one important skill for regulating your emotions is labeling and describing those emotions. When people haven't learned this skill and only know that they feel "bad" or "awful," it can be even harder to manage those feelings or figure out how to make themselves feel better.

So, how does self-harm fit into this picture? Well, some people say that when they see the damage on their skin, it's as if the pain inside them has now been brought outside and put directly on their skin. The cuts, bruises, or burn marks, for example, are external symbols of their internal torment. Because these types of marks are tangible and concrete (unlike emotions, which you can't see or touch), the emotional pain that was swirling around inside of them becomes more clear, concrete, and focused. If you've had this experience, you may have noticed that your emotions feel more manageable when they're clearer and more concrete. It's as if knowing what you're feeling and "seeing" your emotions in front of you makes it easier to deal with them. In fact, this is probably one of the reasons why it helps people to write down how they feel. By writing down your feelings, you take your emotions from inside and put them directly onto paper, where they probably seem more clear, organized, and easier to deal with.

To Punish Oneself

Now, this reason might seem to be almost the opposite of the other reasons we've discussed. To some of you, punishing yourself might seem to be something that would make you feel worse, right? Well, this may be true for some people, but for others, self-punishment can actually lessen emotional pain. People who say that they harm themselves to punish themselves often talk about experiencing incredibly intense guilt and shame. They may blame themselves for problems they have or terrible things that they've been through in the past. And this shame and guilt can be incredibly difficult to tolerate. In fact, some research indicates that intense shame is one of the most painful and intolerable feelings people can have (Tangney and Dearing 2002).

So, what does this have to do with self-punishment? Well, when people who are experiencing a lot of shame and guilt punish themselves, those feelings sometimes disappear (or at least lessen) for a short time. One way to understand this is to think about the criminal justice system. When people commit a serious crime, they're often punished by being incarcerated for a certain period of time. At the end of that time, they are released, and are considered to have "done their time." By accepting the punishment, it's as if they're absolved of their crimes and allowed to move forward in their lives. Self-punishment works in a similar way for some people. It's as if by punishing themselves, they're absolving themselves of all the things they believe they've done wrong. And, what better way to punish oneself than to engage in self-harm?

Of course, the problem with using self-harm to punish yourself is that the relief you feel from your guilt and shame will usually be fairly short lived. This means that you might have to punish yourself over and over again. In the moment, though, right after you've harmed yourself, you may feel a temporary reprieve from shame and guilt, sort of as if you've "set things right." And, like the other reasons for self-harm we've already discussed, immediate relief from painful emotions can make you more likely to self-harm again in the future.

To End Dissociation

Some people say that they self-harm to end episodes of dissociation. You'll recall that dissociation is the experience of being disconnected from the present moment, your body, or your surroundings. It often involves the experience of being "checked out," spaced out, in a foggy mental state, not aware of your surroundings, or feeling as if you're not inside your body. Some people describe feeling as if they're floating to the ceiling and looking down on their bodies and the people around them. In more extreme cases, dissociation can involve a complete break with the here and now. For instance, dissociation can take the form of flashbacks, which involve feeling as if a traumatic experience is happening all over again.

Now, dissociation is sometimes used as a way of coping with emotional distress in the moment. Just like self-harm, dissociation can allow you to temporarily avoid or escape emotional pain by "checking out" or mentally "leaving" the present moment. The problem is that dissociation can take on a life of its own and become more and more automatic, to such an extent that you might begin to feel as if you're always disconnected from yourself and the world around you. At that point, dissociation can become very uncomfortable and distressing, so much so that you might be desperate for a way to end it.

Unfortunately, though, dissociation isn't always that easy to end. Especially when it's severe or takes the form of a flashback, people find it hard to bring themselves back to the here and now. Self-harm, however, is one way that seems to work. Because self-harm can involve physical pain, it can capture people's attention and bring them back to the present moment. And, some people find that self-harm is the thing that ends their dissociation most quickly.

To Get a Rush or a High

Up until now, we've mainly been talking about self-harm as a way to get away from unwanted emotions, but sometimes this behavior can also be a way to feel emotions that you want to feel. For some people, self-harm provides a "high" or a "rush" that can be very exciting or even invigorating. Now, we don't know exactly why self-harm provides a high for some people, but one possible explanation is that cutting yourself or inflicting intense pain can cause a rush of endorphins, your body's natural pain-relieving chemicals. Endorphins are released into the brain after strenuous exercise or when your body gets hurt. And, when they're released, they can result in a natural high. For example, long-distance runners often describe a rush after running long distances, referred to as a "runner's high." Just like the high or rush produced by drugs, however, the natural high produced by endorphins can be addictive, making people more likely to harm themselves again in the future.

To Communicate to Other People

Finally, another common purpose of self-harm is to communicate something to other people. As we mentioned before, some people who harm themselves have difficulty expressing their feelings, or struggle to put their emotional pain into words. Other people who self-harm aren't sure how to open up emotionally to other people, or worry that doing so will make them too vulnerable to being hurt. And still others have tried to communicate how they feel, only to find that people ignore or dismiss what they're saying, invalidate their feelings, or don't understand them. In all of these cases, it can be really difficult to communicate your feelings and needs to other people.

Of course, the problem is that human beings are naturally social beings, and we all have the need to communicate with others. Feeling invalidated or misunderstood is very distressing, and many people will go to great lengths to avoid feeling this way. And, some people find that self-harm is one way to show others just how bad they're feeling and to express the true extent of their pain. In fact, one study that looked at why people self-harm found that half of the participants reported engaging in self-harm in order to communicate with other people (Brown, Comtois, and Linehan 2002). However, almost all of these people said that they also had other reasons for harming themselves and that the desire to communicate something was not the only reason for their self-harm. When self-harm serves many different purposes all at once, it can be even harder to stop.

WHY IT'S IMPORTANT TO KNOW THE FUNCTIONS OF SELF-HARM

So, how can knowing the functions of self-harm help you? Well, there's a couple of reasons why we think it's important for people to know all the purposes self-harm can serve.

Decrease Shame and Increase Self-Acceptance

First, as we mentioned before, many people feel ashamed about their self-harm. Other people who self-harm think there's something wrong with themselves for engaging in this behavior, or that it means they're crazy or sick. And still others think that they are terrible people for harming themselves. Now, we can definitely understand where these thoughts come from. As we discussed in the introduction, self-harm has a large stigma attached to it, and our society tends to judge negatively people who harm themselves. Unlike some other behaviors that people sometimes use to cope with emotional pain, self-harm isn't ever seen as acceptable. Take the case of drinking, for example: Even though alcohol abuse is frowned upon by society, it's generally considered acceptable to drink in moderation in many social situations. In fact, society has a pretty high tolerance for drinking, even when people drink to the point of getting tipsy. This is definitely not the case for self-harm, though. On the contrary, society generally sees self-harm as unacceptable at any level and under any circumstances. Therefore, it's understandable why people who harm themselves might think negative thoughts about themselves.

The problem is that it's not helpful. Thinking all of these terrible things about yourself or feeling ashamed can actually increase your emotional pain, making you even more likely to self-harm again! It's like a vicious cycle where feeling bad leads to self-harm, which (in the long run, after the temporary relief subsides) makes you feel even worse, which then leads to even more urges to self-harm. If you struggle with self-harm and have ever felt terrible about yourself afterward, or have ever beaten yourself up for doing this, we hope that learning all of the important functions that self-harm can serve might help you go easier on yourself the next time you're tempted to (or actually do) harm yourself.

Now, for some of you, this might seem like a strange thing for us to hope for. You might be asking, "Why would I want to go easier on myself when I slip up and harm myself? Isn't beating myself up for this and feeling bad going to help me stop?" Well, the fact is that a lot of evidence suggests that feeling really ashamed about something doesn't actually help people stop doing it. In fact, in many cases, it actually makes people more likely to do it again. This probably has something to do with the fact that shame is such a painful emotion that most people will do whatever they can to try to avoid or escape it.

What all of this means, though, is that by beating yourself up for harming yourself, you might be setting the stage to do it again! In fact, some treatments for self-harm actually teach people to practice self-compassion and be more accepting of themselves. We'll tell you more about these treatments in chapter 8.

Identify Alternative Behaviors

Second, knowing what purposes self-harm serves can help you find ways to stop harming yourself. Some people who self-harm know exactly why they do it, but others are less certain. Now that you know some of the most common reasons for self-harm, we hope that you're a little clearer about what your self-harm does for you. And, once you know what self-harm does for you, you can take a big step toward stopping your self-harm.

How do you do this? Well, one of the best ways to stop self-harm is to figure out what self-harm does for you and the purposes it serves, and then find other ways of getting those needs met. In fact, a lot of treatments for self-harm do just this: the therapist helps you figure out what purposes your self-harm serves and then teaches you other ways to get what you need. We'll tell you more about these treatments in chapter 8. However, the basic idea is that taking self-harm away without giving you a substitute that meets your needs is a recipe for failure. If you stopped self-harming and had absolutely nothing healthy to replace it with (for example, no other way to feel better), then you'd probably have an incredibly hard time staying away from self-harm. Instead, you need to learn other ways to cope with your distress, understand and express your feelings, communicate to other people, and so on. So, the bottom line is this: if you want to stop self-harming, one of the best ways to start is to figure out what purposes self-harm serves for you and then find other ways of getting those needs met that don't have the same negative consequences as self-harm.

Here's something that might help you with this. The next time you have urges to self-harm, stop and think about why you want to harm yourself and what you'd get out of it. Do you want relief from emotional distress? Do you want a way to relieve the tension building up inside of you? Do you want to express to someone how you feel? Do you want to punish yourself for some mistake you have made? Write down all of the different purposes your self-harm may serve. The questions below will help you figure out what you get from your self-harm.

WHAT DOES SELF-HARM DO FOR YOU?

Answer each of these questions with a yes or no.

To feel better

- Do you harm yourself to distract yourself from emotional pain or negative feelings?

- Do you harm yourself to express your emotions?

- Do you harm yourself to express feelings that you can't put into words?

- Do you harm yourself to release built-up tension?

To make emotional pain clearer and more tangible

- Do you harm yourself so that you can "see" your emotions on your skin?

- Do you harm yourself to make your inner pain more concrete and clear?

- Do you harm yourself to move your emotional pain from the inside to the outside?

- Does seeing the marks on your body make it easier to deal with your emotional pain?

To punish oneself

- Do you harm yourself when you feel guilty about something?

- Do you harm yourself to punish yourself for some mistake you have made?

To end dissociation

- ❧ Do you harm yourself to reconnect with the here and now?

- ❧ Do you harm yourself to stop flashbacks?

- ❧ Do you harm yourself to end feelings of being disconnected from the world around you?

To get a rush or high

- ❧ Do you harm yourself to get a rush of adrenalin?

- ❧ Do you get a high or a rush of excitement when you harm yourself?

To communicate to other people

- ❧ Do you harm yourself to show others what you are feeling?

- ❧ Do you harm yourself to express your needs to other people?

- ❧ Do you harm yourself so that other people understand how bad you feel?

Now that you've answered these questions, you probably have a better idea of what your self-harm does for you. And, that's the first step toward stopping your self-harm. To move on to the next step, keep reading!

Next, turn to the questions below to help you figure out what to do instead of harming yourself. These questions will get you to think about what you really want and how you can get it without harming yourself. So, the next time you think about harming yourself, get a piece of paper and write down all the different ways you could get your needs met without harming yourself. Then, choose some of these things and do them *instead* of self-harm. The more you do this, the more you'll get used to doing other things to get your needs met.

OTHER WAYS TO GET YOUR NEEDS MET (INSTEAD OF SELF-HARM)

To figure out what you can do instead of harming yourself, answer the questions below each of the needs your self-harm meets. Try to come up with as many answers as possible for each of the questions.

To feel better

- What else can you do to make yourself feel better?

- What else can you do to express your emotions?

- How else can you release the tension inside of you?

To make emotional pain clearer and more tangible

- How else can you figure out what you are feeling?

- What else can you do to make your emotions clearer and easier to understand?

- What are other ways of getting your emotions out?

To punish oneself

- What are you punishing yourself for?

- What do you think you've done wrong?

- What would be a better way of reaching your goals?

- How else could you make amends for your mistake (if you've made a mistake)?

To end dissociation

- How else can you reconnect to the here and now?

- What else can you do to get in touch with your body?

- What can you do to feel connected to your environment?

To get a rush or high

- 🌿 What else can you do to feel excitement?

- 🌿 What other things might provide you with a sense of stimulation?

- 🌿 What do you find exciting to do?

To communicate to other people

- 🌿 What do you want to communicate to other people?

- 🌿 What do you want them to know or understand?

- 🌿 What can you do to get the message across without harming yourself?

Now that you've figured out other ways of getting your needs met, try these things instead of self-harm. They may not work quite as quickly as self-harm (and, at first, they may not work quite as well), but they also won't have all of the downsides that self-harm has in the long run. And, you might even find that you feel proud of yourself for resisting your urges to self-harm.

Once Susan figured out what purposes her self-harm served, she knew she was moving forward on the road to recovery. She started by asking herself what her self-harm did for her and what needs it helped her meet. Once she realized that she usually harmed herself to feel better when she was lonely, she tried to come up with other ways of relieving her loneliness. She came up with a list of things she could do that usually helped her feel less lonely. Some of the top items on her list were calling a friend, going to the mall, and visiting her brother. Then, whenever she felt lonely and started to have urges to cut herself, she did these other things instead.

SUMMARY

- ✿ Self-harm serves many important purposes for people, and is used to meet very basic human needs.

- ✿ Some of the most common functions of self-harm are to feel better, to make emotional pain more clear and tangible, to punish oneself, to end dissociation, to get a rush or high, and to communicate to others.

- ✿ Knowing the purposes your self-harm serves can help you be more accepting of yourself when you slip up and harm yourself. This, in turn, will help stop the vicious cycle of self-harming, feeling bad about yourself for your self-harm, and then harming yourself again.

- ✿ Knowing the functions of your self-harm can also help you stop this behavior by pointing you toward substitute behaviors. In particular, behaviors that meet the same needs as your self-harm make the best substitutes.

Of course, just as much as self-harm can be very helpful in the short term by meeting some very important and basic human needs, it has some serious downsides in the long term. In the next chapter, we talk about all of the problems that self-harm can cause or make worse, in the hope of helping you get motivated to stop your self-harm (if you aren't motivated already or you simply need more good reasons to stop).

Chapter 6

So, What's Wrong with Self-Harm?

At the beginning, Dave thought that self-harm was no big deal. He only did it occasionally, when he was really stressed out about a work deadline, and all he'd do was go into the bathroom and hit himself repeatedly on the leg. But, over time he discovered other ways to harm himself, like cutting. And, the more often he cut, the harder it was to stop. He spent the whole day at work looking forward to getting home and cutting himself. Dave tried several times to quit, but each time, he couldn't hold up against the overwhelming urge to harm himself. Scared and concerned about Dave, his girlfriend tried to help him but eventually broke up with him when he started harming himself more severely. One day, Dave woke up with a knife in his hand and a pool of blood on the bathroom floor next to him. That was when he realized that he'd better get help.

In this chapter, we talk about some of the problems with self-harm. Although self-harm can be quite alluring and addictive, it actually creates more problems than it solves, and there are many good reasons to stop harming yourself. This is what we mean when we say what's "wrong" with self-harm. We aren't saying that self-harm is morally wrong or inappropriate (we don't believe that, and self-harm is like any other behavior: you do it because it works for you in some way). We're talking about the negative effects of self-harm for people who harm themselves and the people they care about. This chapter goes along with our chapter on getting motivated to stop harming yourself (chapter 10). One of the best ways to get motivated to stop harming yourself is to think about important reasons to stop. If you're having trouble coming up with these reasons, you'll find this chapter very helpful.

SELF-HARM IS ADDICTIVE

One of the biggest problems with self-harm is that it can be addictive. In fact, for many people, self-harm is much like using drugs. People who self-harm often talk about how hard it is to quit, how strong the urges are, and how they can even have uncomfortable physical feelings like agitation and bodily aches when they've gone a long time without harming themselves.

So, what exactly do we mean by addictive? If you're addicted to something, you depend on it. "Addiction" is the more common term to describe what psychologists call *dependence*. Dependence on self-harm means that you're preoccupied with or spend a lot of time thinking about self-harm, you might hurt yourself more than you intend to, you have difficulty stopping self-harm, and you might have symptoms of withdrawal or tolerance (discussed below). People who are dependent on alcohol or drugs have very similar experiences. Below, we discuss how the different aspects of dependence fit with self-harm.

Preoccupation

One aspect of dependency is *preoccupation*. Preoccupation means that you spend a lot of time thinking about and planning self-harm, figuring out when you can do it, or looking for ways to harm yourself (for example, buying or cleaning razors).

Some people are very preoccupied with self-harm. We've seen people who go through the whole day looking forward to the opportunity to go home and self-harm, who think a lot about the next time they might harm themselves, or who bring items to work (for example, lighters or razors) just in case they want to self-harm. We've also seen people who actually take things from work (such as needles, paper clips, and so on) that they can use to harm themselves.

The main problem with being preoccupied with self-harm is that it takes your time and attention away from living your life and dealing with your problems. Basically, instead of working to improve your life, you end up putting your time and effort into trying to escape your problems. Now, at times, you might think, "Sure, what's wrong with that?" And, this is understandable. You've probably noticed that when you escape your problems, you feel emotionally relieved or less stressed out—at least temporarily. The problem, however, is that you can't solve a problem by escaping it. You might have noticed that when you put a lot of effort into escaping your problems, in the end your problems don't normally go away, and sometimes they become worse. So, one problem with self-harm is that you can get so preoccupied with harming yourself and escaping that you have little room left to work on getting the life you want.

As with any addiction, we've seen people become increasingly preoccupied with self-harm over time. In the beginning, you might think of self-harm only when you're really upset. But, the more you do it, the better it seems. And the better it seems, the more preoccupied you'll be. Dr. Thomas Joiner (2002) has said that the more you harm yourself, the more you'll notice the good effects of self-harm (for example, feeling better or tension release) and the less likely you are to notice the negative effects (such as shame and unsightly scars). Even if you're not preoccupied right now, you could become preoccupied with self-harm, so the best time to stop harming yourself is right now.

Difficulty Stopping

Now, it's easy for us to say, "Stop harming yourself," but it's another story when you actually try to stop. Indeed, another part of being dependent is having difficulty stopping self-harm. People who smoke often try to quit many times before they're successful, and this can be true of self-harm as well. Self-harm just seems to be one of those things that really hooks people. And, for that reason, it can be very difficult to quit for good.

But, the good news is that we've seen many people do it. So, there's no reason to believe that you're unable to stop harming yourself. It's just that it can sometimes seem impossible, if you're dependent on self-harm. With smoking (arguably, one of the hardest habits to kick), researchers have found that the more times a person tries to quit, the more successful she or he will be at quitting for good. Self-harm might work in a similar way. So, don't be too discouraged if you've tried to quit time and time again. It might be that the more often you try, the more likely you are to quit for good one day. So, keep trying!

Doing More Harm Than Intended

You might also find that you sometimes self-harm more than you intend to. For example, you might start out only meaning to scratch yourself but, instead, find that you've made a deep cut. This is another part of being dependent—doing more of the behavior than you meant to do.

We think this happens for three reasons: The first reason is that you can get used to self-harm and build up a tolerance for this behavior, so that you need more and more serious or frequent self-harm to get the same effect. The second reason is that the more you self-harm, the more confident you are about harming yourself. When you first began harming yourself, you might have been afraid to cause too much damage. You might have been very careful, making sure to only use clean knives and to only harm yourself to a certain degree. But, some researchers (Joiner 2002) think that the more people self-harm, the more confident and brazen they become about their self-harm. It's basically as if people become daredevils with their self-harm, and are willing to inflict much more damage on themselves than when they first began harming themselves.

The third reason is that many people don't experience pain when they self-harm. If you don't experience pain when you self-harm and you're really upset, you might harm yourself more than you intended to, simply because the pain isn't there to help you put on the brakes. Related to this, many people who self-harm do so in a numbed-out, dissociated state (where you aren't really aware of yourself or your surroundings). Even if you do experience pain when you self-harm, if you hurt yourself while in a dissociated state, you might not even be aware of what you're doing or how much you're harming yourself. The bottom line is that if you have harmed yourself more than you intended to, you might be dependent on self-harm. This is a very good reason to stop, because otherwise you might cause yourself serious damage without even intending to.

Tolerance and Withdrawal

A third part of being dependent is *tolerance and withdrawal*. Although some people think tolerance and withdrawal are unique to drug use, we believe that they play a role in self-harm as well. You build up a tolerance when you need more and more of something to achieve the same effect. When this happens, people can move from relatively superficial cutting to life-threatening self-harm without meaning to or even realizing it. *Withdrawal* involves uncomfortable symptoms that you might experience when you've gone some time without harming yourself.

> *Judith was trying hard in therapy to quit self-harm. She used to harm herself daily but recently stopped for a few days. She felt agitated and uncomfortable, and had very strong urges to harm himself. Her arms (where she normally burned herself) started to feel achy and tense. Judith couldn't stop thinking of harming herself, in part to get rid of these withdrawal symptoms.*

Tolerance and withdrawal are part of the vicious cycle that can keep you hooked on self-harm. The more of a tolerance you have for self-harm, the more seriously you have to harm yourself to get the same effect. And, the more serious your withdrawal symptoms are, the harder it is to resist harming yourself. We've worked with people who sometimes harmed themselves just to stop the uncomfortable nervousness or the urges, cravings, or thoughts about self-harm.

So, one of the problems with self-harm is that it can get you into a vicious cycle of preoccupation, tolerance, and withdrawal. Although it may be hard to stop, the only way to break this cycle is to stop harming yourself. And, as with other addictions, like smoking and drug use, it can take a long time being "off" self-harm before you feel that you have it under control. So, the bottom line is this: Start as soon as possible on the road to quitting! The sooner you stop, the sooner you'll be free. Answer these questions to find out how dependent you are on self-harm.

ARE YOU DEPENDENT ON SELF-HARM?

Answer the questions in each category with a yes or no.

Preoccupation

- Do you think about self-harm a few times a week to a few times a day?

- Do you plan ahead for when you'll next harm yourself?

- Do you think about getting things (knives, and so forth) to hurt yourself with?

- Do you search for things (at home or at work) to hurt yourself with?

- Do you fantasize about harming yourself?

- Do you find yourself wondering what it will feel like the next time you harm yourself?

Difficulty Stopping

- Have you tried more than once or twice to quit self-harm?

- Do you doubt your ability to quit self-harm?

- Do you find that you keep trying to quit and then going back to self-harm?

- When you really want to self-harm, do you try to stop yourself and fail?

Doing More Harm Than Intended

- Do you sometimes hurt yourself more severely than you had intended?

- Do you sometimes hurt yourself more frequently than you had intended?

- Have you ever hurt yourself without even knowing that you had done so?

Tolerance

- Do you hurt yourself more often than you used to?

- Do you hurt yourself more severely than you used to?

- Do you use a variety of methods to hurt yourself (such as cutting, burning, hitting, and so on)?

- Do you find that it takes more severe types of self-harm to give you the same effects?

Withdrawal

- Do you feel strong urges when you've gone for some time without harming yourself?

- Do you feel agitated, tense, or anxious when you're not harming yourself?

- Do you have any uncomfortable sensations in the places where you hurt yourself?

- Do you sometimes feel as if you can't go one moment longer without hurting yourself?

If you answered yes to three or more questions in each category, you might be dependent on self-harm. Keep reading to find out what you can do about this.

Now, sometimes it can be hard to face up to the fact that you're hooked on something like self-harm. The problem is that it's hard to really step onto the road to freedom from self-harm if you're not aware of how seriously dependent you are. Awareness is not a cure itself, but it's a very important first step. The good news is that even if you're dependent on self-harm, you have already taken one important first step toward the life you want (assuming, of course, that you want a life that's free of self-harm). As you read through this book, we hope that you continue to take steps down the road to freedom from self-harm.

Not Everyone Who Self-Harms Is Addicted to It

It's important for us to mention that not everyone who self-harms is addicted to this behavior. There are certainly people out there who harm themselves regularly but aren't preoccupied with self-harm, only harm themselves as much as they want to, and don't experience tolerance or withdrawal. Indeed, some people only harm themselves a few times and then stop altogether. Even so, self-harm almost always causes more problems than it solves. And, even people who aren't addicted to self-harm need lots of help and support in their efforts to stop.

SELF-HARM CAN MAKE YOUR "COPING MUSCLES" ATROPHY

Another problem with self-harm is that it can weaken your coping skills. Your ability to *cope* is your capacity to manage stress and deal effectively with problems in life. Healthy coping skills are those that help you reduce, manage, or accept your emotions and navigate the maze of problems that many of us face in life. When you use healthy coping skills, you feel competent and effective, and you generally respect yourself. Unhealthy coping skills, like engaging in self-harm, might work to make you feel better emotionally, but they don't help you feel better about yourself. In fact, if you harm yourself, you probably feel even less competent and less respectful of yourself afterward. The problem, though, is that self-harm can help you feel better so quickly and easily that it can be hard to imagine anything else that would work as well. And, this means that you might come to rely on self-harm and forget about your other, healthy coping skills.

Basically, coping skills are a lot like muscles: you either use them or lose them. If you work out, you know what we're talking about. If you're used to doing bicep curls every morning, and all of a sudden you stop, your muscles eventually lose their definition, tone, and size. People stuck in hospital beds for long periods eventually find it difficult to walk, because their leg muscles have atrophied (*atrophy* means a wasting or reduction in size due to lack of use). And, our brains even seem to work this way. People who keep their minds active seem to be better able to ward off memory problems in old age (Rebok, Carlson, and Langbaum 2007).

It's the same thing with coping skills. The more you rely on self-harm to cope with emotions or stressors in life, the less you'll use your other coping muscles. And, the less you use your other coping muscles, the weaker they'll become. Eventually, you might forget about all the other ways to cope with emotions or life. You might find that coping without self-harm is as hard as climbing a mountain is for someone who hasn't exercised for months. Basically, because self-harm works so well in the moment and provides such quick-acting relief, it can be really easy to end up relying on it so much that your other "coping muscles" atrophy. Check off the items below to find out whether your "coping muscles" may have atrophied.

HAVE YOUR "COPING MUSCLES" ATROPHIED?

Answer each of these questions with a yes or no.

"Coping Muscles" Questions

- When you're upset, do you have trouble thinking of other ways of coping besides self-harm?

- When you're upset, do you think of self-harm first, before anything else?

- Is it difficult to remember the last time you used a different way of coping?

- Does doing something other than self-harm seem too difficult, or as if it would require too much effort?

- Do you ever try to cope in some healthier way but find yourself unable to do it very well?

- Do you ever find that when you use some other coping strategy, it doesn't work?

- Do you remember being better able to cope with stress before you started harming yourself?

- Do you feel "weak" or "incapable" when you face challenges in life?

- Do you doubt your ability to cope with your emotions?

- Do you feel that you might be obsessed with self-harm (can't stop thinking about it)?

You might be discouraged to find out that your "coping muscles" are weaker than they used to be or weaker than you want them to be. The good news, though, is that as soon as you start using them again, they'll start to get stronger. In chapters 11 and 12, we explain several useful coping skills that you can use to manage emotions and urges to harm yourself. If you start using these skills, you're taking one more step on the road to recovery, and you might find that you feel much stronger and more capable when facing stress in your life.

SELF-HARM DOESN'T SOLVE YOUR PROBLEMS

Another problem with self-harm is that, in the end, it doesn't actually solve your problems. As we described in chapter 5, most people harm themselves to try to solve some sort of problem. If you harm yourself, the problem you're trying to solve could be that you are more stressed out or have more emotional distress than you'd like. You might harm yourself to feel better or less emotional. Or, the problem could be that you're having trouble in a relationship and can't figure out any other way to get your feelings or thoughts across to someone. If this is your problem, you might harm yourself to express just how much pain you're in or because self-harm is the only thing that seems to get people to stop and listen to you. Another problem you may be trying to solve with your self-harm could be that you keep doing things you feel ashamed of. Maybe you harm yourself in order to punish yourself, and punishing yourself actually makes you feel less guilty or as if you've "set things straight" somehow.

Now, the problem is that although self-harm works temporarily to make you feel better, it doesn't actually solve your problems. Self-harm is about as effective at solving problems as chewing bubble gum is. Imagine that you're very anxious about a project you have due at school that's going to determine your final grade. In fact, you're so anxious that all you want to do is avoid thinking about it, because every time you do think about it, you feel sick to your stomach. So, instead of working on it, you decide to distract yourself by sitting in your room and chewing bubble gum all day. You spend time finding the best bubble gum with the biggest bubbles, perfect your bubble-blowing technique, use a webcam to join an online bubble-blowing competition, and learn how to chew gum in such a way that it lasts for a really long time.

Now, even though all of this bubble-gum chewing probably makes you feel better and less anxious in the moment, your project doesn't get done and you fail your class. And, what do you do to cope with your anxiety and shame about failing this class? Yep, you go home and chew some more bubble gum to distract yourself. This is a lot like self-harm. Self-harm doesn't fix your problems; it simply helps you to escape or avoid them.

And, believe us, these problems can be solved. You can learn how to cope with your emotions and solve the problems in your life. We've seen many people make incredible changes in their lives, fixing major problems and learning how to manage their emotions. In chapter 12, we'll teach you some skills for managing your emotions. You can also learn how to communicate your needs and feelings to other people without harming yourself. People do this in therapy all the time. In fact, researchers have developed entire treatments to teach people how to communicate with others. You can also learn to stop behaviors you're ashamed of without punishing yourself, or to stop feeling so ashamed of things you don't need to feel ashamed about.

These and other life problems are very fixable, and self-harm does nothing to fix them. It simply makes you feel better for a short time, until the problems come back again (which they probably will, because they haven't been fixed). And when they come back, guess what you'll feel even more like doing? Harming yourself!

Now, one message you might hear from some people is that you won't be able to stop harming yourself until you've resolved your "underlying issues." We discussed this in chapter 2 but thought it would be helpful to bring it up again here. Basically, some people believe that you shouldn't try to stop your self-harm until you've addressed the underlying problems that made you start to self-harm in the first place. We disagree with this. On the contrary, we believe that stopping self-harm will make it easier for you to solve the other problems in your life. And, self-harm can actually stop you from addressing important issues in your life or solving your problems. So, don't wait until you've addressed your issues to stop self-harm. No matter what problems you're struggling with, the best time to stop is now. And, we've found that the best way to stop is to work directly on stopping self-harm.

SELF-HARM CREATES PROBLEMS AND MAKES YOU FEEL BAD ABOUT YOURSELF

Not only does self-harm not solve your problems, it also creates new problems. Indeed, self-harm comes with a lot of baggage, or unintended consequences, in the form of relationship problems, stigma and disapproval from other people, stress, shame, and negative thoughts about yourself. If you self-harm, you can probably think of times when your self-harm has led to all of these problems and more.

Relationship Problems

Self-harm often interferes with healthy relationships. In fact, we would say that it's nearly impossible to maintain a close relationship with someone if you regularly harm yourself.

Wendy started harming herself when she was twenty-five. Her parents had just gotten divorced, and she was struggling in graduate school. The only thing that seemed to help her feel better was to harm herself, but this really upset her husband. He had no idea how to respond when she harmed herself, and felt scared for her safety. He also started to see her differently. He used to see her as a strong and independent person, but the more she harmed herself, the more he saw her as fragile and incapable. Without even realizing it, he started to treat her that way too. What's more, Wendy and her husband had heated arguments about her self-harm, during which her husband tried to convince her to quit, and Wendy tried to make him understand that it was the only thing that helped her cope. Their relationship started to decline, and her husband became afraid to leave the house, fearing that Wendy would harm herself if he left her home alone.

People we've worked with have often described relationship break-ups, conflicts, and general stress as a result of their self-harm. The fact is, most people simply don't know how to deal with someone who self-harms. Knowing that someone you love is harming herself or himself can be very frightening, and most people just don't know how to respond or help. And, for someone who doesn't understand self-harm, the visible reminders of self-harm (such as scars) can lead to fear, anger, helplessness, and sadness.

Self-Respect Problems

Self-harm can also erode your self-respect, which can affect a variety of areas of your life. It's very difficult to keep a reasonable degree of self-respect if you self-harm. It's almost as if your brain notices that you're self-harming and then concludes that, if you're willing to inflict damage on your own body, you must not really respect or care about yourself. On the flip side, nurturing or soothing yourself in another way (like taking a warm bath or doing something nice for yourself) might communicate to your brain that you do care about and respect yourself. What's more, most people we've known who self-harm struggle with intense shame and negative thoughts about themselves (such as, "I'm weird," "I'm a freak," "I'm mentally ill," "I can't cope with anything," or "There's something wrong with me").

Now, if you feel ashamed and think that there's something wrong with you, you might actually start to act in ways that match these feelings and thoughts. You might start acting as if you're incapable of coping (even if you are capable), treating yourself poorly (not taking care of yourself), or avoiding other people out of fear that they'll find out what you're "really like." You might also start to think that you don't deserve good things in life.

> After harming herself for two years, Wendy started to feel as if she didn't deserve anything good. She'd never felt this way before, but after her birthday one year, she was plagued with the thought that she didn't deserve all of the attention and kind words she'd just received. She felt like a "fake," as if she were just acting like a "normal person" when, deep inside, she was flawed.

Physical Problems

Self-harm also comes with other baggage. If you hurt yourself enough, you may end up with scars. Sometimes the scars go away, but at other times they can be permanent. And at times, you'll probably take steps to conceal these scars from other people. If people do find out that you hurt yourself, most people can't help but look at you differently. As with Wendy, even people who care deeply about you might change their view of you and start treating you differently. And, even if nobody else sees your scars, when you see them, you might feel shame, anger, disappointment, or even urges to harm yourself.

Now, many people who self-harm say that they like their scars at first. Some people look at their scars and see them as a symbol of the relief that came with self-harm. Others see their scars as a sign of strength, or a reminder that they were strong and powerful enough to inflict tissue damage on themselves. And, others think of their scars as a concrete expression of the pain they feel inside and yet struggle to understand or put into words. The problem is that many people who self-harm eventually regret the fact that they have these visible marks on their bodies, and wish that there was a way to get rid of them completely.

> *Maria felt completely out of control most of the time. Especially when it came to her emotions and relationships, she felt as if she were barely hanging on. The only time she felt in control was when she harmed herself. In those moments, she felt strong and powerful. And, later, when she looked at her scars, she was reminded of just how strong she could be. At times, though, Maria regretted having these scars and all the work it took to hide them from her daughters.*

The bottom line is that self-harm comes with a lot of baggage. Although most people harm themselves to feel better, self-harm has a rebound effect, leading to emotional turmoil, relationship difficulties, and other problems. Check off the items below that describe some of the problems you've had as a result of harming yourself. As we'll talk about in chapter 10, identifying the downsides can help you stay motivated to stop self-harm.

PROBLEMS WITH SELF-HARM

Answer each of these questions with a yes or no.

Problems with Self-Harm

- Do people get upset with you about your self-harm?

- Do people tell you that they're concerned about you because of your self-harm?

- Do people seem shocked, upset, confused, angry, or distressed about your self-harm?

- Does your self-harm take you away from your friends or loved ones?

- Do you think a relationship you've had might have ended because of your self-harm?

- Do other people seem to look at you differently since they learned about your self-harm?

- Does thinking about self-harm interfere with your work?

- Do you self-harm at work?

- Do you have scars from self-harm?

- Do you make efforts to conceal your scars?

- Do you ever end up in the emergency room because of your self-harm?

- Have you ever been on a medical floor or intensive-care unit because of your self-harm?

- Do you feel shame about your self-harm?

- Do you feel angry at yourself because of your self-harm?

- Do you have negative thoughts about yourself as a person who self-harms?

- Do you think that you're incapable, mentally ill, strange, or sick because you self-harm?

Becoming aware of the baggage that goes along with self-harm is one important step on the road to recovery. Knowledge of the ill effects of self-harm can fuel your motivation to quit. As we mentioned in chapter 3, one way to use this information is to write down all of the downsides of self-harm and repeat them to yourself until you've memorized them. Then, bring them to mind whenever you feel like hurting yourself, and see if they help steer you in a different direction. We offer more guidance on how to steer away from self-harm in chapter 10.

SELF-HARM CAN BE DANGEROUS AND EVEN LETHAL

Self-harm can also be dangerous. As we discussed before, self-harm is something that people do without trying to kill themselves. And most people who self-harm choose methods that aren't likely to result in death, such as burning, minor cutting, or hitting themselves. In fact, some people think that by harming themselves, they'll feel better and be less likely to try to commit suicide. And, there are times when self-harm works like this. The problem is that self-harm can become more lethal over time.

This is how we think it works. As we mentioned previously, Dr. Thomas Joiner's theory is that the longer a person self-harms, the less shocked or concerned this person is about the negative effects of self-harm. So, the more you self-harm, the less concerned you might be about scars, social disapproval, or how deeply you cut yourself. At the same time, you might need more and more severe or frequent self-harm to get the same effects. So, not only are you less concerned about your safety, but you are also harming yourself more and more severely (more cuts, more severe burns, and so on). Further, the more you self-harm, the more likely you are to pay attention to the positive effects of your self-harm. So, if you self-harm to feel better emotionally, the whole idea of feeling better emotionally becomes bigger and bigger, overshadowing any concern you might have about seriously harming yourself. Over time, you might become blinded to the dangers of self-harm, paying attention only to how it makes you feel better in the moment.

As we mentioned, if you feel no pain when you self-harm (or if you self-harm in a numbed-out, dissociated state), the situation becomes even more dangerous. We've known people who were absolutely shocked at how severely they had harmed themselves without even knowing what they were doing. They hadn't intended to kill themselves but had come very close to doing so.

In short, these are four ingredients that can make self-harm dangerous:

- ❦ You can develop a tolerance, requiring more severe self-harm to get the same effects.

- ❦ You can become blinded to the negative effects or seriousness of self-harm.

- ❦ You can become obsessed with or completely focused on the positive effects.

- ❦ You may not feel enough pain to stop yourself from doing something very dangerous.

Although it was a long, hard struggle, Dave eventually quit harming himself. Before this, he had a couple of other severe episodes of self-harm where he ended up in the ICU. But, he became very skillful at dealing with his emotions and urges to self-harm. The longer he went without harming himself, the less time he spent thinking about self-harm and struggling with urges. His scars began to fade, and his new relationships weren't tainted by his struggles with self-harm. Dave also felt stronger and more capable of coping with life. Even though he went through some extremely stressful events (including the death of his father and loss of his job), he felt capable enough to cope with these events without harming himself.

SUMMARY

- Although self-harm can work well to manage emotions, it comes with many negative consequences.

- Self-harm is addictive.

- Relying on self-harm makes your "coping muscles" atrophy.

- Self-harm does not solve your problems.

- Self-harm creates problems and makes you feel bad about yourself.

- Self-harm can be dangerous and lethal.

We hope that reading this chapter helped you to become more aware of the negative effects of self-harm. Now that you know a little more about the downsides of self-harm (or maybe you knew all of this already, and we just reminded you) and, hopefully, feel a little more ready to step onto the path to recovery, we move on to chapter 7, where we offer some concrete suggestions on how to seek help for self-harm.

PART II

How Do I Get Help for Self-harm?

Chapter 7

Getting Help for Self-Harm

Andrea had been harming herself for the past few years. For most of this time, she never told anyone about her struggles with self-harm, because she was deeply ashamed of this behavior and afraid of what might happen if she told someone about it. After she confided in a friend who was supportive and kind, she started to feel a little more ready to start on the path toward getting professional help. The problem was that she had no idea of where to look.

If you harm yourself, you might have had a similar experience to Andrea's. It's hard enough to confide in someone about your struggles with self-harm, but it can be even harder to figure out how to get help in the first place. In this chapter, we describe how to find help for self-harm, the kind of help that may be available, and the things to keep an eye out for as you determine the best treatment options.

THE INTERNET AND SELF-HARM: A MIXED BLESSING

The Internet is definitely a mixed blessing when it comes to information on self-harm. Although some websites provide good information on available treatments and cutting-edge research, others are fraught with misinformation and bad advice. Some websites even include networking groups that encourage people to harm themselves! This web of options can be very confusing, making it hard to know where to turn for accurate information or help. We can help you with this. Below are some websites that we know and trust, and that will help you start on your journey of learning about self-harm and finding the help you need.

Secret Shame: Self-Injury Information and Support (crystal.palace .net/~llama/psych/). This website is one of the most extensive, informative resources for self-harm on the Internet. Included are links to information on the causes of self-harm, co-occurring disorders and problems, and treatments, as well as self-help information for individuals who harm themselves and quotes from people who struggle with this behavior. Also offered is some information on coping strategies, and on what family members and friends can do to help. Although it appears as if this website has not been updated since 2004, much of the information is still relatively current and will probably be useful.

BUScentral (BUS stands for "bodies under siege.") (buslist.org/). This website is also quite informative, with fact sheets on self-harm, links that allow you to get involved in a "bodies under siege" e-mail list, and links to other helpful sites. Everything on this site is free, and the fact sheets are informative, including a variety of general information on self-harm, as well as some specific coping strategies that you can use to avoid harming yourself. BUScentral also has a Web-based bulletin board, where you might find it useful to learn coping strategies from other people who self-harm or who have stopped self-harming.

Bristol Crisis Service for Women (www.users.zetnet.co.uk/BCSW/). This organization is devoted primarily to helping women who self-harm. Based in the United Kingdom, the Bristol Crisis Service has a national "helpline" for people who self-harm, and puts on a variety of workshops and educational events for treatment providers and others. If you click the "leaflets" link, you'll find some brochures with useful information on self-harm, as well as information on how to cope with anger and flashbacks. Some of the materials on this website are offered in a variety of languages other than English. In addition, the Bristol service has a bibliography of different self-harm resources and books that you might find helpful.

FirstSigns Voluntary Organisation (www.firstsigns.org.uk/). A very informative website, FirstSigns has frequently updated links and information on the home page, including letters from people who self-harm, articles, and videos. FirstSigns includes frank discussions of difficult topics, such as the use of masturbation as a coping strategy to avoid self-harm, and other such topics. The website also includes disclaimers when information or videos in the links could potentially be upsetting or might increase viewers' urges to self-harm.

S.A.F.E. (Self-Abuse Finally Ends) Alternatives (www.selfinjury.com /index.html). The S.A.F.E. Alternatives website describes a specific treatment program for self-harm developed by two experts in the area, Karen Conterio and Dr. Wendy Lader. Refer to the website for more information on this specialized treatment. The website also offers some useful resources for people who self-harm, including general information about self-harm, as well as a self-harm blog, references for articles on self-harm, and links to other websites that address mental health issues.

OTHER WAYS TO FIND INFORMATION ON SELF-HARM

Although the Internet is a good resource, there are other ways to learn about self-harm and how to begin the journey toward recovery. One way is to read books on self-harm, like this one. On the websites above, you'll find lists of different books as well, some written by people who've struggled with self-harm and others written by professionals like us to help people who self-harm. We recommend that you read through some of the material in these books just to make sure that you're not purchasing a book with a judgmental tone, or one that *pathologizes* people who self-harm (or makes it seem as if people who self-harm are flawed or defective in some way). Local bookstores, public libraries, and university libraries can also be useful places for finding information and books on self-harm.

There's also a variety of other ways to get information on self-harm:

> ❧ Go to a community or university mental health center, and look for brochures, handouts, or other educational materials on self-harm.

❧ Contact a local psychology or psychiatry professor who does work on self-harm. Such individuals might be able to give you information on self-harm, or recommend therapists in your area.

❧ Search for a local self-harm support network. Be cautious, however, because some of these support networks involve a lot of discussions about self-harm, self-harm methods, scars, and so on. Although some people find that these discussions can make them feel less alone in their self-harm, many people find that too much discussion of ways to self-harm and of self-harm itself (rather than of effective coping strategies) can bring on urges to self-harm and make it hard to stay "clean" from self-harm.

TREATMENTS FOR SELF-HARM

A variety of different types of treatments provided by different types of mental health professionals is available for people who self-harm. As you work on finding the treatment that's right for you, you'll find it useful to know what types of treatments are out there and who generally provides these treatments.

Types of Professionals Who Treat Self-Harm

Many different types of mental health professionals can provide treatment for self-harm. Following is a list of different types of mental health professionals:

Psychologists have extensive training in the treatment of mental health problems. A psychologist can have a Ph.D. or a Psy.D. in clinical psychology, or a Ph.D. in counseling psychology. Unlike psychiatrists, psychologists cannot prescribe medications (although this is changing in some places in the United States).

Psychiatrists are medical doctors with specialized training in the treatment of psychiatric disorders. Psychiatrists can prescribe medication treatments. However, many provide psychotherapy as well.

Social workers are mental health professionals who've had training in a variety of areas, such as counseling, therapy, and mental health and social policy, among others. Normally, a social worker has a master's degree in social work.

Counselors are individuals with training in professional counseling who may have a variety of different types of degrees.

Psychological Assessments

Normally, your first visit with a mental health professional will involve a psychological assessment. Often, in a psychological assessment, you complete a face-to-face interview, answering a lot of personal questions about your life. This is an initial get-to-know-you phase, where the clinician works to figure out why you're seeking treatment, your current problems, how long you've struggled with your problems, your history, your goals, and the types of treatments you've had in the past. Clinicians are also often interested in what your relationships with family members and friends are like, how you did in school, and your family history of mental health problems. The main purpose of an assessment is to help determine the goals and focus of treatment, as well as the type of treatment that may be best for you.

Now, one of the difficult things about being someone who self-harms is that you might feel nervous, ashamed, and unwilling to talk about your self-harm. It might feel as uncomfortable as talking about past traumas or masturbation. Because society generally views self-harm as an unacceptable behavior, you might be afraid that this information might leak out and come back to hurt you in some way. Or, you might be concerned that the clinician will think you're crazy or try to get you committed to a hospital. If you have these concerns, we suggest that you bring them up with the person who's doing the assessment. To get help for self-harm, it's incredibly important that you open up about your self-harm—as hard as it is to do.

Hospitalization, Partial Hospitalization, and Outpatient Treatment

Depending on where you live, a variety of different treatments might be available. Some of these treatments are very intensive, in that they involve many hours of treatment per week or even a hospital stay with round-the-clock care. Other treatments are less intensive and simply involve meeting once or twice per week with a therapist or counselor. Although all these different types of treatments can be helpful, experts often say that it's best to choose the least intensive treatment possible (Gunderson et al. 2005). Basically, the more your treatment can be integrated into your real life, the better off you are—and the more time you have to live your life! This brings us to the issue of hospitalization treatment.

HOSPITAL OR NO HOSPITAL? PROS AND CONS OF HOSPITALIZATION

The most intensive treatments are those that involve hospital stays. These programs provide round-the-clock care twenty-four hours per day, usually for one to a few days, depending on what problems you come into the hospital with. Usually, inpatient treatment programs are for people who are in a crisis or at risk of killing themselves.

As we mentioned, however, people are sometimes admitted to inpatient hospital programs after they harm themselves. Often, this is because concerned family members encourage the individual to go to the hospital or because the self-harming person shows up at the emergency room, is evaluated, and then is admitted to the hospital. The goal of hospitalization is usually to get you through a crisis and reduce your suicide risk.

It's important for you to know about some of the pros and cons of hospitalization-based treatments. We've often seen people who thought they required a long hospital stay to "get over" their self-harm. Family members often think this way as well. In their desperate desire to get help for their loved ones, they often think that the only solution is an intensive, long-term hospital stay that can get the self-harm out of the person's "system" once and for all.

The problem with this approach is that there's no evidence that hospitalization is better than less intensive treatments, such as meeting with a therapist on a regular basis. Although hospitalization has some advantages under certain circumstances, it also has some serious downsides. Below is a list of some of the pros and cons of hospitalization.

PROS AND CONS OF HOSPITALIZATION

There are several pros and cons of hospitalization for self-harm treatment. If you've been in the hospital, you might relate to some of these pros and cons.

Pros

- Your treatment team might refer you to a good treatment provider in the community who can help you with your self-harm over the long term.

- You might receive a medication evaluation to see if medications may be helpful to you.

- You may receive individualized attention and treatment from hospital staff.

- You might get to interact with other people who have similar problems.

- You might feel safe and secure.

- You might get a temporary break from some of the problems in your life.

- You might have the space or time to come up with a plan for how to deal with your problems, including self-harm.

Cons

- Hospitalization is not the treatment of choice for self-harm; there's no evidence that hospitalization is better than outpatient treatment.

- You can't work while you are in the hospital, so you may have to take a leave or use up vacation or sick days.

- In the hospital, you're removed from your normal social network, family, and friends (although, sometimes, this could be a "pro"!).

- Depending on the particular hospital, you might not actually get the individualized time and attention you need.

- You might feel more like a "mental patient" (because, technically, you are).

- If you go repeatedly to the hospital, your self-respect might take a downturn.

- You can get "hooked" on the hospital as a temporary vacation from your problems.

- Hospitalization may not actually reduce suicide risk.

- You might learn other ways to harm yourself by talking with other patients.

- Hospitalization for self-harm isn't really necessary; it's like using a wrecking ball to hammer a nail.

Think through your own experience with hospitalization (if you've had such experiences), and add pros or cons to the list. Then, think through the pros and cons the next time you wonder whether hospitalization is the right choice for you.

PARTIAL HOSPITALIZATION

Another type of treatment program is a *partial hospitalization program*. In this type of program, you go to the hospital for several hours of treatment per day, for one or more days per week. Because you go home each night and are not under direct supervision twenty-four hours per day, these programs often help people make the transition from being on an inpatient unit to being in outpatient treatment. Partial hospital programs are becoming more popular and are available in many communities. For people who need more support and structure than outpatient treatment can provide, partial hospitalization programs provide an option other than inpatient hospitalization, and are often the preferred choice.

OUTPATIENT TREATMENT

Finally, the most common and well-known type of treatment is *outpatient treatment*. Outpatient treatment is the least intensive type of treatment and generally involves seeing a treatment provider in the community (or in a hospital or private practice) for about one to five hours per week. The major advantage of outpatient treatment is that you get to continue living your life and facing your problems while you get help from a therapist.

If you want to learn how to live your life better in some way, it often works best to get help while you're living your life—rather than while you're in the hospital taking a reprieve from life. Learning how to live your life better while you're in the hospital is a lot like trying to learn how to play hockey without actually playing hockey. Instead of taking a break from hockey and spending a lot of time talking about it and how to play it (which is like going to the hospital and talking a lot about how to cope more effectively), it works best to actually join an amateur team, go to the practices each week, and play the game.

What's more, outpatient treatment doesn't have some of the draw-backs of hospitalization. For example, in outpatient treatment, you can still work and see your loved ones (if you want to), and you're less likely to feel like a "mental patient." Also, most of the treatments shown to be helpful for self-harm are outpatient (rather than inpatient) treatments.

Specific Types of Psychological Treatments for Self-Harm

Several different types of treatment may be helpful for self-harm, including the following:

Cognitive-behavioral therapy (CBT): CBT helps people learn new skills for managing their emotions, thoughts, and behaviors. CBT is often a fairly structured treatment, with a clear agenda for each session. Often, the sessions focus on changing thinking patterns and behaviors that cause problems for you, and learning how to cope with stress, emotions, or interpersonal situations. In CBT, the therapist often gives you homework assignments to practice new skills and change behaviors outside of therapy sessions.

Dialectical behavior therapy (DBT): DBT, developed by Dr. Marsha Linehan (1993a), is a type of CBT that combines the kinds of things described above (for example, learning skills, and changing behaviors and thinking patterns) with strategies for helping clients learn how to accept themselves, their lives, and other people. We'll tell you more about DBT in chapter 8. Also, we include some DBT skills in chapters 11 and 12, where we talk about how you can deal with self-harm urges and overwhelming emotions.

Psychodynamic therapy: In psychodynamic therapy, the therapist helps you figure out why you self-harm and the underlying issues that might drive your self-harm. Usually, psychodynamic therapists pay a lot of attention to your childhood experiences and how these experiences influence you today. Unlike CBT or DBT, psychodynamic therapies are normally not especially structured, and sessions usually flow along with whatever you bring up in therapy. Some psychodynamic therapists focus a lot on your childhood, and others pay more attention to how you're doing in the present.

Right now, DBT has the best scientific evidence in the treatment of self-harm, but there are also some useful CBT and psychodynamic therapies. In chapter 8, we'll tell you more about some of the treatments that studies have shown help people with their self-harm.

INDIVIDUAL THERAPY

Most treatments for self-harm include individual therapy. Most often, individual therapy occurs for one to five hours per week. As we discussed above, the focus of these therapy sessions may differ widely depending on the type of treatment you're receiving, ranging from more to less structured, and having more or less of a focus on your current difficulties versus the past difficulties that you've had. Normally, after the psychological assessment (the get-to-know-you phase), you and your therapist will agree on how therapy will proceed, what the goals of therapy are, and what you'll spend time working on in your sessions.

Certain therapists might also ask you to make specific agreements before you start therapy. For example, if you self-harm, a therapist might ask you to commit to working on stopping your self-harm. Other therapists might have you sign a crisis agreement, stating that you agree not to attempt suicide, or that you agree to call the therapist, a crisis line, or go to the hospital if you're at risk of attempting suicide.

GROUP THERAPY

Treatments for self-harm often involve some kind of group therapy. Sometimes, the group therapy is your primary treatment, and at other times, it supplements what you do in individual therapy. Group therapy can be very useful for people who self-harm. If you go to a group, you'll find out that you're not alone, and you might learn from the experiences of others. People sometimes also find that groups help them to feel less ashamed of self-harm.

There are three main types of group therapy. One type is a *psychoeducational group*, where the main goal is to give you education or information that might help you in your recovery process. For instance, the therapist might give you information about self-harm, its risk factors, and the types of problems that often accompany this behavior, as well as information on emotions, coping, or stress. The idea behind this kind of group is that you'll be better able to move forward on the road to recovery if you're armed with information.

Psychoeducational groups are probably most helpful if you don't know much about the problems you're struggling with, and are just beginning to explore ways to help yourself. Although it's always nice to be knowledgeable about your problems (indeed, that's one of the goals of this book!), keep in mind that no research has shown that having more information alone is enough to "cure" self-harm. Sometimes, you have to learn how to actually use new coping skills rather than simply get more information about your problems.

This brings us to the second type of group: a *skills-oriented group*, where the main goal is to teach you skills or strategies that will help you reduce self-harm. DBT, for example, includes a skills-training group designed to teach you how to pay attention to the present moment, manage your emotions, tolerate emotional distress, and deal with interpersonal relationships (Linehan 1993b). In other groups, the therapist might teach you how to accept your emotions and move forward in your life in ways that matter to you (Gratz and Gunderson 2006). Yet other skills-oriented groups might teach you how to manage stress or anxiety. Keep in mind that skills-oriented groups (like psychoeducational groups) are somewhat like classes, in that the focus of the group is primarily on teaching you new skills, rather than having group members talk extensively about their experiences, the past, or daily life.

In contrast, the third type of group, a *process-oriented group*, does involve a lot of discussion about your emotions, your past, and your daily life or interpersonal problems. Process-oriented groups are usually not nearly as structured or classlike as skills-oriented or psychoeducational groups. Normally, you spend time discussing your current problems, patterns of behaviors, and past experiences with other group members while the group leader encourages and facilitates the discussion. People often develop emotional attachments to other group members, and part of the point of many process groups is to discuss the interactions that group members have with one another in the group (and to learn more about themselves in the process).

Now, process groups can be helpful, but a few words of caution are necessary:

- ❦ Sometimes, process-oriented groups involve a lot of discussion of self-harm, which can bring up urges to self-harm and make it hard for you to refrain from harming yourself.

- ❦ Group members might also discuss events (such as past childhood sexual abuse) that you find very distressing. Although you might feel less alone with your problems, you might also find this to be emotionally overwhelming, triggering urges to harm yourself, or even flashbacks and nightmares (if you've had similar childhood experiences).

🦋 In some self-harm groups, the group members show their "battle scars" or talk about what they used to do to harm themselves and how much they miss it. There's the risk that, through this process, you might start to miss self-harm, learn new ways to hurt yourself that you had never considered before, or both.

Mary had gone for three months without hurting herself when she joined a self-harm group. She'd been in individual therapy for about a year but sometimes thought her therapist (who had never self-harmed) couldn't fully understand where she was coming from. So, she joined the group in hopes of connecting with people who had been through similar experiences with self-harm. At first, she felt comforted by the stories of other group members and realized that she wasn't weird, sick, or abnormal. Over time, however, she found it harder to attend the group. On one occasion, all of the group members showed up in T-shirts with the word "freedom" printed on them, with their arms and scars clearly visible. Mary left the group with overwhelming urges to hurt herself, and spent most of the next week thinking about how she wished that she'd hurt herself enough to produce the dramatic scars that other group members had. That was when she started wondering if this wasn't the right group for her at this stage in her recovery.

Medication Treatment

To pursue medication treatment, you normally have to meet with a physician or psychiatrist. First, you would get an evaluation to see what types of medication might work for you. Then, you would receive a prescription, try out the medication, and meet with the psychiatrist regularly to monitor your symptoms and any side effects that you might be experiencing. Please see chapter 9 for more details on medication treatments for self-harm.

For now, it's important for us to point out that experts on the treatment of self-harm generally agree that it's best to use medication treatments only in combination with psychological treatments. Medications alone just don't seem to do the trick when it comes to a behavior like self-harm. Now, for some people who self-harm, certain medications are very helpful. But there's not a lot of good hard evidence that medication alone works for self-harm.

It's also important for you to know that if you're seeing a professional just to get medications (and not for individual therapy as well), you can probably expect that the sessions will be fewer, shorter, and focused mostly on symptoms and possible side effects of the medications. Although the first couple of sessions with a psychiatrist or physician may be longer, later sessions may be only fifteen to thirty minutes. These sessions will probably focus primarily on the symptoms you're having, any changes in symptoms you've experienced, and any side effects of the medications that you're noticing. This is especially likely if you also have an individual therapist.

That said, most people who provide medications are also trained to provide psychological treatments. Therefore, if you don't have an individual therapist and are seeing someone for medication treatment only, we would still encourage you to ask this professional for support when you're struggling, as well as advice about possible coping skills that may be helpful for you.

IMPORTANT STEPS WHEN YOU'RE SEEKING HELP

Hopefully, you now have a better idea of where to find information on self-harm, the types of resources that are out there, and some of the treatments for self-harm. Below, we turn our attention to the specific ways in which you can go about finding help in your area, as well as some important things to keep in mind during this process.

1. Seek Someone with Training and Experience in Treating Self-Harm

This is an important step, because many therapists don't actually have much experience or training in the treatment of self-harm. In fact, it's unfortunate, but some therapists actually refuse to treat people who self-harm, or they might require that you stop self-harming before they will treat you. This is like saying, "Get rid of your problems, and then I'll help you." Most therapists aren't like this, but it's important to know that this does happen to some people.

If possible, one of the things to look for is a therapist who's comfortable treating people who self-harm, and has a good amount of training and experience with this type of work. There are several different ways to seek out someone like this. For example, you can:

- Contact a hospital psychiatry department and ask about treatment providers in your area.

- Go to a mental health clinic and set up an informational meeting with a clinician.

- Contact a university counseling or psychology clinic and ask for referral information.

- Search your area, state, or provincial registry of psychologists or psychiatrists.

- Get in touch with your area's psychological association and ask for a referral directory, or ask how you might find treatment providers who can help you.

- Search local university websites for psychology faculty members with expertise in self-harm or BPD, and ask if they know of any therapists in your area with expertise in self-harm.

Now, it's not always easy to figure out whether the person you're seeing has the background and training to help you. Because of this, you might have to take charge of this process by asking questions, such as the following:

- Have you ever treated someone who self-harms before?

- What kind of training or experience have you had in treating people who self-harm?

- How well do people who self-harm do in treatment with you?

- How do you feel about working with someone who self-harms?

- Do you think you can help me?

2. Get a Thorough Psychological Assessment

As we mentioned above, a thorough psychological assessment is the first step in treatment. Without knowing what kinds of problems you're dealing with, it's hard for anyone to help you with self-harm. A psychological assessment can also help the clinician get a good sense of the other difficulties you might have, and this information can help determine the best kinds of treatments for you. Treating someone for self-harm without a thorough assessment is like going to a new country and trying to find your way around without a map. You might find your way around eventually, but not before going in the wrong direction, getting lost, and so on. And, if you self-harm, you really can't afford to have someone try to help you find your way without a good map.

So, how do you get a psychological assessment? Well, normally, this is done at the beginning of treatment, so once you've found someone to help you, this professional will often start out with an assessment. But, you might also be interested in simply getting an assessment to learn more information about yourself before you seek treatment. In that case, you might consider searching (using the strategies we mentioned above) for mental health professionals in your area and setting up an appointment for an assessment. We sometimes see people who are not interested in starting treatment right away but simply want to know exactly what diagnoses they have (if any) and what treatment options are available. If you're not sure whether you're ready for therapy or if you can't afford it, you might consider doing this as well, as a way of giving yourself a direction once you are ready.

3. *Take an Active Role in Your Treatment*

The first step in taking an active role in your treatment is to determine the kind of treatment you want and the type of person you'd prefer to work with. Depending on your personal preferences, certain types of psychological therapies might be a better fit for you than others. For example, do you want a more active, problem-solving approach? If so, maybe CBT or DBT would be a better fit for you than psychodynamic therapy.

It's also important to consider the characteristics you prefer in a therapist. Some people prefer to work with a therapist of a particular gender. Others prefer therapists who are older or younger than they are, and still others prefer to work with someone of a similar (or not) ethnic or racial background. Consider your personal preferences, and then decide whether the person with whom you're meeting is a good fit for you.

Now, in some cases, you may not have much of a choice in the matter. For example, you may live in an area where there are very few treatment providers to choose from. Or, your insurance company may only cover the services of a few therapists. If this is the case, you may need to decide if you're willing and able to be flexible regarding some of your preferences. If you do, however, have a couple of different options and, for whatever reason, aren't comfortable with or interested in working with the person you're meeting with, it's perfectly acceptable to tell the professional about your preferences and ask for a referral.

The next, and perhaps most important, step in taking an active role in your treatment is to ask questions. Below are some questions you may want to ask your treatment provider.

Questions to Ask Your Treatment Provider

- What kinds of credentials do you (or does this program) have? What's your educational background and training? Are you licensed?

- How long have you (or has this program) been treating people who self-harm?

- Do you have specialized training or experience in the treatment of self-harm?

- What kind of treatment is provided (for example, CBT, DBT, or psychodynamic)?

- What types of treatment are available (for example, individual, group, or family therapy, or medications)? Will I have access to more than one type?

- How long does treatment normally last?

- How many hours per week does this treatment involve?

- What will I be expected to do in this treatment (for example, homework, or attending a group)?

- What's the cost of the treatment? Do you accept private insurance, Medicare, or Medicaid?

- What's the name of the therapy we're going to do?

- What kinds of changes can I expect to see as a result of this treatment?

- What are the risks of this treatment?

- How often will we meet?

- How long do you think this therapy will last?

- How do we decide when to stop therapy?

- What's your policy on emergencies?

- Do you take phone calls from clients?

- What's the plan if I'm having urges to harm myself or kill myself?

- What do you do with clients who hurt themselves or are suicidal?

- What happens when you're on vacation or away for business?

4. Don't Get Discouraged

Now, we know that this is much easier said than done. Seeking treatment for self-harm and working to stop self-harm can be discouraging. This is perfectly normal. When you begin to feel discouraged, the most important thing is to remember that this process is challenging and sometimes takes a long time. Although there are many reasons why you might feel discouraged now and then, we want to talk about two of the most common reasons people give for feeling discouraged when trying to get help for self-harm. These include difficulties finding treatment and the persistence of self-harm urges even after you've been in treatment for some time.

WHAT IF I LIVE IN AN AREA WITH NO EXPERTS IN SELF-HARM TREATMENT?

One question we've heard several times is, "What do I do if I go through all of the steps you described, only to find that there isn't anyone in my area with experience in the treatment of self-harm?" Unfortunately, as much as we wish this weren't the case, many areas of different countries simply don't have many clinicians with training or experience in treating self-harm. In fact, sometimes finding treatment of any sort can be a challenge. Now, as frustrating as it may be to spend a lot of time trying to find someone with experience in treating self-harm only to discover that the closest person to you is four hours away, the good news is that all is not lost.

Although we believe it's best to work with someone with experience in the treatment of self-harm, clinicians can learn how to treat self-harm by working with you. Even clinicians who are now experts at treating self-harm had to start somewhere, and learned a lot about how to treat this behavior by working with people who self-harm. So, if you can't find a clinician who specializes in self-harm, look for someone who's willing to learn, and who really tries to understand your experience and what self-harm does for you. Basically, you and your clinician can work together to figure out what needs your self-harm meets for you and how to get them met in other ways.

Now, you might be thinking, "I don't want to have to teach my clinician about my self-harm! Aren't therapists supposed to be the experts?" Well, on the one hand, this is true. Many therapists do come to the table with lots of training, knowledge, and experience. In the end, though, you aren't a "textbook case" (you're a real person!), and you aren't exactly like everyone else who self-harms. Because of this, all therapists must learn from their clients. What works for other people might not work for you. So, as therapists, we're always trying to figure out the best ways to meet the needs of the person sitting across from us. Even therapists with little experience in treating self-harm can work with you to understand what self-harm does for you.

So, if you go through all the steps above and don't find anyone who has a lot of experience treating self-harm in your area, these are some things to look for when trying to choose the right therapist for you.

- Does this person ask you why you self-harm and the functions it serves for you?

- Does this person seem open to your own understanding of your self-harm behavior?

- Does this person seem to understand that you don't harm yourself to try to kill yourself?

- Does this professional seem willing to work with you and stick with you as you try to stop your self-harm, or does this person demand that you stop it before starting therapy?

FEELING STUCK IN TREATMENT

Another thing that can be very discouraging is the feeling that you just can't get rid of your urges to self-harm. This can make you feel stuck in treatment, or as if treatment isn't working well enough or quickly enough. We've both worked with people who have made great progress but felt extremely demoralized when their urges and thoughts about self-harm didn't disappear completely. This is perfectly normal. Remember that if you have hurt yourself repeatedly, you've taught your brain to expect self-harm. It's a lot like teaching your brain to expect coffee in the morning with your breakfast. If you've ever tried to give up having coffee in the morning, you know that the urges and cravings for coffee take some time to diminish.

In the case of self-harm, people often have urges to harm themselves once in a while months or even years after they've stopped self-harming completely. Usually, people find that these urges and thoughts become less frequent and less intense the longer they abstain from self-harm, but they often don't go away completely. We haven't found any silver bullet that blows away self-harm urges and thoughts for good, and believe us, we would tell you if we had! So, don't measure your progress by how often you think about or feel like hurting yourself. The true measure of how well you're doing is whether you're moving away from self-harm (reducing the behavior, not necessarily the thoughts and urges) and forward in the directions that are important to you in life.

SUMMARY

- ❧ There are several ways to get information on self-harm, including the Internet, books, and mental health professionals.

- ❧ Be careful when using the Internet, and choose only trusted sites that provide accurate information and don't encourage self-harm.

- ❧ Get a good psychological assessment before starting treatment for self-harm.

- If you have an option, choose the least intensive treatment available. Outpatient and partial hospitalization programs are usually preferable to inpatient treatment programs. Remember that it's always helpful to stay in the game while you learn how to play it.

- Although DBT has the strongest scientific evidence in the treatment of self-harm, other treatments have also been shown to be helpful. We'll tell you about these in chapter 8.

- Consider your therapy expectations and preferences before you start treatment.

- Use caution when considering a process group. If you go to a process group focused on self-harm, make sure you have an individual therapist who can help you cope with any self-harm urges that arise as a result of group discussions. Remember that process groups aren't always the best option, especially for people in the early stages of recovery.

- Consider not relying solely on medication. If you're taking medication, see a therapist as well, or find a way to get psychological treatment from your prescribing psychiatrist.

- Find a therapist who's a good fit for you, and take an active role in your treatment.

- Remember that feelings of discouragement are a natural part of trying to find and use treatments for self-harm. Focus on ways to move past these feelings, and don't allow them to keep you from moving forward. Remember that overcoming self-harm takes a lot of time and work.

We hope that you'll walk away from this chapter with some specific ideas about ways to find help for self-harm, as well as information on the type of help that's out there. In our next two chapters (chapters 8 and 9), we give you a lot more information about the types of psychological and medication treatments that can be helpful for self-harm.

Chapter 8

Psychological Treatments

Brad was really making progress in stopping his self-harm. Because he was a student, the idea of researching self-harm and learning more about it just made sense to him. And, he was happy to find some really useful coping skills in some of the books he was reading. Yet, even with all of this new information and some good skills under his belt, he felt as if he needed more. Recovering from self-harm just seemed like too large of a task to accomplish on his own. That's when he started to look into the treatments for self-harm available in his area.

This chapter is all about psychological treatments for self-harm. As we mentioned before, many people find that it's easier to stop self-harm if they get help from a therapist. Having a therapist and being in treatment means that you don't have to go through this process on your own. A therapist can teach you skills for stopping your self-harm, support you as you try to give up this behavior, and help you use the skills we'll teach you in chapters 10, 11, and 12. Having a therapist can be like having a coach and cheerleader rolled into one person. So, if you're having trouble stopping your self-harm or even finding the courage to consider stopping, we recommend that you seek treatment from a professional. And, as we mentioned in chapter 7, we suggest that you begin by looking into psychological treatment before you consider medication.

The good news is that there are several psychological treatments out there that have been shown scientifically to help people with their self-harm. These treatments differ in length, take different forms (for example, some involve group therapy, and others are one-on-one), and focus on different things. They also differ in terms of how narrow or broad their focus is. For instance, manual-assisted CBT and Dr. Gratz's emotion regulation group therapy were developed just to treat self-harm. They are short, focused treatments whose main goal is to help people reduce their self-harm immediately. DBT and *mentalization-based treatment* (MBT), on the other hand, were developed to treat BPD, so they are broader and more comprehensive. In addition to focusing on self-harm, DBT and MBT focus on many other difficulties that go along with BPD. They're also longer than the other two treatments (lasting at least a year), and involve at least a couple of treatment sessions per week. Yet, despite these differences, the one thing these treatments have in common is scientific evidence that they are helpful for self-harm.

Below, we tell you a little more about each of these treatments and how they go about treating self-harm.

MANUAL-ASSISTED COGNITIVE BEHAVIOR THERAPY

Manual-assisted cognitive behavior therapy (MACT) was developed by two clinical researchers in England, Drs. Ulrike Schmidt and Kate Davidson (2003). Their goal was to develop a brief, structured, practical treatment for self-harm that could be used in any community mental health clinic in the United Kingdom. Therefore, this treatment is different from DBT and MBT, because its sole purpose is to help people reduce their self-harm as quickly and efficiently as possible.

To do this, they incorporated elements of DBT and other problem-solving skills into a series of six booklets, and these six booklets form the basis of the treatment. For some clients, MACT consists of the booklets alone, in which case it's a form of *bibliotherapy*, or the use of books to help people understand and work through psychological problems. In other cases, clients receive six individual therapy sessions corresponding to each of the booklets.

Like the next two treatments we'll tell you about, MACT is a cognitive behavior therapy. Therefore, the basic goal of this treatment is to teach you problem-solving skills and other strategies for understanding what you're getting out of self-harm, managing your emotions and negative thoughts, preventing future episodes of self-harm, and learning healthier behaviors. In addition, a lot of the strategies included in the MACT booklets come straight out of DBT.

What the Booklets Teach You

Below we describe the types of skills covered in each of the six booklets (and during each of the corresponding therapy sessions).

Booklet 1: The first booklet helps you learn what leads you to self-harm, what you get out of your self-harm, and what happens after you harm yourself (for example, emotional relief or support from other people) that keeps your self-harm going, or *reinforces* your self-harm. You will also be asked to come up with a list of the pros and cons of harming yourself. Making this list will help you get in touch with the purposes your self-harm serves, as well as the downsides of your self-harm. By the way, if thinking through the pros and cons of your self-harm sounds as if it could be helpful, you'll be happy to know that we will teach you this skill in chapter 10.

Booklets 2 Through 4: The second booklet teaches you basic problem-solving strategies. These strategies are meant to help you solve the life problems that make you want to self-harm. The third booklet will help you learn how to monitor your emotions and thoughts. This is a common cognitive behavioral strategy for increasing your awareness of how your thoughts, emotions, and behaviors influence each other. If you have a better understanding of how your feelings and thoughts influence your self-harm (or put you at risk for harming yourself), you'll be in a better position to "catch" yourself early and do something other than self-harm. The fourth booklet helps you tackle your emotional problems. It teaches you skills for coping with emotional distress and contains some of the DBT distress tolerance skills we'll tell you more about below. These skills are all about helping you manage your emotions and tolerate distress without making your problems worse.

Booklet 5: This booklet is a bit different from the first four, because it focuses on alcohol and drugs. Although this might seem a bit strange for a treatment that's meant to reduce self-harm, fear not—there is a method to their madness! They included the fifth booklet because some people only harm themselves when they've been drinking or using drugs. So, for those people, helping them stop (or reduce) their drinking and drug use should also help them reduce their self-harm. Even if you don't normally self-harm when you're high or drunk, using substances can make you more likely to harm yourself impulsively (without thinking it through), and may cause you to harm yourself more seriously than you intended. Therefore, it makes a lot of sense to help people who harm themselves get their drug and alcohol use under control.

In terms of specific skills, this booklet teaches you some of the downsides of drinking and drug use, and some strategies you can use to cut down on your use of alcohol and drugs. And, just as with self-harm, this booklet will help you identify the pros and, most importantly, the cons of your drinking and drug use.

Booklet 6: The final booklet helps you plan how to handle urges to self-harm in the future. This is really a wrap-up booklet. It will walk you through identifying what skills you need to work on and how to stop future episodes of self-harm. The goal of this final booklet is to make sure you have the skills you need to prevent self-harm in the future.

So, Does MACT Work?

As we mentioned before, MACT was developed to be as brief and practical as possible. In fact, the goal was to develop a treatment for self-harm that could be used in any mental health setting. And, this is an incredibly important goal. The more comprehensive treatments that we will tell you about later in this chapter (DBT and MBT) aren't always easy to get up and running in a lot of mental health centers. They require a lot of training and a real time commitment on the part of clients and therapists. And that means that these treatments aren't always available in all communities and for all clients. So, having a treatment for self-harm that's quick and inexpensive, and that could be used anywhere would be very helpful.

Yet, just as there are some upsides to having a short and focused treatment for self-harm, there are also some downsides. Any treatment that's as short and focused as MACT may not be enough to help you completely stop a behavior as serious as self-harm. As we've mentioned many times, self-harm is a hard behavior to give up, and many people rely on this behavior for years. So, it's difficult to imagine that just reading six booklets and completing some exercises could make you stop self-harm completely. If this were the case, there'd be no need for treatments like DBT and MBT (and we could have ended our book after chapter 6!).

Therefore, it's probably not surprising that studies on MACT have found that the six booklets (together with a few individual therapy sessions) are somewhat helpful, but not significantly better than the treatments people usually receive for self-harm. For example, the first study of MACT found that the rate of self-harm episodes was lower for clients who received MACT than for clients who received standard treatment in the community, but not *significantly* lower (Evans et al. 1999). The word "significantly" refers to statistical tests that researchers use to see if one treatment is better than another. When studies find that two treatments aren't significantly different from one another, it means that these treatments are equally helpful. So, in this case, the study found that even though MACT may help people with their self-harm, it's probably not more helpful than the treatments people typically receive for self-harm.

In a larger follow-up study, the researchers uncovered some important information about the types of clients MACT may help and the types of clients who might be better off with another treatment (see Tyrer et al. 2004). Specifically, the researchers found that MACT has some benefits for clients who don't meet criteria for BPD. For these clients, MACT led to fewer self-harm episodes and cost less than the treatment clients typically received in those part of the United Kingdom. Unfortunately, though, this wasn't the case for clients with BPD. These clients actually harmed themselves more quickly and had higher health care expenses than clients who received the usual treatments provided in the area.

Now, the reason MACT works differently for these different groups of people probably has something to do with the fact that it's such a brief and focused treatment. Think about it: if you're not struggling with a lot of other problems in addition to your self-harm, it makes sense that a short treatment focused specifically on self-harm could give you some of the skills you need to start getting your self-harm under control. On the other hand, if you have to deal with all of the problems that go along with BPD, a few booklets focused on your self-harm probably won't do the trick. You're simply going to need more help than that, not to mention a wider range of skills and a longer treatment. The more problems you're struggling with, the more help you need to recover. So, for those of you who meet criteria for BPD or think that you might be struggling with this disorder, we suggest that you look into some of the other treatment options we describe below. All of these were developed just for people with BPD, although they may also help even if you don't meet the criteria for BPD.

EMOTION REGULATION GROUP THERAPY

One of the authors (Dr. Gratz) also developed a short-term treatment for self-harm. Unlike MACT, this treatment was specifically developed to help women with BPD reduce their self-harm. And, partly because of this, it's a little longer and a little more intensive than MACT. The treatment lasts fourteen weeks, and each session is about an hour and a half long.

Unlike MACT, DBT, and MBT, this treatment is a group therapy and doesn't include individual therapy. Instead, this group was developed so that clients could add it onto whatever individual therapy they were receiving at the time. So, it's different from the rest of the treatments we describe in this chapter because it's an *adjunctive*, or add-on, treatment. The goal in developing this treatment was to come up with some way to supercharge people's standard treatment and really focus on decreasing self-harm immediately. And, since that's the whole purpose of this treatment, the goal of reducing self-harm doesn't have to compete with other important goals in therapy.

You see, even though many individual therapists focus a lot of time and attention on helping clients stop self-harm, they also have to help them with other problems. As many of you can probably relate to, people often come to treatment struggling with a number of different problems. And, let's face it, sometimes life just happens and new problems come up unexpectedly! So, therapists often have to split their attention between several different problems that their clients are struggling with, which means that stopping self-harm can't always be the number-one priority. The nice thing about this group therapy is that stopping self-harm is the only priority, so there's never a need to focus on something else. And, this means that we can focus all of our attention on helping people stop self-harm.

So, how does this treatment work? Well, this treatment was developed to get at one of the primary reasons why people self-harm: to regulate or avoid their emotions. Given how many people say that they harm themselves to feel better, Dr. Gratz thought that teaching self-harming women healthier ways of responding to their emotions would decrease their need for self-harm. Basically, this was the idea: if self-harm helps people regulate their emotions (which seems to be the case), and if people learn other ways of regulating their emotions so that they don't feel as overwhelmed by them, then they shouldn't really need to self-harm as much. So, this treatment is all about stopping self-harm by teaching you how to regulate your emotions in healthy ways.

Now, an important and unique part of this treatment is *how* it teaches you to regulate your emotions. Instead of teaching you to control your emotions or keep them in check, this treatment helps you learn to accept your emotions. As we mentioned in chapter 6, a lot of people who harm themselves say they do so to avoid or escape their emotions. Basically, their emotions feel so intolerable and overwhelming that they want to get rid of them as quickly as possible.

So, if this is the problem, how do you treat it? Well, one way would be to teach people how to get rid of their emotions quickly. The problem is that this just isn't possible, and trying to do this can actually make you feel worse in the end. As we've mentioned before, trying to avoid your emotions or get rid of them altogether will probably make your emotions even stronger and longer lasting. In other words, trying to avoid your emotions often backfires. So, that doesn't seem like a good way to try to treat self-harm.

Now, another way to help people who feel really overwhelmed by their emotions is to teach them skills to accept their emotions so that their emotions don't feel as awful or overwhelming. The basic idea is that the less you fight your emotions, the better you'll feel. So, a big part of this group therapy teaches you skills for responding to your emotions in ways that will help you feel better in the long run. For example, instead of fighting your emotions or trying to get rid of them, this treatment teaches you skills for identifying your emotions, figuring out what information they are providing you, and figuring out how to use this information to make your life better. This treatment also teaches you how to be open to your emotions and willing to experience them as they come up. And, on a similar note, this treatment teaches you to be more accepting of your emotions and, in particular, not to judge yourself for feeling certain ways. Finally, a big part of this treatment is teaching you to do the things you need to do and to move forward in your life no matter what emotions you experience or how you feel. Many of the skills in this group come from DBT, and others come from another acceptance-based behavioral therapy called *acceptance and commitment therapy* (*ACT*; Hayes, Strosahl, and Wilson 1999). You can think of this group therapy as a streamlined version of many of the emotional acceptance skills from these other two therapies—rolled up into one treatment and designed to help people stop self-harm.

Content of the Group

So, what exactly do you learn in this treatment each week? Below we tell you more about the skills you learn in this group.

Week 1: During the first week, you learn more about what self-harm does for you and what exactly you get out of your self-harm. You also start to identify the downsides of your self-harm and the ways in which it hurts your life in the long run.

Week 2: This week focuses on teaching you why you have emotions and what your emotions do for you. Since so many people who self-harm really hate their emotions, we thought it would be a good idea to teach you all of the benefits of emotions and why human beings still have them today. During this week, you also begin to identify your own negative beliefs about your emotions (for example, "Some emotions should never be felt" or "Having certain emotions is a sign of weakness") that make you feel even worse when you're upset.

Weeks 3 Through 6: The next few weeks are all about helping you learn to identify and label your emotions. You are taught to identify the thoughts that go along with your emotions, how your body responds to these emotions, and the things you do when you experience different emotions, so that you can figure out exactly how you're feeling. In fact, this is one of the skills we teach you in chapter 12. You also learn how to tease apart whether the feelings you are having are about something that just happened (*primary emotions*), or about your beating yourself up or being hard on yourself for feeling a certain way (*secondary emotions*). And, you learn different skills for managing your primary and secondary emotions. Finally, you learn how to identify what your emotions are trying to tell you, and how to act on this information in a healthy and adaptive way.

Weeks 7 Through 8: During these two weeks, you learn all about the downsides of avoiding your emotions and trying to get rid of them. You also learn skills for accepting your emotions and being open to them. For example, you practice observing your emotions instead of pushing them away, and you learn to let go of the struggle with your emotions, to take yourself out of the fight, so to speak, so that you can focus instead on living your life and doing the things that matter to you (Hayes, Strosahl, and Wilson 1999).

Weeks 9 Through 10: During week 9, you are taught basic coping strategies for managing your emotions without avoiding them (for example, by focusing your attention on your five senses, taking the time to figure out what you're feeling, or expressing your emotions). Then, during week 10, you are taught some basic strategies for controlling your self-harm and other impulsive behaviors. For example, you learn to replace your self-harm with other behaviors that meet the same needs as your self-harm, but in a healthy way. For example, if you self-harm to release pent-up frustration or tension, you could go for a run, sing along to loud music, or do some kickboxing instead. You also learn to reward yourself for resisting your urges to self-harm (so that you can get some benefits from stopping self-harm in the short run).

Weeks 11 Through 14: The last four weeks of the group are all about helping you figure out where you want to go in your life, and the things that matter to you most. You learn how to start moving forward in the directions you want in life immediately! A lot of people feel as if they can't start moving forward in their lives until they feel better and have gotten their self-harm under control. This group teaches you that you don't need to wait to start moving forward in your life. Instead, you can start doing things that matter to you right now, in the moment. In fact, doing these things might very well make it easier to stop self-harm. A lot of these skills come from Dr. Steve Hayes and colleagues' (1999) acceptance and commitment therapy (ACT). If you'd like to learn more about ACT or some of these skills, check out his book, *Get Out of Your Mind and Into Your Life: The New Acceptance and Commitment Therapy* (New Harbinger, 2005).

Does Emotion Regulation Group Therapy Work?

To see if this group therapy would help people stop their self-harm, we took a group of self-harming women with BPD and had half of them participate in this group. Everyone in the study was already receiving individual therapy, and many people were also receiving other group therapies, additional sessions of individual therapy, or individual skills training. However, half of these women also received the emotion regulation group therapy, in addition to their other treatments.

And, the good news is that the group worked! The clients who received this group therapy in addition to their other treatments had fewer episodes of self-harm; were less likely to try to avoid or suppress their emotions; and had less depression, anxiety, and stress (Gratz and Gunderson 2006). In addition, the clients who received the group therapy were more accepting of their emotions, had a better understanding of what they were feeling, were better able to control their impulsive behaviors when they were upset, and felt as if they had healthy ways of managing their emotions. In fact, their emotion regulation skills improved so much over the course of the group therapy that, by the end, most of them scored in the normal range on a measure of emotion regulation. Another, larger study is currently under way to see if this treatment will be just as helpful with another group of clients, and to see how long the positive effects of the treatment continue after the group therapy ends.

DIALECTICAL BEHAVIOR THERAPY

Dialectical behavior therapy (DBT) was developed by Dr. Marsha Linehan in the 1980s. She originally sought to develop a treatment for suicidal women but soon realized that many of these women also harmed themselves without trying to kill themselves, and that many of them met criteria for BPD. So, she ended up developing a treatment for BPD and many of the problems that go along with this disorder. However, she never lost sight of her goal of treating suicidal and self-harm behaviors, and, in fact, helping people stop self-harm is a big focus of this treatment. That may be why DBT is so helpful in reducing self-harm. In fact, many people consider DBT to be one of the best treatments for self-harm out there, especially since it has more scientific evidence than any other psychological treatment for self-harm.

Unlike the two treatments we've told you about so far, DBT was developed to treat all of the problems that go along with BPD. And what this means is that it's a very comprehensive treatment. DBT includes individual therapy (where you meet one-on-one with a therapist) and group skills training (where you attend a group therapy session to learn a bunch of different skills). In addition, DBT therapists have their own group each week, called a *consultation team*, where they provide support and assistance to one another and work together to become better therapists. In some ways, the consultation team is like therapy for the DBT therapists!

So, what exactly do you do in DBT, and how does it help you stop self-harm? Well that depends on which part of DBT you're talking about.

Individual Therapy

As we said, individual therapy is an important part of DBT. In fact, this is the place where you set treatment goals and really prioritize what you are going to work on in treatment. Obviously, this is an incredibly important thing to do, since it would be incredibly overwhelming (not to mention impossible!) to try to solve all of your problems at once. Therefore, DBT has something called a *hierarchy of treatment targets*, which is a list that helps you and your therapist figure out the most important thing to focus on in any given session. And, the first thing on that list is stopping any self-harm or suicidal behaviors (called *life-threatening behaviors* in DBT). What that means is that if you are struggling with self-harm urges or have harmed yourself that week, then self-harm will be the number-one priority during your therapy session that week.

And, this means that you and your therapist will work together to understand what led to your self-harm, what you got out of your self-harm, and what you could have done at various points along the way to stop yourself from engaging in self-harm. Your therapist will also figure out if there are any skills that could have helped you resist the urge to self-harm and, if so, will either teach you these skills or (if you know them already) help you figure out what got in the way of using them. By the time the session is done, you'll have a much better idea of all the places along the chain where you could have prevented self-harm, as well as a plan for stopping self-harm in the future. You may also have learned some new skills that could help you stop your self-harm or solve the problems that led you to self-harm in the first place.

What's more, because DBT is tailored to help with the problems that go along with BPD, individual therapy helps you with many problems in addition to self-harm. Your therapist may help you with relationship problems, work stressors, anxiety and depression, problems with drinking or drugs, and unhealthy eating behaviors, among others. Individual therapy also helps you stay motivated to move away from unhealthy behaviors (such as self-harm or substance use) and toward the goals in life that are meaningful to you.

Group Skills Training

The skills-training group is the second major part of DBT. The goal of skills training is to help you learn the skills you need to improve your life, stop self-harm and other problematic behaviors, and reach your goals in life. These skills are broad enough to address a lot of the problems that people with BPD often struggle with, and aren't specific to self-harm. In fact, unlike DBT individual therapy, you don't normally talk much about self-harm in a DBT skills group. Instead, the skills training is really just that: a group that teaches you skills that you and your individual therapist will then apply to your own specific problems.

So, what skills do you learn, and how do they help with self-harm? The DBT skills include *emotion regulation skills*, *distress tolerance skills*, *mindfulness skills*, and *interpersonal effectiveness skills*. Each of these sets of skills probably plays a role in stopping self-harm; however, some may be more helpful than others, especially if they help you meet the same needs that your self-harm meets.

EMOTION REGULATION SKILLS

Not surprisingly, the emotion regulation skills in DBT help you manage your emotions in ways that work for you and don't cause other problems in your life. For example, these skills help you identify your emotions; the types of events (and the ways you think about these events) that lead to different emotions; and the aftereffects of different emotions on your thoughts, behaviors, and mood. Other emotion regulation skills teach you to figure out why you have your emotions and what information these emotions provide you. And still other skills teach you to change or accept your emotions when necessary, and to make yourself less vulnerable to negative emotions by increasing pleasant events in your life and taking care of your physical and emotional needs.

DISTRESS TOLERANCE SKILLS

Distress tolerance skills are all about making it through difficult times and stressful events without making things worse. Basically, they help you learn to deal with overwhelming emotions without doing something to try to escape them that you'll eventually regret. Given that self-harm is often used to escape overwhelming emotions, it's probably not surprising that these distress tolerance skills could help you reduce your self-harm. Specifically, distress tolerance skills teach you to accept your emotions without trying to change them, to accept reality for what it is, and to control your behaviors even when you are really upset (for example, by using distraction and self-soothing techniques rather than acting impulsively). Finally, other skills teach you to think about the long-term consequences of your behaviors, so that you aren't focusing just on the positive short-term consequences of actions like self-harm.

MINDFULNESS SKILLS

Mindfulness skills teach you to pay attention to what's happening in the here and now, and to be fully awake and present in the moment. These skills are also about participating fully in your life, not letting it slip by because you are up in your head or distracted by worries, fears, intense emotions, and so on. A very important part of mindfulness is not judging yourself or your experiences. You are taught to pay attention to what's happening around you (in addition to what's happening inside you, for example, your thoughts and emotions) without judging these experiences. Instead, you simply observe these experiences and describe them for what they are. For example, you are taught to "stick to the facts" and be objective, instead of adding on evaluations and judgments, as most of us do sometimes. Given how large a role shame plays in self-harm, you can imagine how the ability to observe your thoughts, feelings, and behaviors without judging them could help reduce self-harm. Other mindfulness skills involve noticing sensations (sights, sounds, smells, or tactile sensations) that are happening in the here and now, throwing yourself fully into whatever you're doing in the moment, focusing on one thing at a time, and doing what works.

INTERPERSONAL EFFECTIVENESS SKILLS

Interpersonal effectiveness skills are designed to help you manage your relationships with other people in an effective manner. These skills teach you to keep your goals for your relationships in mind as you interact with the people around you. They are all about making sure that when you say or do something in a relationship, it will help you meet your needs and reach your goals. Some of the interpersonal effectiveness skills teach you to ask others to do things, or say no to their requests, in an effective way (without being too passive or too aggressive). Others teach you to validate other people's feelings and to be honest, truthful, and fair with others. If you have ever harmed yourself because you were upset about a fight you had with someone else, because your relationships are painful, or because you don't know how to ask for support in other ways, then interpersonal effectiveness skills could be just what you need.

To learn more about any of these skills, check out Dr. Linehan's *Skills Training Manual for Treating Borderline Personality Disorder* (The Guilford Press, 1993).

Scientific Evidence for DBT in the Treatment of Self-Harm

As we mentioned before, DBT has been studied more than any other treatment for self-harm, and the results are clear: DBT works! For example, the very first study (Linehan et al. 1991) compared DBT to "treatment as usual," which was the kind of treatment that clients with BPD normally got in the area. DBT was better at reducing self-harm and suicide attempts, not to mention hospital and emergency-room visits. Since then, researchers have conducted several other studies of DBT. A recent study (Linehan et al. 2006) compared DBT to treatment provided by a group of therapists in the area who were considered experts in treating BPD (but who didn't provide DBT). Although both treatments helped reduce self-harm, DBT wasn't better at reducing the number of self-harm acts than the treatment the experts provided. However, DBT was better at reducing the medical risk of suicidal and self-harm behaviors. In addition, findings from several other studies have shown that DBT is a useful treatment for reducing suicidal behavior, impulsive behavior, depression, and anger (see Robins and Chapman 2004).

The other great thing about DBT is that other studies have shown that it can help with other problems as well, such as drug abuse (Linehan et al. 1999) and eating disorders (Safer, Telch, and Agras 2001; Telch, Agras, and Linehan 2001). As you may remember from chapter 4, these are all problems that often go along with self-harm. So, if you struggle with one of these problems in addition to self-harm, DBT might be a great treatment for helping you with all of your problems.

MENTALIZATION-BASED TREATMENT

Mentalization-based treatment (MBT; Bateman and Fonagy 1999) is another treatment for BPD that has been shown to reduce self-harm. MBT was developed by Drs. Anthony Bateman and Peter Fonagy in

England. Unlike the other treatments we have described so far, MBT is not a cognitive behavioral treatment. It's a psychoanalytic treatment. This means that MBT is more of a "talk therapy" than the other treatments we've described. In MBT, most of your time is spent talking with your therapist and learning about yourself and your relationships with others, rather than doing homework assignments, learning new skills, and working to change your behaviors, as you would in cognitive behavioral therapies.

What's more, MBT has a different focus than the other treatments we've discussed. All of the treatments we have described so far are based on the idea that people use self-harm to cope with emotional distress, unwanted feelings and thoughts, and problems in life. Therefore, one of the main goals these treatments have in common is to help people figure out what their self-harm is doing for them, replace their self-harm with other (more adaptive) coping behaviors, and learn new skills to use instead of self-harm.

MBT, on the other hand, focuses more on people's sense of who they are, or their "sense of self." MBT is based on the idea that BPD and the problems that go along with this disorder (like self-harm) are the result of a *weak self-structure*, or an unstable sense of self and poor understanding of the self. According to MBT, people often use self-harm to develop a stronger or more cohesive sense of self. In fact, self-harm is seen as a desperate attempt to maintain some sense of self during stressful times.

And, what exactly causes this weak self-structure? Well, according to MBT, the biggest culprit is the failure to develop *mentalization*. Mentalization is the ability to understand that your own behaviors, and the behaviors of people around you, arise from internal mental states such as thoughts, feelings, and desires. In other words, mentalization means being able to see that the things you do result from your thoughts, feelings, or desires.

If, on the other hand, you haven't learned how to mentalize, you might be confused about why you do the things you do and how your behaviors are related to your mental states. For example, you may find yourself engaging in self-harm with no idea why you started doing this or what was going on inside of you that led you to start harming yourself. You may feel as if your self-harm "just happens" or "comes out of the blue." Yet, as much as it may seem this way, this isn't usually what happens. Instead, you might not be aware of the feelings or thoughts you were having before you started harming yourself, or you might not see the connection between your mental states and self-harm. The fact that you can't see this connection doesn't mean that it isn't there; it just means that you aren't aware of it. And, MBT can help you understand this connection, and see the link between your mental states and your behaviors (including self-harm). In fact, the most important goal in MBT is to increase mentalization.

So, how exactly does MBT help you learn to mentalize? Well, like DBT, MBT is a comprehensive treatment that involves both individual and group therapy. In fact, MBT was first developed as a partial hospital program. As we described in chapter 7, partial hospital programs require a greater weekly time commitment than outpatient treatment, often involving multiple hours of treatment a few days a week. The MBT partial hospital program involves six hours per week of structured treatment, including one hour of individual therapy, three hour-long sessions of group therapy, one hour of expressive therapy, and a community meeting. Yet, the good news for people who aren't looking for a treatment this intensive is that Drs. Bateman and Fonagy are working to develop an outpatient version of MBT involving one individual therapy session and one group therapy session per week. Although no studies have been published on this outpatient version of MBT as of summer 2008, this is sure to become a popular option, because outpatient therapy is, by far, the most common type of treatment.

Individual Therapy

In MBT individual therapy, your therapist works with you to understand why you do the things you do and how others might react to those actions. For example, your therapist might ask you to think about how she or he would feel about something you did, and how these thoughts and feelings might then lead to different actions. Your therapist might also spend time talking about how your behaviors stem from your thoughts, feelings, and desires. All in all, an MBT therapist will work with you to help you understand that everyone's behaviors stem from, or are related to, some internal experience, like thoughts, feelings, or desires.

Your therapist also spends time trying to understand how your actions are related to the actions of others (and to your feelings and thoughts about their actions). In fact, your therapist might try to understand how your actions are related to your thoughts and feelings about her or his own actions in therapy. For example, let's say that your therapist was a few minutes late for your session, and you yelled, "You must not care about me at all!" Well, in MBT, your therapist would try to understand how your yelling was related to the thoughts (for example, "I'm not important!") and feelings (for example, disappointment and hurt) you had about your therapist's lateness. The idea is that your therapist's efforts to understand these connections will help you start to learn them too. In other words, they will help you learn how to mentalize. According to MBT, the more your therapist tries to understand how all of these things are related, the more you will learn how your actions are linked to the things that happen around you, and to your reactions to these things.

Another important part of MBT individual therapy is taking a position of "not knowing." Basically, this means that you and your therapist don't assume that either one of you has all the answers or completely understands what the other person is experiencing. This stance of open curiosity, or "not knowing," is thought to play a key role in helping you develop mentalization.

Group Therapy

Interestingly, MBT group therapy looks a lot like MBT individual therapy. In fact, in some ways you can think of MBT group therapy as the same as MBT individual therapy—just with more people in the room! We say this, because many of the things you find in MBT individual therapy can also be found in MBT group therapy. For example, as we discussed above, all members of an MBT group (and the group leader) are asked to take a position of "not knowing" and to try their best to understand how group members' behaviors are related to the behaviors of other members of the group, as well as to their own feelings, thoughts, and desires. In particular, all members of an MBT group are encouraged to consider the mental states of the other group members, as well as their own mental states. Because of the focus on mentalization (which really involves thinking about other people in relation to ourselves), group therapy provides a great opportunity to practice this skill.

Scientific Evidence for MBT in the Treatment of Self-Harm

Just like DBT, MBT has been shown to help people with BPD stop their self-harm. Although MBT hasn't been studied as much as DBT (mostly because it's a newer treatment), the existing studies show that MBT helps reduce self-harm. In the first study of MBT, Drs. Bateman and Fonagy (1999) compared the eighteen-month-long MBT partial hospital program to the treatment clients typically received in the community. They found that MBT was better at reducing suicide attempts and self-harm (in addition to depression and anxiety). What's more, clients who were treated with MBT continued to have less self-harm and fewer suicide attempts eighteen months after the treatment had ended (Bateman and Fonagy 2001). Even more exciting, in the longest follow-up study of any treatment for BPD, Drs. Bateman and Fonagy (2008) found that clients who received MBT continued to have fewer suicidal behaviors and better overall functioning five years after completing the treatment.

FIGURING OUT WHICH TREATMENT IS RIGHT FOR YOU

There are many things to consider when choosing the right treatment for you. Do you prefer an active, problem-solving approach that teaches you new skills and helps you find ways to replace your self-harm with healthier behaviors? If so, you probably want to consider MACT, DBT, or the emotion regulation group treatment. Or, would you prefer a less structured treatment where you spend most of your time talking with your therapist about yourself and your relationships? If so, MBT may be your best bet.

You'll also want to consider whether you want a short, focused treatment or a longer, more comprehensive one. Are you interested in finding a treatment that will focus just on your self-harm and provide you with some new skills to stop your self-harm right away? If so, MACT or the emotion regulation group therapy may be a good choice. If, on the other hand, you're interested in finding a comprehensive treatment that will address all of the different problems you struggle with (in addition to your self-harm), DBT or MBT may be a better choice.

Other considerations to keep in mind when choosing a treatment include:

- Whether or not you want to be in group therapy (which is a part of DBT and MBT, and the entire format of the emotion regulation group)

- If you also struggle with BPD, in which case MACT may not be the right option for you

- What treatment makes the most sense to you and seems to address why you self-harm

Finally, it's important to keep in mind that even if some (or all) of these treatments aren't available in your community, you can still get the help you need. In chapter 7, we suggested some steps you can take if nobody in your area offers these treatments. In addition, it's important to keep in mind that many therapists who work with people who self-harm know about the different treatments we described here and use some of the strategies from these treatments in their own practices. Therefore, even if none of these treatments is available in your area, the therapist you work with could very well end up teaching you some of the skills from these treatments and covering a lot of the same information. So, the more you know about the treatments that studies have shown to work for self-harm, the better off you'll be when it comes to choosing a therapist who's right for you.

SUMMARY

- Several psychological treatments have been shown to be helpful for self-harm.

- These treatments range from short, focused treatments, like MACT and the emotion regulation group therapy, to comprehensive treatments for BPD, like DBT and MBT.

- MACT is the shortest of these treatments, and consists of reading six booklets (and, for some people, meeting with a therapist for a few sessions). MACT teaches you some basic distress tolerance and problem-solving skills, and could be a good first step in stopping your self-harm. However, it doesn't seem to work for people with BPD, and it probably works best if you don't have a lot of other problems in addition to your self-harm.

🌿 Dr. Gratz's emotion regulation group therapy is a fourteen-week treatment for self-harm developed for women with BPD. This group therapy teaches you a variety of different emotion regulation skills, and was designed to be added on to the therapy you are already receiving. This could be a good option if you already have a therapist but are interested in adding on a brief treatment just for your self-harm.

🌿 DBT and MBT are comprehensive treatments for BPD that have been shown to help people reduce their self-harm. Longer lasting, and including individual and group therapy, they are good options if you want a treatment that will help you with all of your problems (not just self-harm) and if you're looking for a longer-term treatment.

🌿 A lot of different factors go into choosing the right treatment for you. The most important thing is to find a treatment that makes sense to you and that addresses your needs.

Now that you know more about the psychological treatments that research has shown to be helpful for self-harm, we will turn our attention to some medication treatments that may be useful.

Chapter 9

Medication Treatments

Wendy was a nurse who had been self-harming for the past seven years. She'd gone back and forth in her mind about whether she really wanted to stop self-harm, but one day (after hurting herself way more than she had wanted to), she decided that now was the time to stop. The first thing she did was to contact a therapist in her area who specialized in the treatment of self-harm. And, within just a few weeks she started to feel that she was developing new coping skills. Being a nurse, however, she soon found herself wondering, "Are there any kinds of medications that might help me?" So, she booked an appointment with a psychiatrist to discuss her medication treatment options.

You may already know that many people who self-harm are on psychotropic medications of some sort. *Psychotropic medication* is simply medication designed to influence your mental states, emotions, behaviors, or psychiatric symptoms. Between 21 and 50 percent of people who harm themselves take some kind of psychotropic medication (Houston et al. 2003; Nada-Raja et al. 2004). Perhaps you are on medication to help with your self-harm (or one of the problems that tends to go along with self-harm), or maybe you're simply wondering if you should consider medication as an option.

Because so many people who harm themselves take medications, this chapter is devoted to giving you accurate information on medication treatments in general, as well as the types of medications that may be most useful for self-harm. We'll also give you some helpful hints of things to consider before taking medications, questions to ask the person who's prescribing your medication, and ways to keep track of how well your medication is working for you.

HOW DO MEDICATIONS WORK?

Before we talk about the medications that may help with self-harm, it's important for you to know a little about psychotropic medications, how they work, and how scientists test them to see if they work.

Changing Your Brain Chemistry

To put it simply, medications are designed to change your brain chemistry. The idea is that problems with brain chemistry cause or influence some psychiatric problems; therefore, if you correct these brain-chemistry problems, your psychiatric problems should improve as well.

Now, before we get into exactly how medications change your brain chemistry, it's helpful to know a little about how your brain chemistry works. The first thing to know is that we call the main chemical messengers that activate your neurons (brain cells) *neurotransmitters*. And this is how neurotransmitters work; imagine that there are two islands separated by a narrow channel of water: Pre Island and Post Island. Each island has a big marina where a bunch of boats dock after traveling from one island to the next. This is a lot like the neurons in your brain. In this example, the islands are neurons, and the channel between them is a synapse. The boats are the neurotransmitters. The neurotransmitters travel from one neuron (technically called the *presynaptic neuron*) to another neuron (the *postsynaptic neuron*), and then bind to the other neuron (like how a boat docks in the marina).

Now, let's say that a bunch of people get onto a boat on Pre Island and travel over to Post Island. Once the boat gets there, a few different things can happen. One thing that might happen is that the boat arrives, and the people get out, explore the island, buy things, and cause a lot of activity to happen on the island. Similarly, some neurotransmitters cause the postsynaptic neuron to fire, or to become active. We call these *excitatory neurotransmitters*, because they "excite" activity in the postsynaptic neuron.

A second thing that might happen is that the neurotransmitter might prevent the postsynaptic neuron from firing. Some neurotransmitters work in this way; that is, they make other neurons less active or block their activity. For instance, a pirate ship might travel from one island to the next, and then the pirates might get out and loot the island, turn off the electric-power plant, or steal things so that the little town on the island can't function. Neurotransmitters that block the activity of a neuron are called *inhibitory neurotransmitters*, because they inhibit the activity of other neurons.

A third thing that might happen is that a bunch of boats might just sit in the docks at the marina, preventing other boats from docking. Some neurotransmitters work like this. They block the receptors of other neurons so that no other neurotransmitters can "dock" and activate the neurons.

Another important thing to know about how neurons work is that, sometimes, neurotransmitters leave the presynaptic neuron and never make it to the postsynaptic neuron. This can happen for a couple of reasons:

- One reason that a neurotransmitter might not make it to the other neuron is called *reuptake*. Basically, reuptake happens when chemicals in the synapse pull the neurotransmitters back into the presynaptic neuron before they can get very far. This is like boats leaving Pre Island, only to be captured by the Coast Guard and taken back to Pre Island before they make it to Post Island.

- Another reason is that certain *enzymes* (molecules that speed up chemical reactions in the body) in the synapse might break down the neurotransmitter chemically before it reaches the postsynaptic neuron. This would be like a stormy sea battering and destroying the boats before they get to Post Island.

So, how does all of this relate to medication treatments for self-harm? Well, for example, some researchers have suggested that self-harm may be caused by too little serotonin activity (remember this from chapter 3?). Too little serotonin activity could be due to too little release of serotonin, enzymes that break down serotonin before it reaches the postsynaptic neuron, reuptake, or the presence of other neurotransmitters that block the receptors at the postsynaptic neuron.

Scientists have designed medications to correct problems related to neurotransmitters. Next, we give you some information on the most common medications used to treat self-harm, how they're supposed to work, and some of the side effects to watch out for.

TRICYCLIC ANTIDEPRESSANTS (TCAS)

Tricyclic antidepressants (TCAs) work primarily by blocking the reuptake of norepinephrine, serotonin, and (to a lesser extent) dopamine. This means that more of these neurotransmitters are available in the synapse and, as a result, they have a better chance of activating another neuron. This is like getting rid of the Coast Guard so that more boats make it to Post Island. As we mentioned in chapter 3, serotonin is a neurotransmitter that regulates mood, hunger, temperature, sexual activity, sleep, and aggression, among other things. *Norepinephrine* (sometimes called *noradrenaline*) is a neurotransmitter involved in alertness, concentration, aggressiveness, motivation, and the fight-or-flight system. *Dopamine* is a neurotransmitter involved in mood, pleasure, and body movement.

Some of the common side effects of TCAs include dry mouth, fatigue, urinary retention, dizziness, blurred vision, hand tremors, constipation, and nausea. Some common examples of TCAs include Elavil (amitriptyline), Norpramin (desipramine), Tofranil (imipramine), Aventyl (nortriptyline), and Anafranil (clomipramine).

SELECTIVE SEROTONIN REUPTAKE INHIBITORS (SSRIS)

Selective serotonin reuptake inhibitors (SSRIs), such as Prozac, work in a similar manner as TCAs. Like TCAs, SSRIs prevent the reuptake of serotonin. The difference is that TCAs prevent the reuptake of serotonin, norepinephrine, and dopamine, whereas SSRIs prevent the reuptake of serotonin only (that's why the term "selective" is used).

Although the side effects of SSRIs are often quite mild, many are possible. Some of the most common side effects include nausea, diarrhea, headaches, anxiety, nervousness, sleep disturbance, restlessness and agitation, fatigue, dizziness, light-headedness, sexual problems (including lower sex drive), tremor, dry mouth, sweating, possible mania for people who struggle with bipolar disorder, weight loss or gain, rashes, and seizures.

Some common examples of SSRIs include Prozac (fluoxetine), Zoloft (sertraline), Luvox (fluvoxamine), Celexa (citalopram), Lexapro (escitalopram), and Paxil (paroxetine).

ANTIPSYCHOTIC MEDICATIONS

Originally used to treat people with schizophrenia, treatment providers often prescribe antipsychotic medications to help people who have trouble controlling impulses, such as the impulse to engage in self-harm. There are many ideas about how antipsychotics work, but the most common explanation is that they block activity of dopamine areas in the brain. Some research shows that *too much* dopamine activity might lead to some of the symptoms that people with schizophrenia experience, such as delusions and hallucinations. Different antipsychotic medications work in different ways, but most of these medications block dopamine receptors. This would be like having a bunch of big boats sitting in the docks at the marina, preventing any other boats from docking on Post Island. When the dopamine receptor is blocked, dopamine can't bind with the receptor or cause the neuron to fire.

There are two main types of antipsychotics: *first-generation antipsychotics* and *second-generation antipsychotics*. First-generation antipsychotics aren't used very often (except for people with serious psychosis who don't respond to other medications) because of their side effects. A downside of first-generation antipsychotics is that the amount of medication that tends to be enough to help with patients' symptoms is very close to the amount of medication that tends to produce troublesome side effects.

For second-generation antipsychotics, however, you need to take a much higher dose of medication before dangerous side effects occur. For these medications, the *therapeutic dose* (the dose that produces good effects) is normally lower than the dose that produces troubling side effects. Nevertheless, even second-generation antipsychotics have several common side effects, including sedation and fatigue, low blood pressure, weight gain, temperature increases or decreases (for example, feeling hot a lot of the time), changes in the activity of your heart or cardiovascular system, and changes in your skin pigmentation, among others. In addition, certain second-generation antipsychotics (such as clozapine) require you to take special steps in order to avoid serious side effects. For example, if you take clozapine, you need to have your white blood cells monitored regularly.

Severe side effects of antipsychotic medications include involuntary movements in your face and other body parts (called *tardive dyskinesia*), and *neuroleptic malignant syndrome* (NMS). Although tardive dyskinesia is much more common if you're using first-generation antipsychotics, it's a possible side effect of second-generation antipsychotics as well. NMS is the most serious side effect of all, and can occur if you're taking any antipsychotic. NMS consists of muscular rigidity, elevated temperature, blood-pressure increases or decreases, agitation, delirium, and even coma. If you have any of these symptoms, you must see your doctor immediately, and you will need to be taken off the medication.

Some common examples of second-generation antipsychotics include Loxitane (loxapine), Clozaril (clozapine), Risperdal (risperidone), Zyprexa (olanzapine), and Serlect (sertindole).

HOW WELL DO MEDICATIONS WORK FOR SELF-HARM?

In this section, we tell you about some of the medications that may work for self-harm. First, we tell you a little about how people test and study medications in the first place, and then we go on to tell you about some of the findings on certain medications for self-harm.

How Do You Know If a Medication Works?

As you might have guessed, determining whether a medication works is a very complicated question. It's also a very important question, though. In fact, it's just as important for you to know the answer to this question as it is for your doctor to know the answer. We want you to have the information you need to be able to evaluate the advertisements for medications you see all over the place these days: on TV, in magazines, and even in your doctor's waiting room!

To make sense of all the information out there on medications, you need to know how people study medications, and what type of evidence is the "best" and most reliable. Therefore, we'll start by telling you how researchers figure out whether a medication works.

Researchers use a variety of different methods to study medications.

Case studies: In a case study, a researcher usually gives an individual a particular medication for self-harm and then publishes information on how well that medication seemed to work for that particular person. Case studies can be useful when people are trying out new medications, but there's a big problem with them: We simply can't assume that all patients are alike. For instance, we can't assume that just because a medication worked for Sally Smith in Nebraska, it will work for you.

Open-label trial: For an open-label trial, the researcher gets a group of patients to take one or more medications. In this kind of study, both the patients and the researchers know which drug the patients are receiving. Quite often, researchers use open-label trials to test new medications or to try out existing medications for different types of problems. One major problem with open-label trials is that they are ripe for *placebo effects*, which refers to the tendency for people to get better simply because they know they're taking a medication and *expect* to get better. Another problem with open-label trials is that the researcher knows who's getting the medication. Because the researcher sometimes wants the medication to do well, researcher bias might influence the findings. A third problem is that patients might get better just because their symptoms naturally improve over time, not because the medication actually works. Although open-label trials can be helpful, we all need to be a little skeptical about any medication that has only been studied in open-label trials.

Double-blind, placebo-controlled trials: In a double-blind, placebo-controlled trial, the researchers randomly assign the patients to get either the drug (like Prozac) or some kind of placebo (usually a sugar pill). Also, these studies are "double-blind" because both the researcher and the patient are "blind" to (they don't know) which drug (placebo or Prozac) the patient is taking. These studies basically get rid of the possibility that a placebo effect could explain the findings. Also, if the medication does better than the placebo, this is probably not just because the patients get better over time—because both placebo patients and medication patients are given the chance to get better over time. It's more likely that something about the medication itself causes the improvement. This type of study is one of the best ways to test a medication, so you can have the most confidence in medications that researchers have tested in double-blind, placebo-controlled trials.

How Well Do Medications Work for Self-Harm?

Well, we would like to be able to say that there's a fabulous medication out there that will help you stop your self-harm once and for all. Unfortunately, this isn't the case. So far, there haven't been very many studies of medications for self-harm. And, because many of the existing studies have been case studies or open-label trials, it's not clear what to make of their findings. So, with that in mind, we turn now to what we do know about specific medications for self-harm.

STUDIES OF SSRIs

SSRIs seem to have the most evidence going for them when it comes to medication treatments for self-harm. For instance, one study examined Prozac (fluoxetine) for 15 women who repeatedly picked their skin (Bloch et al. 2001). In an open-label trial, 8 out of the 15 patients showed a 30 percent or greater improvement in the frequency of their skin picking. Of the 8 patients who showed these improvements, 4 were randomly assigned to continue fluoxetine, and 4 went on a placebo. The findings showed that the 4 patients on fluoxetine kept up their improvements, whereas the 4 patients on the placebo went back to the same amount of skin picking that they had been doing before the start of the study. Up to 30 months after the study, the patients who continued taking fluoxetine were doing better than the patients who didn't. Other studies have also found that fluoxetine (Simeon et al. 1997) and other SSRIs like Lexapro (escitalopram; Keuthen et al. 2007) are useful for skin picking.

Other studies have tested different SSRIs for other kinds of self-harm behaviors. For instance, one open-label trial found that female patients who took Luvox (fluvoxamine) showed improvements in a behavior called *excoriation* (Arnold et al. 1999), which is a type of self-harm that involves picking at or removing scabs or wounds. In this study, 4 out of the 14 patients showed at least a 30 percent reduction in their excoriation behaviors.

Overall, these studies tell us that SSRIs may be a useful medication for people with skin-picking and similar forms of self-harm that involve picking rather than cutting or burning. Interestingly, both skin picking and excoriation are *compulsive behaviors*, or repetitive, habitual behaviors that people find very hard to stop (like fidgeting, biting your nails, pulling your hair, or other types of activities). And, as it turns out, SSRIs also work quite well for another disorder that involves compulsive behaviors, obsessive-compulsive disorder (OCD). So, it makes sense that SSRIs might work best for types of self-harm that are a lot like the repetitive behavior that occurs among people with OCD.

STUDIES OF TCAs

A few studies have investigated the use of TCAs for self-harm. The problem is that these studies have generally only involved case studies and have largely focused on people with mental retardation or other developmental disabilities, such as autism. To our knowledge, there have been no well-controlled studies of TCAs for self-harm as of July 2008. Of course, given that studies have found that TCAs are very helpful for depression (Van, Schoevers, and Dekker 2008), it's definitely possible that a TCA could be helpful for self-harm as well. That is, if you experience improvements in depression, you might find it easier to stop harming yourself. But, the evidence that TCAs specifically help people stop self-harm is far from conclusive.

STUDIES OF ANTIPSYCHOTIC MEDICATIONS

Some studies have examined antipsychotic medications for self-harm. Much of this research has focused on patients (mainly female patients) with BPD or individuals with cognitive deficits (low IQ, or mental retardation). One study of BPD patients with psychotic symptoms found that Clozaril (clozapine) was helpful in reducing self-harm behaviors (Chengappa et al. 1999). Another study (an open-label trial), however, found that patients with BPD who took Risperdal (risperidone; a second-generation antipsychotic) showed improvements in aggression and hostility but not necessarily self-harm (Rocca et al. 2002). Another study examined outcomes among adults with cognitive deficits who had taken risperidone, quetiapine, or olanzapine (Ruedrich et al. 2008). The findings revealed that patients who struggled with aggression showed some improvement in aggressive behaviors, but patients who also self-harmed didn't show improvements. Therefore, the jury is still out on whether antipsychotics can actually help reduce self-harm. In addition, it's important to remember that if you don't have BPD and you have normal cognitive functioning, there's not much evidence to support using antipsychotics to help you with your self-harm.

STUDIES OF OTHER MEDICATIONS AND SUPPLEMENTS

Researchers have also studied other medications and supplements for self-harm. One such medication is *naltrexone*. Something else researchers have started studying is not a medication but a dietary supplement, *omega-3 fatty acids*. In our experience, physicians prescribe supplements and naltrexone less often than antidepressants and antipsychotic medications, but it's still useful for you to know something about what they are and whether they are helpful for self-harm.

Naltrexone is a medication that blocks opioid receptors in the brain so that the natural (endogenous) opioids cannot bind with and activate the postsynaptic neuron. This would be like a bunch of boats docking at Post Island, preventing other boats from docking and, thus, preventing people from entering the island and doing touristy activities. Remember when we told you about the possible role of natural opioids in self-harm? The idea is that people who self-harm might get a lot of emotional relief when they have an injury because their natural pain-relief system (the opioid system) is overactive. Well, if naltrexone blocks your opioid receptors, then you are less likely to get this emotional relief when you self-harm. Over time, if continuing to harm yourself doesn't bring any relief, you might stop harming yourself.

Several studies have examined naltrexone for self-harming patients. Many of the studies have shown reductions in self-harm among patients who take naltrexone (Rénéric and Bouvard 1998). The problem is that most of these studies have been case studies or very small open-label trials. Now, a few double-blind, placebo-controlled trials have examined naltrexone, but these studies have found mixed results. Some of these studies have found improvements in self-harm, whereas others haven't. As a result, it's not entirely clear whether naltrexone is helpful for self-harm. It could be that people who self-harm partly because of excessive opioid activity might benefit most, but psychiatrists don't yet have the technology to determine whether their patients have excessive opioid activity in their brains.

As we mentioned, researchers have also begun to study the effects of omega-3 fatty acids on self-harm and suicidal behaviors. Omega-3 fatty acids are found in fish, certain types of nuts, flaxseeds, and other foods, and have many beneficial effects, such as reducing cholesterol and blood pressure as well as the risk of heart disease. In fact, these health benefits are one advantage of the omega-3 fatty acids over standard psychotropic medications. Another advantage is that they have very few side effects. The jury is still out, however, on whether omega-3 fatty acids can actually help with self-harm. One study compared a placebo to omega-3 fatty acids in the treatment of women with BPD and found that women who took omega-3 fatty acids showed greater improvements in aggression and depression (Zanarini and Frankenburg 2003). However, taking the omega-3 fatty acids didn't really seem to help with self-harm, because equal percentages of patients in each group (placebo and omega-3) harmed themselves during the study (10 percent). In addition, another placebo-controlled trial compared omega-3 fatty acids to a placebo in the treatment of patients who went to a hospital emergency department in Ireland after having harmed themselves (Hallahan et al. 2007). Patients who took omega-3 fatty acids showed greater improvements than patients who received the placebo in depression, stress levels, and suicidal thoughts, but not in self-harm behavior. Therefore, it seems that omega-3 fatty acids can help with emotional symptoms (such as depression and stress) and aggression, but studies have yet to show that omega-3 fatty acids reduce self-harm any more than a placebo does.

THE BOTTOM LINE ON MEDICATIONS FOR SELF-HARM

The bottom line is that medication is not the gold-standard treatment for self-harm. These are probably the best conclusions we can make so far:

- There's some evidence that SSRIs may be helpful in reducing self-harm behavior that involves repetitive picking of the skin.

- TCAs might be helpful for people with cognitive disabilities, but we don't know enough to say whether they are useful in general for people who self-harm.

- Antipsychotics might help with some of the symptoms of BPD, but there's little evidence that antipsychotics actually reduce self-harm.

- Naltrexone has had mixed findings, with some studies showing good effects and others not showing changes in self-harm.

- Certain supplements, such as omega-3 fatty acids, might help with stress, depression, or aggression, but they probably won't directly help with self-harm.

Now, if you self-harm, this summary probably isn't the most encouraging thing you've ever read. Keep in mind, though, that there are effective treatments for self-harm; it's just that these treatments tend to involve psychotherapy. So, your best bet will probably be to find a psychological treatment like the ones we discussed in chapter 8. As for medications, even if a medication doesn't reduce self-harm, it might still help you with some of the other problems that often go along with self-harm, such as depression or anxiety disorders in particular.

In summary, although medication may play a role in your recovery process by helping you with other emotional problems or psychiatric difficulties, we strongly recommend that you seek counseling or psychotherapy to help you with your self-harm, because medication alone probably won't do the trick.

TAKE AN ACTIVE ROLE IN YOUR TREATMENT

Whether you're on medication now or simply considering starting a medication, you will probably receive greater benefits if you take an active role in your treatment. When it comes to medication treatments, there are three important ways to take an active role: (1) Get information about the medication and ask questions, (2) think through your decision regarding whether to take the medication, and (3) monitor how you are doing on the medication. Below, we give you practical suggestions for accomplishing each of these steps and taking an active role in your treatment.

Get Information About Medications and Ask Questions

Before you start taking a medication, the first step is to gather as much information as possible. One way to do this is to read self-help materials like this book. Another way to do this is to talk with your psychiatrist or physician about the medication and ask any questions you have. Below, we list some important questions you may want to ask your prescribing physician before starting a medication.

WHAT TO ASK YOUR PRESCRIBER BEFORE STARTING A MEDICATION

Questions about how well the medication works:

- How do your patients do on this medication?

- Does this medication work for people with my problems?

- How many people seem to get better on this medication?

- What are the chances that this medication will help me with my problems?

- What can I do, if anything, to make the medication work better for me?

- How long will it take for me to notice a difference in my symptoms?

- How does the medication work?

- Why do you think this medication will work for me?

Questions about things to watch out for:

- What's likely to happen if or when I go off the medication? Do people often have a relapse if they stop taking this medication?

- What happens if I miss a dose?

- What are the side effects of the medication?

- Will this medication interact with my other medications?

- Which side effects are common, and which ones are rare?

- Which types of side effects do I need to be most concerned about?

- What kinds of side effects might tell me that there's an emergency?

- Are there any foods or drugs (including alcohol) that I need to avoid if I'm on this medication?

> **Other important information to gather:**
>
> - How expensive is the medication?
>
> - Will my insurance plan cover it?
>
> - How will we figure out how well the medication is working?
>
> - What will we do if this doesn't work? Will we stop this medi-
>   cation and try another one, or will we keep this medication
>   and add another one?

Your physician is the best source of information on medications, and has the added benefit of being able to answer your specific questions. Other sources of information on medications include the Internet and a book called the *PDR Drug Guide for Mental Health Professionals* (Thomson Healthcare Products, 2008). When it comes to the Internet, many companies that produce medications actually have websites that provide information on the effects and side effects of their medications, how they work, and what dosages are normal or optimal. Some websites are even devoted entirely to one particular medication. For instance, there's a website for Prozac (www.prozac.com) and similar drugs. These websites can be a good source of information on medications. Keep in mind, however, that the companies that produce these medications want people to buy them. Therefore, even though the information on these websites is often detailed and accurate, it's probably a good idea to remember that the companies have a financial interest in having people use their medications.

The *PDR Drug Guide* (mentioned above) is another source of information on a variety of medications. The *PDR* is a big, heavy book that provides physicians with information on specific medications, including their effects, how they work, side effects, and the evidence in support of using the medications for particular disorders or problems. The *PDR* is very technical and could be hard to read if you are not very familiar with medications, but it does include pertinent details about medications, and you can trust that the information you read is accurate.

Think Through Your Decision

After you've gathered all of the information you need, it's very important to give yourself some time to think through your decision to take medication. As you may have noticed, physicians often work very quickly and efficiently. You might see someone for a very brief appointment and end up on your way to the pharmacy before you've really thought through whether taking the medication is right for you. You might feel so desperate for help that you would take anything that someone offers. Therefore, we suggest that you ask as many questions as possible (as noted previously) and then give yourself some time to think through the pros and cons of taking the medication before making your decision.

PROS AND CONS OF MEDICATION

One of the best ways to think through decisions like this is to come up with a list of the pros and cons of going on the medication. In the pros category, put all of the positive things that might come from being on the medication. In the cons category, put all of the negative things that might go along with taking the medication. Then, look at your lists and decide whether you want to go ahead and try the medication.

We've included some examples of pros and cons below.

Pros of the Medication	Cons of the Medication
❧ I might feel better emotionally.	❧ I would have to avoid certain foods.
❧ My depression might improve.	❧ I wouldn't like the side effects.
❧ It might be easier to stop my self-harm.	❧ I can't afford it, and my insurance doesn't cover it.
❧ I might feel less anxious.	❧ There's no good scientific evidence for this medication for self-harm.

Monitor How You Are Doing

Another way to take an active role in your treatment is to monitor how well it's working. If you are on a medication, you'll probably meet with your physician or psychiatrist for brief appointments to determine how you are doing and whether you are having any notable side effects. The thing is, these appointments might only happen once every couple of weeks or months. Therefore, it can be very helpful for you to monitor how you're doing on a daily or weekly basis. That way, you can keep track of any improvements, difficulties, or side effects that you are having. What's more, you can share this information with your prescribing physician so that she or he has as much accurate information as possible when it comes to monitoring how you are doing on the medication, and making decisions about your dosages and so on.

Next, we include a symptom-monitoring form that you can use to monitor how you're doing on a particular medication. With some small modifications, this is the same form that we published in our previous book, *The Borderline Personality Disorder Survival Guide* (New Harbinger Publications, 2007).

SYMPTOM MONITORING LOG

Instructions:

Use this log to keep track of your symptoms or experiences and to communicate how you are doing to the person who prescribes your medication. You can also use this log to keep track of how you do when your medication changes, or when you don't take your medication as you are supposed to. You might modify this log according to your own specific symptoms or problems. For instance, you might consider adding columns for emotions or behaviors that you're especially interested in keeping track of.

Fill this out at the end of the day, every day, so that the information is still fresh in your mind. For each column that asks you for a 0–10 rating, please make a rating based on the highest or most intense experience for that day. For example, if the column asks you about self-harm urges, please write in the number that matches your highest self-harm urges for that day (not your average). Here's the scale: 0 = none (no emotional distress, self-harm urges, and so on), and 10 = highest possible (emotional distress, self-harm urges, and so on).

For the Self-Harm column, please write in how many times you hurt yourself each day.

Day	Emotional Distress	Self-Harm Urges	Suicidal Thoughts	Self-Harm	Took Meds as Prescribed	Side Effects
	0–10	0–10	0–10	# of times	Yes or No	0–10
Mon.						
Tue.						
Wed.						
Thur.						
Fri.						
Sat.						
Sun.						

Important Notes (write down any important information about self-harm, side effects, or other important information):

SUMMARY

- Neurotransmitters are chemicals in your brain that affect the activity of brain cells (neurons).

- Medications change the activity of your neurotransmitters.

- In trying to figure out whether a medication is helpful, we are most confident in the findings from studies that use double-blind, placebo-controlled trials.

- The medications most commonly used to treat self-harm include tricyclic and SSRI antidepressants, and antipsychotic medications.

- SSRIs have shown some benefit for people whose self-harm involves repetitive picking of their skin.

- Antipsychotics and tricyclic antidepressants have been studied in very specific types of patients (for example, people with cognitive disabilities or BPD), and most studies don't show that these medications actually help reduce self-harm.

- Naltrexone has had mixed findings when it comes to treating self-harm, and could be helpful for some people.

- Omega-3 fatty acids might help you with some of the problems that often go along with self-harm (in particular, mood and emotional problems), but this supplement probably won't help you with your self-harm behavior.

- Take an active role in your treatment by seeking out information on medications, giving yourself the time to think through your decision of whether or not to take a medication, and working with your prescribing physician to monitor how well the medication is working for you.

Now that you know more about psychological and medication treatments for self-harm, we move on to the coping skills section of this book. In the next few chapters, we teach you skills to help you (1) get motivated to stop self-harm (or, for those of you who are already motivated, to supercharge your motivation) and make success more likely (chapter 10), (2) cope with self-harm urges (chapter 11), and (3) manage your emotions (chapter 12). We hope that the practical suggestions in the next three chapters will help you move forward on the road to recovery and toward freedom from self-harm.

PART III

COPING STRATEGIES FOR MANAGING SELF-HARM

Chapter 10

Getting Motivated to Stop Self-Harm and Increasing Your Chances of Success

Steve finally understood just what he was struggling with. For so long, he couldn't understand how or why he could harm himself on purpose, and sometimes wondered if he were going crazy. But, after reading and learning more about self-harm, he finally felt as if he had a grip on his behavior. And, for a couple of weeks, this new awareness and knowledge really helped. Knowing what he was up against and having the facts about self-harm made him feel better equipped to handle his self-harm. He finally felt that he might just be able to kick this behavior. The problem was that whenever a bad mood came on, he still found himself turning to self-harm like an old friend. He soon realized that knowledge and understanding was only the first step on the road to recovery. He wondered what the second step was.

At this point, you've probably learned a lot about self-harm. We have given you a lot of information on what self-harm is, why it occurs, and the purposes it serves. We've also told you about the kinds of psychiatric problems that often go along with self-harm, and some psychological and medication treatments that have been found to help people stop self-harm. And, as we mentioned before, understanding what you are struggling with is the first step on the road to recovery. In this chapter, we'll help you take your second step by providing you with skills to get you motivated to stop your self-harm and increase your chances of successfully doing so.

SKILLS FOR INCREASING YOUR MOTIVATION TO STOP SELF-HARM

As you probably know, stopping self-harm isn't the easiest thing to do. Just when you think you're ready to give it up, something happens to pull you back in. As we mentioned before, self-harm serves a lot of important purposes, and can be a very quick and powerful way to get relief. And, any behavior that works that well in the short term will be very hard to give up. What this means is that many people who struggle with self-harm aren't always sure that they want to stop. For example, you might have noticed that you feel really motivated to stop your self-harm when you think about all of the downsides of harming yourself. But, at other times, you might question whether you want to give up one of the only ways you have of making yourself feel better. Because self-harm works so well in the short term, it's hard to stay motivated to stop it.

The good news is that there are skills that can help get you out of this dilemma by increasing your motivation to stop self-harm. Now, this doesn't mean that you will never again question whether you want to stop, or wonder if you should allow yourself to do it "once in a while" or keep it as an option "just in case." However, these skills can get you motivated to stop self-harm now, and can even help if your motivation wavers in the future.

Identifying Pros and Cons of Self-Harm

One of the first steps to increase your motivation to stop self-harm is to list all of the pros and cons of self-harm, both short term and long term. One reason it can be so hard to stop self-harm is that people tend to remember the short-term consequences of their behaviors much more than the long-term consequences. Our minds actually make the strongest connections between events that happen close together in time. So, you are much more likely to remember the feeling of relief that usually comes right after you self-harm than you are to remember your feelings of shame, disappointment, or self-loathing that come much later.

The problem is, when it comes to a behavior like self-harm, those negative long-term consequences that you tend to forget are exactly the ones that you need to keep in mind. If you never think about the negative long-term consequences, and focus only on the positive short-term consequences, why would you want to give it up? The only thing you would be aware of is how well it works. So, you need to find some way to make the negative consequences of self-harm just as memorable as the positive short-term consequences.

One way to do this is to list all of the pros and cons of self-harm (you can learn more about this skill in Dr. Linehan's *Skills Training Manual for Treating Borderline Personality Disorder,* published by The Guilford Press, 1993). Use the following table to come up with as many consequences as you can. Make sure you fill in each of the four boxes in the table. Now, some of you might be wondering how listing the pros of self-harm could increase your motivation to stop doing it. You might think that focusing on the benefits of self-harm would make it harder to stop, and you might be tempted to ignore those cells of the table. Resist that temptation! It won't help you to pretend that self-harm doesn't have some positive consequences in the short term. It does, and pretending they don't exist isn't going to work.

To make the best use of this table, you need to make sure that you have all the facts in front of you. Only then can you make an informed decision about whether or not self-harm is worth it in the long run. If you don't list all of the things it does for you in the short run, you aren't going to believe your list. You may feel as if you are trying to trick yourself into giving up self-harm, and this just isn't going to work. So, make sure you write down all of the consequences you can think of— positive and negative.

Consequences of Self-Harm		
	Positive	Negative
Short-Term Consequences		
Long-Term Consequences		

Make a copy of this table and carry it around with you. Then, the next time you find yourself considering self-harm as an option, take this table out and focus on all of the downsides of self-harm. Use this table (especially the right-hand side) whenever your motivation to stop self-harm wavers.

After you come up with as many consequences as you can, take a long, hard look at this table. Do you notice anything? One thing people often notice is that many of the negative long-term consequences are mirror images of the positive short-term consequences. Any relief self-harm provides in the short term is usually reversed in the long term. For example, even though self-harm might make you feel better or less upset in the short term, it probably makes you feel even worse in the long term. Realizing this can get you motivated to stop self-harm. In fact, the next time you find yourself thinking about all of the benefits of self-harm, take out this table and focus on all of the downsides of self-harm. Pay particular attention to the bottom, right-hand corner and really think about all the ways self-harm makes your problems worse in the long run.

There are two other important things to keep in mind when you use this strategy. First, be sure to come up with important pros and cons. It probably won't be hard to come up with important pros, but you might have a hard time coming up with important cons. If that's the case, ask yourself, "Does this make me feel more like stopping self-harm?" each time you come up with a con. If the answer is yes, then that's probably a good con to write down. Think of things you really hate about self-harm—things that make it hard for you to keep harming yourself. You may even want to underline or put a star next to the really important cons.

Second, memorize your list of cons. Sit down and really cement these cons in your mind so that you can come up with them easily in the heat of the moment. When you're upset, you will probably remember the pros more than the cons, so you need to find a way to make sure that the cons come to mind just as easily. One way to do this (and one we strongly suggest, especially when you're just learning these skills) is to carry your pros and cons table around with you and read it whenever you feel the urge to self-harm.

Identifying Reasons Not to Harm Yourself

Another skill that's a lot like the first one is to come up with as many reasons as you can to not harm yourself. Some of these will come from the previous table. For example, if you find that self-harm actually makes you feel even sadder or lonelier in the long run, those are two good reasons not to harm yourself. Or, if you're embarrassed about the scars you get from self-harm, that can be another reason not to self-harm.

The reason we have this listed as a separate skill, though, is that many people can come up with other reasons for not harming themselves that might not be included in the previous table. The following list contains some of the reasons people sometimes give for not harming themselves. Look through this list and see if any of these reasons is important to you.

Reasons Not to Harm Yourself

- You could scare your loved ones or make them worry.

- You could harm yourself more seriously than you intended.

- You might have to go to the emergency room.

- You could accidentally kill yourself.

- Each time you harm yourself, it's harder to resist your urges the next time.

- You could get into trouble at school or work.

- People may disapprove or think poorly of you.

- Self-harm can take on a life of its own.

- Self-harm makes you feel even worse about yourself in the long run.

- Self-harm can actually make you more upset and cause more emotional pain.

- Self-harm makes your "coping muscles" atrophy.

Then, come up with your own personalized list of reasons not to harm yourself. For instance, think about how harming yourself will affect the people you care about. Imagine how scared or worried your parents, partner, or friends would be if they saw the cuts on your arm or the burns on your skin. Think about all the ways self-harm can go awry and how you can hurt yourself more severely than you intended. And, think again about the pros and cons table you just completed, and all the ways self-harm can make you feel even worse than before.

Once you've come up with a list of all of the reasons not to harm yourself, make copies of the list and put them all over. Carry one in your pocket. Put one in your car or your locker at school. Tape one to the mirror in your room. Put a copy anywhere you may be tempted to harm yourself. Thinking clearly about anything can be hard when you are really upset, and thinking of reasons not to do something that would give you some relief in the moment (like self-harm) can be even harder. Therefore, if you have a copy of your list with you at all times, you won't have to depend on yourself to think of these reasons "on the fly," when you're in no state to do so. Instead, whenever you consider harming yourself, just take out this list, read it over, and focus on all of the important reasons not to harm yourself.

Write All the Positive Consequences of Stopping Self-Harm

This is a lot like the last skill, but instead of focusing on all of the downsides of self-harm, this skill is all about focusing on the benefits of not self-harming. See the difference? Thinking of all of the good things that will come along with stopping self-harm is just as important as thinking of all the not-so-good things that go along with harming yourself. In fact, both this skill and the last one work better when you use them together. So, once you've come up with a list of all of the reasons not to harm yourself, come up with another list of all the reasons to work on stopping your self-harm. You'll quickly see that these lists balance each other out and work to increase your motivation in different ways.

The following list contains some of the positive consequences of stopping self-harm. See if you can think of any others.

Benefits of Stopping Self-Harm

- You won't have to worry about hiding your arms or other parts of your body where you harm yourself; no more need for long-sleeve shirts in the middle of July!

- You may feel proud of yourself for resisting self-harm.

- Your tolerance for your emotions will grow.

- You will have more time and energy to spend on the things in your life that matter to you.

- You may have more self-confidence when talking to other people.

- No more new scars!

- You won't end up in the emergency room because of your self-harm.

- You can learn other ways of solving your problems and coping with your emotions.

These are just some of the benefits of stopping self-harm. Come up with as many others as you can. Once you have a complete list, carry it around with you at all times and read it whenever your motivation to stop self-harm wavers!

Enlist the Support of Other People

As we mentioned before, your motivation to stop self-harm will probably wax and wane. Therefore, it can be really helpful to bring other people into this process and get their support in stopping self-harm. You know the saying, "Two minds are better than one"? Well, two motivated people are better than one, too. If you have the support of people who care about you, then their motivation for you to stop self-harm could help carry you though the times when your own motivation falters.

In fact, the idea that people can motivate one another to change their behaviors can be seen in some common techniques for promoting healthy behavior change. For example, a common strategy to help people exercise more regularly is to find a gym buddy, or someone to work out with. The idea behind this strategy is that people are more likely to resort to old patterns and give up the commitment to exercise when they're left to their own devices. On the other hand, people are more likely to follow through on their commitment to change when they're accountable to someone else and can rely on other people's strength and commitment when their own motivation wavers. The clinicians and researchers who encourage people to use social support like this know how hard it can be for people to keep up a constant and unwavering motivation to change, especially when the change in question involves a lot of hard work and some discomfort in the short term.

So, how can this help you with your motivation to stop self-harm? Well, there are two important reasons why having the support of other people will help you stay motivated to stop your self-harm. The first is that human beings are more likely to follow through with something when other people know about it. Being accountable to someone else just makes it harder to get out of something. And, this can be a good thing when you're trying to make positive changes and stop your self-harm.

The second reason it can be helpful to enlist the support of other people in your recovery is that you can rely on their motivation when yours falters. And, because it can be so hard to see someone you care about engage in self-harm, your loved ones will probably be extremely motivated for you to stop self-harm. In fact, their motivation to help you stop self-harm probably won't waver very much. Unlike for you, your self-harm doesn't have a lot of positive short-term consequences for your loved ones, so there's not much that will get in the way of their motivation for you to stop. And, that means that your loved ones can be powerful allies in your battle to stop self-harm.

So, if you are having a particularly rough day and are considering harming yourself, ask one of your support people to help you think up reasons not to self-harm. Rely on that person's strength and motivation to get you through hard times. Or, ask a support person to be your "cheerleader," giving you encouragement when you're feeling down or when your motivation to stop self-harm wavers. You could even ask some members of your support system to help you complete the self-harm pros and cons table in this chapter. Other people sometimes have really good ideas about some of the downsides of self-harm and can help you come up with some that you never would have thought of.

Next is a list of some of the ways you can begin to enlist the support of other people in your decision to stop self-harm.

Ways to Enlist the Support of Others

- 🌱 Tell your loved ones that you want to stop self-harm; say this aloud to anyone you trust.

- 🌱 Share your list of pros and cons with members of your support system.

- 🌱 Ask a support person to help you come up with a list of reasons not to self-harm.

- 🌱 Share your list of reasons for not harming yourself with others; give each of your support people a copy to keep.

- 🌱 Ask a support person to be your "cheerleader" when your motivation to stop self-harm wavers.

- 🌱 Tell your support people about the types of things that put you at risk for self-harm so that they can be on the lookout for them too. Two sets of eyes are better than one!

- 🌱 Let members of your support system know the best way to respond to you when you're at risk for self-harm. Tell them what will and won't work for you.

- 🌱 Ask a support person to "check in" with you every now and then to see how you are doing, just in case you're feeling down and not seeking support.

- 🌱 Work with your support person to come up with milestones on your journey to recovery. Then, each time you meet one of these milestones, take some time to celebrate with your support person. Stopping self-harm is no easy task, and encouragement along the way can be the fuel that keeps you going.

Try some of these today, and see if they work! Or, ask some of your support people to help you come up with other ways to use their support in this process. Just knowing that you're not alone can help you find the courage you need to consider stopping self-harm.

Use Guided Imagery to Motivate Yourself to Stop Self-Harm

When thinking about stopping a behavior like self-harm, it's easy to focus on all of the downsides of stopping. You might worry about how you'll cope with your emotions without self-harm, or you might question your ability to resist your urges. This is perfectly normal, but it also makes it hard to get motivated to stop self-harm. So, you might find that you need some special strategies to really connect with just how much your life will improve without self-harm. A lot of people have told us that guided imagery, or using the power of their imaginations, is one of the best ways to do this.

One way to do this is to imagine your life without self-harm:

1. Start by getting into a relaxed state. Find a quiet room with no distractions. Sit in a comfortable chair, close your eyes, and pay attention to your breathing. Notice what it feels like when the air enters and then leaves your body. Try to slow down and deepen your breathing by slowly counting to five as you breathe in, and again as you breathe out (you'll find deep breathing described in more detail in chapter 12). Do this for a few minutes until you begin to feel more relaxed.

2. Now, imagine that it's one year into the future. Try to come up with as vivid an image as you can in your mind. What are you wearing? Where do you live? What's the weather like outside? Do you have a new hairstyle? What kind of job do you have? Who are your friends? Ask yourself as many questions as you can to create a picture of what your life will look like one year from now. Try to bring in as many senses as you can, to make the picture as realistic as possible. What do you see? What sounds do you hear? What scents are in the air? Paint an elaborate picture in your mind.

3. Next, remind yourself that you are now living a life without self-harm. What does that mean for your life? Think about the pros and cons list you completed earlier in this chapter. Imagine what

your life will be like without those long-term negative consequences. Imagine yourself handling a crisis without self-harm. Pay attention to how you feel. You might feel satisfied and proud of yourself for making it through a difficult situation without relying on self-harm. Imagine feeling free of the shame or guilt of having engaged in self-harm. Imagine what it's like to get ready for a party or date without having to worry about hiding your injuries or getting blood on your clothes.

4. After you've pictured this for a while, bring your attention to your feelings. In thinking about your future without self-harm, how do you feel? Hopeful? Excited? Proud? It would also be normal if you felt just a little sad about the loss of your self-harm. Just notice whatever feelings are there.

Imagining a future without self-harm can be a great way to get in touch with the positive aspects of stopping self-harm. It can also help bring the future into the present moment and allow you to catch a glimpse of what your life might look like without self-harm. Practice this exercise whenever you want to boost your motivation to stop self-harm.

Another way to use guided imagery to boost your motivation to stop self-harm is to get back in touch with the moment when you made the decision to stop harming yourself. You can use this strategy when you have the time to sit down and really focus on this moment (as we described previously), or you can use it "on the fly" to get yourself through those moments when your motivation to stop self-harm wavers.

Think back to where you were when you decided to work on becoming free of self-harm. Close your eyes, and imagine that you're back there again. Imagine all of the sights, sounds, smells, and sensations that you were having at the time. Really dive into that moment, remembering the thoughts and feelings you had at the time. Maybe you were fed up with all the trouble caused by your self-harm. Perhaps you "hit rock bottom" and hurt yourself more than you had intended to, or maybe some people close to you found out about your self-harm and got really upset. Maybe you simply had a moment of resolve and found yourself saying, "That's it! No more!" Whatever your experience was, bringing it to the forefront of your mind by using imagery can help give you the same motivated feeling you had back when you decided to work on stopping self-harm.

INCREASING YOUR CHANCES OF SUCCESSFULLY STOPPING SELF-HARM

Now that you've learned some skills to increase your motivation to stop self-harm, we want to teach you some ways to be more successful in your efforts to quit. Even if you're really motivated to stop harming yourself, it can be hard to do so. But, there are certain things you can do to increase your chances of success.

Making It Harder to Harm Yourself Impulsively

One thing to keep in mind when it comes to stopping self-harm is that your motivation to stop self-harm will probably wax and wane. It's not as if you are suddenly home free once you make the decision to stop. Instead, even after you've gotten in touch with all of the important reasons not to harm yourself, you might still have moments when the urge to self-harm will feel overpowering. For example, most people find that their motivation to stop self-harm becomes weaker when they're really upset. In those moments, you'll probably be so focused on feeling better that self-harm will start to look pretty good. And, at those times, you may be at risk of harming yourself *impulsively*, or on the spur of the moment. The good news is that there are things you can do to make it harder to harm yourself impulsively.

GET RID OF THE OBJECTS YOU USE TO HARM YOURSELF

One way to make it harder to harm yourself impulsively is to get rid of anything you typically use to harm yourself. Throw out lighters, candles, razor blades, or anything else you've used to harm yourself in the past. Go through your bedroom, bathroom, car, office, locker, and anywhere else you have stored these objects in the past, and make sure to throw them out.

Of course, it may not be possible to throw out everything you could use to harm yourself. For example, some of these items may belong to other people in your home or may be things you need in your daily life. In those cases, the best strategy is to take steps to make sure that these items are difficult to get to or find on the spur of the moment. For instance, you could lock these items up in a box or a filing cabinet, and put the key someplace where it's hard to find or difficult to get to right away. One strategy you could use is to freeze the key in a block of ice so that you have to wait a while for the ice to melt in order to get the key. Or, you could give the items to a friend, family member, or partner for safekeeping (and tell this person not to give the items to you unless you schedule the time in advance). Or, you could ask that your family members or roommates keep their items locked up or hidden so you can't find them.

Now, even if you take all of these steps, it probably won't be possible to limit your access to everything you could use to harm yourself. And that's okay. The goal of this skill is not to make it impossible to harm yourself. That's just not realistic. Instead, the goal is to make it harder to harm yourself impulsively, on the spur of the moment. People often find that if they can just resist urges to self-harm for a little while, these urges will lessen so that they can focus on the reasons not to self-harm and the downsides that go along with self-harm. So, the most important objective of this skill is to make it harder for yourself to get to the objects you typically use to harm yourself so that it's harder for you to self-harm impulsively. Remember that delaying self-harm, even for a few minutes, can help you avoid harming yourself and can give you enough time to use the other skills in this book.

CHANGE YOUR ENVIRONMENT

Another way to give yourself some time to think about what you really want, focus on the downsides of self-harm, and use some of the other skills in this book is to change your scenery. In fact, you'd be amazed at what a difference it can make simply to get out of the environment you're in and go to a different place. So, if you're at home and thinking about harming yourself (and it isn't the middle of the night!), one thing you can do to make it harder to harm yourself is to leave your house and go someplace else, preferably somewhere with other people around (for example, a restaurant, coffee shop, mall, library, university, and so on). On the other hand, if it's late at night or you can't leave your home, simply changing rooms or going to a different part of the house may help. For example, if you're in your bedroom, go to the living room or a communal part of the house, where it would be harder to harm yourself.

And, remember: if you do decide to change your environment, do it fully. This skill will only work if you really notice the new environment you're in and pay full attention to all of the sights, sounds, and smells around you. Leaving your old environment but remaining stuck in your head isn't exactly changing your environment, is it? No, because you're still stuck in your head! So, make sure you focus your attention on your change of scenery, and pay attention to your senses.

Tell Your Loved Ones What You Need and How to Respond to You

Another way to increase your chances of successfully stopping self-harm is to let your loved ones know what you need from them to help you in your efforts to stop self-harm. It's important to keep in mind that most people have no idea how to respond effectively to someone who self-harms. Indeed, you may have noticed that your loved ones have a variety of reactions when you self-harm, ranging from warmth and concern to fear, shock, disgust, or anger. And, at those times when your loved ones get upset with you or don't seem to know how to do or say anything that feels helpful to you in the moment, it's important to keep in mind that this is normal! It doesn't mean that they don't care about you or don't want to help; it's just that most people have never received any advice or guidance on how to support someone who self-harms. So, this means that it will probably be up to you to tell your loved ones what you want and need, and how best to respond to you if you go to them for help.

Now, what exactly you want and need depends on who you are and the types of things that work best for you. However, we do have some

of things you may want to share with your loved ones. The
you may want to make are described next. Of course, if you
re these with your loved ones, make sure to put them into
rds! We describe them here just to give you a sense of some
s you may want to say:

*e do your best not to act shocked or dismayed when I
tell you that I want to self-harm. Try to be as calm as possible,
try to understand where I'm coming from, and help me find
other ways to cope with my problems. I'll do my best to listen
to what you have to say, even if I'm upset."*

- *"Although I want you to be kind and supportive of me (and
  I appreciate your concern!), it's important that you don't give
  me more attention or love after I self-harm than you normally
  do. I know you do this because you care, but the more you
  give me attention and support after I self-harm, the harder it
  will be for me to stop (because I will see that it's a good way
  to get your support when I need it). So, don't be mean to me
  or ignore me after I self-harm, but make sure not to lavish me
  with too much attention or kindness either."*

- *"Don't act shocked or dismayed if I tell you that I've self-
  harmed. Try to be as calm as possible, and help me figure out
  whether I need medical attention. The most helpful thing you
  can do is to be supportive and then, later, when the storm
  has passed, help me figure out how I can avoid self-harming
  next time (this might involve calling my therapist, using coping
  skills, or any number of other things)."*

- *"Please don't blame me for self-harming, or tell me that you
  think I'm sick or that I must be mentally ill. I might need help,
  but a lot of people self-harm, and it's not because they're sick
  or mentally ill. It's mainly because self-harm, like alcohol or
  drugs, works to meet some of my needs (like, to feel emotionally
  better). I just need to find other ways to meet those needs."*

SUMMARY

Stopping self-harm is never an easy thing to do. Yet, as natural as it is to question whether you want to give up your self-harm (and as much as you might find yourself wondering this many times throughout your recovery process), the skills in this chapter will go a long way in helping you get and stay motivated to stop your self-harm, and in making you more successful in your efforts to do so. Below is a summary of the skills we discussed:

- Come up with a list of the pros and cons of your self-harm. Make sure to include both the long-term and short-term consequences of self-harm. Once you've come up with a list of all of the consequences of your self-harm, focus your attention on the downsides of self-harm.

- Come up with a list of important reasons not to self-harm. Try to think of as many reasons as you can. Then, come up with a list of all the positive consequences of stopping self-harm! Once these lists are complete, make several copies of them and put them in your bedroom, bathroom, car, and other places.

- Enlist the help of other people in your journey to recovery. Rely on them to help you get motivated to stop self-harm and to stay motivated when you're having a bad day.

- Practice imagining your life without self-harm. You can also try imagining the moment when you made the decision to work on stopping your self-harm.

- Get rid of anything you typically use to harm yourself, or do something to make it harder to get to these items on the spur of the moment. Make sure to search your home, car, work, and school.

- Change your environment. If you're thinking about harming yourself, go out and do something else, or go sit in another room of your house. Focus all of your attention on your new environment and the change in scenery.

🌿 Let your loved ones know what you need from them to help you in your efforts to stop self-harm, as well as the best way to respond to you if you turn to them for help.

Now that you are more motivated to stop self-harm (or know the steps you can take to get more motivated), the next step is to learn how to manage your urges to self-harm. The next chapter will teach you skills for resisting these urges and continuing to move forward on your journey toward recovery.

Chapter 11

Coping with Self-Harm Urges

Melia came home from work feeling pretty good and even happy. She had gone to lunch with some friends and had finally gotten caught up on a couple of tasks she had been avoiding at work. However, when she walked into the kitchen to start making dinner, her urge to harm herself hit her like a truck. It came on suddenly and with an intensity that sent her reeling. Even worse was that she couldn't figure out where it had come from. She'd had such a good day and hadn't even thought about self-harm for the past few days. Yet, as she stood in the kitchen, the urge felt like a hollow aching in her arms and ankles (where she normally cut herself). She felt pulled toward the kitchen knife, and gripped the kitchen counter thinking, "What on earth is wrong with me?"

In this chapter, we go through some helpful skills you can use to manage urges to harm yourself. Urges to self-harm can make quitting very difficult. It's almost as if these urges were flashing signs convincing you to take an exit (at least temporarily) off the road to recovery. If you self-harm, you might have found that coping with urges to hurt yourself is a major challenge. Because of this, we thought you'd find it helpful to learn some skills that can help you to cope with and even reduce your urges to harm yourself. Now, it's important to mention that any of the skills we teach you in this book will probably help most if you also have a therapist or other professional to guide you in your efforts to stop harming yourself. But even if you don't have a treatment provider, these skills are quite straightforward and relatively easy to use. They are also skills that you can use to help resist urges to do other behaviors that may not always be healthy, such as urges to use drugs or alcohol. We hope that after reading this chapter and practicing some of these new strategies, you'll find it easier to steer yourself away from self-harm.

WHAT ARE URGES?

As we mentioned, strong urges are a very common experience for people who harm themselves. An urge is simply a desire or craving to do something. Many of the people we treat have told us about unbearable urges to harm themselves. You might have experienced these urges yourself.

Urges can come in many shapes and sizes. Sometimes, urges feel like a burning sensation. One of our clients described her urges as a burning sensation in her arms, where she normally harmed herself. Other people have described urges that felt like a tightening of the muscles, a hollowness or empty feeling in the place where they normally harmed themselves, or a feeling of "screaming" or tightness in their heads. When you're feeling urges, you might feel tense, agitated, or hot, or have a pounding heart. Sometimes urges are mild. At other times, they might hit you like a truck, sending you reeling and feeling out of control. Other urges build slowly over time, gradually becoming more and more intense, and lasting for a really long time.

Urges can be very upsetting for many reasons. Some of our clients have told us that having urges makes them feel as if they're abnormal, going crazy, out of control, and unable to cope. It's important to know that urges are perfectly normal. They don't mean that you're going crazy or that you're out of control. They are simply your body's way of telling you, "I want you to hurt yourself!"

Some people find it helpful to keep track of when they experience their strongest urges to harm themselves. Over time, if you keep track of your urges, you might be able to figure out what seems to trigger them. For instance, one of us worked with a woman whose urges seemed to peak right around 3:00 or 4:00 p.m. each day. During those times, she had the hardest time avoiding self-harm, and most of the time, she hurt herself between the hours of 2:00 and 5:00 p.m. After we discovered this, we figured out that she seemed to be most vulnerable to self-harm during the "afternoon lull" that many of us feel, that time of day when our moods and energy levels seem to be low. So, she joined a gym and scheduled a time to work out every day from 3:00 to 4:30 p.m. Not only did this help her get through a hard time of the day, but it also helped her increase her energy and physical fitness. Use the following chart to keep track of when you experience your urges to self-harm.

KEEP TRACK OF YOUR URGES TO SELF-HARM

What are your urges like? Below, write down what your urges normally feel like, so that you can identify them when they happen. For example, you might write, "Tingling feeling in arms. Jittery feelings. Achy sensations."

_____

_____

_____

Track your urges: Next, in the chart below, write down the number that fits how strong your strongest urges were in each period of time for each day. Use a 0–10 scale, where 0 = no urges at all, 10 = the strongest urges you've ever had, and all the other numbers are somewhere in between (for instance, 5 would indicate an urge that's about half as strong as the strongest urge you've ever had). Feel free to modify this chart according to your own sleep schedule (we realize that a lot of people are up well past 10 p.m. or awaken well before 8 a.m.!).

Day	8-10 a.m.	10 a.m.- noon	noon-2 p.m.	2-4 p.m.	4-6 p.m.	6-8 p.m.	8-10 p.m.
Mon.							
Tue.							

Wed.							
Thur.							
Fri.							
Sat.							
Sun.							

Comments: In this section, write down what you were doing during those times when you had the highest urges. Look at the chart above, and see if you can identify any patterns. You could even make a graph if it helps you figure out what the patterns are (see the following example). For example, do you have the strongest urges at certain times of the day? What are you doing and feeling at those times? Then, schedule time to use the skills we describe in this chapter during those peak times when you have the strongest urges.

_____

_____

_____

Sample Self-Harm Urges Graph

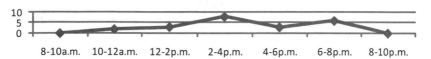

Monday

| | 8-10a.m. | 10-12a.m. | 12-2p.m. | 2-4p.m. | 4-6p.m. | 6-8p.m. | 8-10p.m. |

WHY DO PEOPLE HAVE URGES TO HARM THEMSELVES?

If you struggle with self-harm, you may very well have asked yourself why people have such urges. The fact of the matter is that urges are not only annoying, but they also make it very hard to stop self-harm. Next, we'll explain why you have these urges in the first place.

Self-Harm Causes Chemical Changes in Your Body

Well, we think people have urges for a few reasons. One reason is that harming yourself is a lot like using drugs. When people use drugs, they change the chemical activity in their brains and bodies. Over time, their brains and bodies get used to having the drug, and it becomes very uncomfortable not to have it around.

For an alcoholic, simply the thought of using alcohol, or the sight of a bottle of beer or a bar might lead to very strong urges to drink. Some research says that this is because people's bodies prepare them to drink or use drugs. It's a lot like having a craving for chocolate. If you love chocolate, and a big piece of dark-chocolate cake is in front of you, your body gets ready for the chocolate by producing saliva, which makes it easier to eat the chocolate cake. With self-harm or drugs, it's as if your body's trying to do you a favor. Unlike chocolate, however, this is a favor that you don't need!

It seems to work like this: Let's say you have trouble with drinking, and you walk into a bar. As soon as your brain realizes that you're in a place where you normally drink, it starts getting you "ready" to drink. What actually happens is that your brain makes your body do the opposite of what it does when you drink. So, if your body relaxes, your heart rate and temperature go down, and you start to feel calm whenever you drink, your body will do the opposite to prepare you for drinking. In other words, your temperature and heart rate will go up, and you'll start to feel nervous. And, because one way to get your body back to "normal" is to drink, it becomes harder for you to resist alcohol.

We think a very similar thing happens with self-harm. If you're in a situation in which you normally hurt yourself, your brain probably starts to get your body "ready" for you to hurt yourself. And, as we mentioned in chapter 3, just as with alcohol, there's some evidence that self-harm triggers the release of chemicals in your brain (natural opioids, which work a lot like drugs such as morphine) that make you feel calm and maybe a little euphoric. Therefore, just as with the example of alcohol we just mentioned, if your brain gets reminded of self-harm, it might start making your body feel the opposite of how self-harm makes it feel: agitated, nervous, and craving self-harm. This might be because your brain and body are preparing for the chemical release that happens with self-harm.

Self-Harm Feels Good in the Moment

Another reason that people probably have urges is that self-harm can be quite a pleasant experience sometimes. As we've discussed, many people say that they feel pleasure when they harm themselves. The feeling might be mild euphoria, excitement, invigoration, or calmness. It can be a lot like eating chocolate. Those of us who love chocolate often get cravings to eat chocolate, probably because it tastes so good and gives us a mild, pleasant "rush." If self-harm does this for you, it's not surprising that you might feel urges at times.

Self-Harm Can Take Away Negative Feelings

Self-harm is also very good at reducing unpleasant or unwanted emotions very quickly. So, not only can it be pleasurable, like eating chocolate, but it also gets rid of pain. If you're in a lot of emotional pain, you will probably feel like doing something to escape or reduce that pain. And, if you have learned that self-harm works, then, of course, you'd feel like harming yourself. What's more, because self-harm does work so immediately and completely in the moment, it makes sense that your desire to harm yourself might come in the form of an intense urge.

The bottom line is that having urges to harm yourself is normal. It doesn't mean that you're "sick," "flawed," "pathological," "weird," or anything else. It's simply a normal, if annoying, part of dealing with self-harm. If you had never harmed yourself in the first place, you might never have experienced these urges. But, once you started harming yourself, and your brain and body got used to it, the urges were going to come along for the ride. This is one of the things that makes self-harm so addictive and hard to overcome. But, we've seen many people learn to cope with these urges and overcome self-harm. The remainder of this chapter will give you some skills to help you do just that.

SKILLS TO DEAL WITH URGES

There are several ways to cope with urges. You might find that some of these skills lessen or get rid of your urges, whereas others just make it easier to cope with these urges without actually harming yourself. Many of the skills we discuss next come directly from Dr. Marsha Linehan's work with dialectical behavior therapy. If you believe these skills may be helpful, you might also be interested in checking out Dr. Linehan's *Skills Training Manual for Treating Borderline Personality Disorder* (The Guilford Press, 1993).

Accept That You Have Urges

Urges can be very uncomfortable and hard to deal with. You might resent the fact that you have urges, struggle constantly to get rid of them, get angry with yourself for having them, or wish that you didn't have them. As you might have noticed, the more you hate, get angry at, or struggle with your urges, the more upset you get. And, the more upset you get, the more likely you are to harm yourself. The more you refuse to accept that you have urges, the more difficult it becomes to deal with them. We've both seen clients who struggle with this exact problem.

Betty hated the fact that she had urges. Sometimes these urges would strike her by surprise at inopportune times, such as when she was driving or getting ready to prepare a meal for guests. At other times, she felt intense urges when she was sad, angry with herself, or feeling ashamed. Whenever she felt an urge, she'd think, "Oh, no! Why do I keep having these urges? What's wrong with me? Why can't I just be normal?" The problem was that this type of thinking just made her more and more upset, which made her urges even worse. She tried everything she could think of to get rid of her urges, but nothing seemed to work. In fact, it seemed as if the more she struggled with them, the more intense and frequent they became.

So, if you can't fight your urges or "will" them away, what can you do? Well, the first step in dealing with urges is to simply work on accepting that you have them in the first place. Imagine that you live in a beautiful but very rainy place and that you hate the rain. If you refuse to accept that it rains a lot, what will you do? You might grumble about the rain, complain about it, pretend it's not raining, or refuse to wear a jacket or use an umbrella. The problem is that if you do these things, you'll only end up all wet and even more upset about the rain. Accepting the fact that it rains a lot is the first step in dealing with the rain (for example, buying a good raincoat or moving somewhere else), just as accepting the fact that you have urges to self-harm is the first step in dealing with those urges.

So, how do you work on accepting your urges to self-harm? First, notice that we say "work on" accepting your urges, because acceptance is never something you do once and for all. It's not as if you say, "I accept this," and then magically never struggle with it again. Just as becoming a professional piano player takes years of practice, acceptance takes a lot of practice as well. You have to keep on accepting things over and over again. The good news is that it does become easier over time, and each time you accept your urges, you'll probably feel even better able to cope with them in the future. Please see our suggestions that follow (some of which come from Linehan 1993b) to learn how you can actively practice acceptance of your urges.

Learning How to Accept Your Urges to Self-Harm

Below, we've listed different ways that you can practice accepting your urges to self-harm. When you first start to use these strategies, it can be helpful to keep track of how much they affect your acceptance of urges.

To do this, first rate your urges on a scale of 0 (no urges at all) to 10 (the strongest urges ever), and put your rating in the Urges column. Then, rate how much you accept your urges, from 0 (refuse to accept them) to 10 (completely willing to have them) in the Acceptance Before column. Then, after you use each strategy, think about how much you accept that your urges are there, and rate your acceptance again in the Acceptance After column. After you've done this a few times, you might notice that some strategies work better for you than others, in that they give you a bigger boost in your acceptance levels.

Acceptance Strategies	Urges 0–10	Acceptance Before 0–10	Acceptance After 0–10
Say to yourself over and over again (in a calm and neutral voice, or in your head): *I have urges to hurt myself.*			
Describe the urges by finishing this sentence: *The urges feel like* _____ .			
Repeat to yourself: *I accept that I'm having urges to hurt myself.*			
Tell yourself: *It's okay that I'm having urges. This is perfectly normal for people who harm themselves.*			
Tell yourself: *This is just my body doing its thing, making me feel like hurting myself.*			
Tell yourself: *These urges will pass. I don't need to act on them.*			

Distract Yourself

Sometimes, the best way to deal with your urges to self-harm is to pay attention to something else. You can imagine your attention being like a searchlight. It's as if you're a lighthouse, and you can shine this searchlight wherever you want to. Let's say that one of the boats out there on the ocean has "Hurt yourself!" written all over it. Distraction is like moving the searchlight onto some other boat or some other part of the ocean. This is basically what distraction is all about—moving your attention toward something else (Linehan 1993b).

One of the authors has had years of martial arts training, and sometimes in martial arts you have to hold a painful stance for a long time. For instance, you might have to do something like a wall sit for ten minutes. When the urges to stand up (or fall down and collapse!) become unbearable, the instructor may say something like, "Pretend that you don't have any legs. Focus on something else. Look at the ceiling, pay attention to your arms, or count backward from two hundred." Distraction takes your mind away from the painful urges, at least for a little while.

Now, you don't want to distract yourself all the time. If you distract yourself all the time, you might never learn more effective ways to stop self-harm, like dealing with the emotions or stressful events that caused the urges in the first place. But, you're much better off distracting yourself than harming yourself. Therefore, next we describe some specific things you can do to distract yourself from your urges to self-harm. Together with the other skills we talk about in this chapter and the next two chapters, these skills can help you begin to recover from self-harm. Many of these skills come directly from Dr. Linehan's work on DBT (Linehan 1993b).

GET YOUR MIND BUSY

One of the best ways to distract yourself from urges is to get your mind busy, to "fill it up" so that there's not much room left over for your urges. The best activities to keep your mind busy are those that really attract your attention, or that force you to think hard or figure out something. The idea is to crowd out the urges and thoughts about harming yourself. Here are some suggestions.

Make your mind work: Count backward. Start at 119, and keep subtracting 7 until you get to 0. Do a crossword, a difficult puzzle, or some math problems. Play a word game with a friend or family member, or on your computer. Balance your checkbook. Play a stimulating computer game that really makes you think. Try to solve a complicated problem of some kind. Count the holes in the ceiling tiles. Count the number of floorboards in the room. Count the number of clicks of a second hand on a clock. Try to come up with the name of an animal or a city that starts with each letter of the alphabet.

Think about something else: Think about a time when you weren't having these urges. Think about food you like or about doing something else you really want to do. Think about work or about playing your favorite game.

Use your imagination: Imagine that you're in your favorite vacation spot (such as, on the beach in Hawaii or the Caribbean). Think of a fantasy that you've got, and really get into it (provided that it doesn't involve harming yourself). Imagine that you are successfully dealing with your problems. Imagine that you're in a very peaceful place, such as sitting on a grassy field by a gently flowing stream on a dry, warm day. Imagine all of the sights, sounds, smells, tastes, and touch sensations that you might have in this scenario. Imagine someone you're very attracted to. Imagine going out with some celebrity that you like.

> *Whenever John felt the urge to hurt himself, he'd get his mind busy thinking about doing something else. John was a big fan of Sudoku, so whenever he felt like hurting himself, he would break out a Sudoku puzzle and start working on it. He'd choose the hardest puzzle that he could handle, while still being able to complete it, and he'd keep going until he felt more capable of coping without hurting himself.*

CREATE STRONG SENSATIONS

If you want to distract yourself from an intense urge, it can help to experience a strong sensation that really captures your attention. Creating a strong sensation can give you a jolt that pulls your attention away from your urges. When you use this skill, think about activating each of your five senses.

Taste: Suck on a strongly flavored candy or mint. Good choices are strong cinnamon or ginger candies, or sour lemon drops. Another option that some people find helpful is to eat salt-and-vinegar potato chips, placing a chip on the edge of the tongue and just leaving it there for a while. If you can handle spicy foods (or even if you can't!), bite into a raw jalapeño pepper.

Touch: Focus on things that have a distinct texture or temperature. Run cold or very warm water over your hands. Hold a piece of ice in your hand until it melts. Hold ice against your neck or forehead. Put a bunch of ice cubes in a plastic bag and hold onto them until you can't take it anymore. Hold ice to the place on your body where you feel the urges most intensely. Stand under a very hard, hot shower. Take a hot or cold bath. Take a shower, and turn the temperature back and forth from hot to cold. Run outside on a really cold day with light clothing on. Grab your chair and hold it as tightly as you can; feel the tension building in your hands and arms. Touch various objects around you, such as keys, a zipper, or upholstery. Notice how the textures feel against your fingers. Dig your heels into the floor, and notice what sensations you feel. Notice the tension in your legs and the pressure against the soles of your feet.

Smell: When using this skill, look for smells that are really strong. Slice an onion and breathe in the fumes. Go to your spice rack and start smelling the different spices. Spray a generous amount of perfume or cologne on a piece of paper and smell it. Burn incense. Brew a fresh pot of coffee and smell the aroma.

Hearing: Listen to loud music. Select music that will pull you out of your current state. For example, listen to loud and energizing music if you are sad or feeling down, and listen to soft, soothing music if you are feeling anxious, tense, or angry. Blow a horn or buzzer several times. Blow on a whistle.

Sight: Focus your attention on a really captivating image. This could be something beautiful in nature (such as a gorgeous sunset or a beautiful flower). It could also be a picture of a loved one, a favorite painting, or an inspirational poem or saying that really speaks to you. Focus your attention on every aspect of the image.

Strong sensations worked very well for Betty. When she felt urges to harm herself, she found that activities that stimulated her sense of touch worked best. She'd ask her boyfriend for a deep-tissue massage; hold a piece of ice in her hand; take a soothing, warm bath; or squeeze a stress ball, or a handful of clay or putty. Often, her urges would drop quite significantly while she was doing these activities (from a 9 to a 5 on a scale of 0 to 10).

GET ACTIVE

Another way to distract yourself from urges is to get active. Making yourself very active can leave little room for urges or thoughts about self-harm. Running, working, or doing some other engaging activity will make it harder for the urges to overcome you. Being active gives you something else to focus on.

Do some work: Find some work you have to get done and throw yourself into it completely (for example, cleaning your house, washing the dishes, buying groceries, helping someone with something, doing yard work, or doing your laundry). When you are doing this chore, make sure you focus all of your attention on it. Pay attention to just that chore and nothing else. Immerse yourself in it.

Do something you enjoy that keeps you busy: For example, you could do arts and crafts (even if you're not the artsy-craftsy type!). Keep in mind that this doesn't have to mean that you paint a picture worthy of Monet. It can be as simple as coloring in a coloring book, sketching a picture, or doing a collage. If you're into martial arts or some other kind of physical activity, go ahead and do that. Go out for your favorite walk, go to your favorite restaurant or coffee shop, spend time with (or call, instant-message, or e-mail) someone whose company you really enjoy.

Watch a television show or movie that grabs your attention: Consider choosing something that goes against the emotion that you're feeling. For example, if you're feeling sadness or some other emotion that makes you feel low in energy or motivation, watch a show or movie that's exciting (like a suspense movie) or funny. On the other hand, if you're feeling angry, agitated, tense, or stressed, watch something that might be more soothing, like a nature special or ballet.

Go out and do something: Change your environment. If you're at home, leave your house and go outside, to the mall, or simply for a walk. Go to a movie. Call up one of your friends and go out with that person to get your mind off your problems for a little while. Go to a local fair, and ride the roller coaster. Go skiing, or do something else that gives you a thrill.

*Rick used this skill very well. When he had strong urges, he immedi-
ately left and changed his environment. If he was in his apartment,
he'd leave quickly (before he could talk himself out of it) and go to a
public place, like the mall, a café, a restaurant, or the gym. When he
was in these public places, he felt safe from hurting himself, and could
distract himself by observing the people around him, having a snack,
or working out (if he was at the gym).*

Practice Mindfulness and Urge Surfing

Another way to deal with urges is to be mindful of your urges.
To be mindful is simply to pay attention to what's happening in the
present moment. When you're practicing mindfulness, you are bringing
your full attention to your experiences in the present moment, whatever
those experiences are. As you may remember from chapter 8, mindfulness is an important part of some treatments for self-harm, especially
DBT (Linehan 1993a, 1993b).

One way to be mindful is to simply observe, or notice, the sensations
you're having in the present moment. If those sensations involve urges,
then the skill is to observe these urges.

This probably sounds like the last thing you'd want to do when
you're feeling urges to harm yourself, right? Urges to self-harm can be
very uncomfortable, not to mention scary, so why would you want to
focus on them? Well, some people think that observing urges actually
takes away some of their power and helps them pass more quickly than
they do when you fight them. In fact, some treatments for people who
struggle with drugs and alcohol are based on this very idea (mindfulness-
based relapse prevention; Witkiewitz, Marlatt, and Walker 2005), and
actually involve teaching people to observe their urges. Because these
treatments work so well, we believe that this could also help you with
self-harm. Developed by Dr. Alan Marlatt (a psychology professor at the
University of Washington), the skill is called "urge surfing," and this is
how you do it:

Urge Surfing: A Mindfulness Skill to Cope with Urges

Find a quiet place where you will be relatively free from distractions and unlikely to be bothered by anyone. Sit in a comfortable position. Write down how strong your urge is on a scale from 0 (no urge at all) to 10 (the strongest urge you've ever had). Then, write down how much you feel as if you can handle your urge on a scale from 0 (can't take it for one more second) to 10 (could handle it for ten hours straight if you had to).

Imagine that you're standing on a surfboard on the ocean in a warm, tropical place. You can see the white, sandy shore in front of you, there's a slight breeze, and you can smell the salt of the ocean. There are a few fluffy, white clouds overhead, and the sun feels warm on your back. Really transport your mind to this scene. Now, imagine that your urge to harm yourself is the wave that you're riding. Really notice what the urge feels like in your body. Zero in on the sensations you feel (for example, tightness in your muscles). Now, imagine that you're surfing the wave, and the wave is your urge. As your urge rises and becomes stronger, the wave gets higher, but you keep on surfing on top of it. Imagine that you're an excellent surfer who can handle any wave that comes your way. As the urge gets stronger and stronger, the wave gets higher and higher until it crests. Imagine that you're riding the wave to shore. As you watch and surf the wave, notice what happens to it. Notice if it gets higher and stronger, or if it starts getting lower and weaker. When it gets weaker, imagine that you're sliding with your surfboard in to shore. When it starts to build again, imagine that you're back out there on the wave, just riding it. Keep doing this for about ten minutes or so. Or, keep doing it until you feel as if you have a handle on the urge and will not act on it.

At the end, write down how strong your urge is on a scale from 0 to 10 and how much you feel as if you can handle your urge on a scale from 0 to 10.

Also, keep in mind that if using the imagery of a wave on an ocean doesn't work for you (or isn't your cup of tea!), you can also do this exercise by simply noticing how the physical feelings and sensations of the urge come and go.

Now, one nice thing about urge surfing is that you can actually do it in many different places. Although we suggested that you practice first in a quiet place with no distractions, this isn't always necessary. In fact, you can practice urge surfing just about anywhere: at work, while walking, while shopping, or while sitting at home. And you don't have to use imagery all the time. You can simply notice the sensations of your urges and watch them come and go. The most important thing is to practice this skill when you're struggling with urges. So, how does all of this surfing help you with your urges? Well, one way it may help is by giving you some perspective on your urges. One of the things that make it hard to cope with urges is the sense that they will never end unless you harm yourself. The good news, however, is that urges are actually fairly short lived. Just like cravings for food or drugs, they come and go, and don't last forever. Urge surfing can help you see that urges do not last forever, but rise and fall like waves. And, this means that you don't have to act on your urges, because they'll probably go away anyhow. Why put yourself through the trouble of self-harming when your urge will go away regardless of what you do?

Urge surfing can also help you reduce your urges over time. Urge surfing is a lot like exposure therapy (see chapter 3). As mentioned earlier, in exposure therapy, clients are repeatedly exposed to emotions or events that they fear. For example, a person who's afraid of heights might be taken up to a high place, and told to stand there and look down for an hour. A person who's afraid of snakes might spend time watching or holding a snake. The effects of exposure therapy are almost like magic. Over time, the fear almost always goes down. The more you approach things that you're afraid of (as long as these things aren't really dangerous), the less fear you'll feel.

We think that urge surfing might work in a similar way. The more you sit with and watch your urges (without acting on them), the less intense they'll be over time. It's almost as if the urge is a child throwing a tantrum in the grocery store when his mother says no to his request for a cookie. If his mother says no and then gives in when the child starts screaming, what do you think will happen the next time the mother says no? That's right, the child will start screaming, because he has learned that screaming works to get the cookie. If, however, the mother ignores the child's tantrum and doesn't give in, the child will learn that throwing a tantrum doesn't work and will eventually stop screaming in the grocery store.

The situation is similar with urges. Having a strong urge is like having a child throw a tantrum inside you, screaming, "Hurt yourself!" If you give in to the urge, what do you think will happen the next time you're in the same situation? You'll probably feel urges again! But, if you repeatedly ignore the urge's request and don't harm yourself, your brain will learn that urges don't work, just as a child learns that throwing a tantrum won't work. Over time, you will be less and less likely to have urges, and they will probably be weaker and weaker.

> *Jane became an expert in urge surfing. She was a yoga instructor, so sitting and observing her urges was a skill that worked well for her. She would do the urge surfing exercise for thirty minutes at home whenever she was having strong urges at night, or for brief periods if she was out and about. With practice, she found it easier to step back and become unstuck from her urges. She no longer felt as if her urges were controlling her. She was in the driver's seat. The urges gradually became less frequent until one day she realized that she hadn't had any urges for a whole month.*

Do Something Physical

An urge is a very physical experience for a lot of people. For some people, urges feel like aching pains in the places where they normally harm themselves. For others, urges feel like a hollow sensation, or take the form of a persistent agitation (such as feeling irritable and keyed up at the same time). Because urges are so physical, sometimes the best way to cope with them is to engage in some sort of physical activity.

Next is a list of the different types of physical activities that might help reduce urges. We've collected this list from a variety of sources, including the *Skills Training Manual for Treating Borderline Personality Disorder* (Linehan 1993b), suggestions from colleagues who work with clients who self-harm, and our clients themselves. When you do these activities, take ratings of your urges (on a scale from 0 to 10) and your belief in your ability to cope with these urges (on a scale from 0 to 10) before and after the exercise, and see if there's any change. Remember that not all of these activities have to work in order for you to get some new skills for managing your urges. Even if only a couple of these activities help lessen your urges to self-harm, you will have added some new tools to your toolbox and be much more capable of resisting urges to harm yourself.

EXERCISE YOUR MUSCLES

Working your muscles can help counteract the uncomfortable physical sensations that often go along with urges.

Do intense physical exercise: Go for a run. Lift weights. Do push-ups or sit-ups. Practice martial arts. Do jumping jacks. Climb a long staircase. Go for a bike ride. Go to the gym and do an intense workout. Work out with a tension band. Go for a hike. The point is to do intense exercise that gets your muscles working and your heart pounding. Keep up the exercise for twenty minutes or so.

Do some other intense physical activity: Engage in sexual activity with your partner or alone. Clean your house from top to bottom. Do gardening or yard work. Paint a room in your home. Shovel snow. Work on your home.

TENSE AND RELAX YOUR MUSCLES

One way to deal with urges, and sometimes to reduce them, is to do something called *progressive muscle relaxation* (*PMR*). PMR basically involves tensing and then relaxing all of the various muscles in your body. One big advantage of this skill is that it also can make you feel less tense, less anxious, and more relaxed. In fact, PMR is so helpful in reducing anxiety that it is a part of many different treatments for anxiety and other emotional difficulties. Therefore, not only can PMR help you manage the physical sensations that often go along with self-harm urges, but it may also help you feel better emotionally. Follow the steps below to practice PMR:

1. First, find a quiet place where you won't be disturbed, and get into a comfortable position. You can do this lying down, sitting up, or even standing up, but you might find that it works best if you're lying down.

2. Next, find a place on your body to start. We suggest that you begin by focusing on the part of your body where you feel the urges most strongly. If there isn't one particular place on your body where you're feeling the urges, then just start with the top of your head or the tips of your toes.

3. Next, bring your full attention to that part of your body. Let's say that you've started with your forearms. Imagine that your whole brain is being drawn down to your forearms. Then, put your hands into fists and squeeze to about 75 to 80 percent of your maximum strength, and hold them tense for about five to ten seconds.

4. Then, let them go and relax your muscles. Notice the difference between how they felt when they were tense and how they feel now. Just notice any sensations of relaxation or warmth, or anything else you might experience.

5. Repeat that process again, first tensing the muscles in your forearms, holding that tension for five to ten seconds, and then relaxing those muscles.

6. Then, move to another area of your body. For instance, people often feel urges in their abdomens. Pull in your belly and clench your abdominal muscles. Hold them for five to ten seconds again, and then let it go, relaxing your abdomen. Repeat this process again to really relax those muscles.

7. So, that's it. Just keep going through different muscle groups in your body, doing exactly the same thing. Each time, just tense your muscles about 75 to 80 percent for about five to ten seconds, and then relax them, focusing on the difference you feel. Do PMR for anywhere from five to twenty-five minutes, depending on how much time you have. Even doing it for five minutes can make a difference.

What About Substitutes for Self-Harm?

Some people do things that are similar to self-harm (but don't actually cause any physical damage) as a way to make it easier to move away from self-harm. These activities are substitute activities, and they usually involve producing some kind of pain without actual physical damage. The idea is that these activities might reduce urges because they trick your brain into thinking that you're harming yourself. Now, although some therapists recommend these strategies (and you might see them on some of the websites you visit), we actually don't recommend using them.

Why do we say this? Well, there are two main reasons. First, self-harm substitutes don't help you learn to stop craving self-harm. It's a lot like the situation where the child throws a tantrum in the grocery store. Let's say that you're taking care of a child who throws a big tantrum when you tell her that she can't have a chocolate bar. Your goal is to keep her from having any treats right now. But, she keeps throwing a fit and getting more and more upset, kicking her legs, screaming, and flailing her arms. You decide that you can't take it anymore, and say, "Okay, you can't have a chocolate bar, but you can have a chocolate-chip cookie." She sputters and groans a bit but eventually calms down, and things are more peaceful for both of you.

What do you think she has learned? Exactly, she has learned that if she throws a tantrum, she'll get something, whether it's a chocolate bar or a cookie. And, if the tantrums work in this way, she'll keep throwing them. This can be one of the problems with self-harm substitute activities as well: you never quite teach your body and your brain to stop producing these urges (throwing a tantrum, basically), because when you experience urges, you give your body and brain what they want (something much like self-harm).

A second downside to these activities is that you can easily take them too far. Although self-harm substitutes seem safe, it can be easy to take these actions too far and actually cause tissue damage. You might also start to rely on them just as you rely on self-harm. Therefore, for these two reasons, we don't recommend that you use substitute activities. Instead, we suggest that you try some of the other skills in this chapter and see if they work for you.

TROUBLESHOOTING: ONE PROBLEM TO WATCH OUT FOR

The skills we just described will make it easier to tolerate your urges and may even help lessen these urges. However, there is one problem to watch out for as you begin to practice these skills. It has to do with your expectations about the use of these skills.

Don't Expect Your Urges to Vanish

The problem some people have when they start to use these skills is that they expect their urges to vanish completely. They hope that, by using these skills, their urges will go away forever and never return. And, although there may be times when you use these skills and find that your urges do disappear in that moment, this isn't always going to happen. What's more, none of these skills will make your urges disappear forever. So, if you're coping with urges, you can normally expect these skills to work *while you are using them*. But, don't be surprised if the urges return later on, when you've stopped using the skills. We don't measure success by whether or not the urges return—they almost always do. We measure success by whether you use these skills and avoid harming yourself in the moment.

> *After learning some skills to cope with her urges, Melia came up with a plan that she would put into action whenever her urges became too strong. First, she'd slow down her breathing and just pay attention to what was happening in the moment. Next, she'd practice accepting whatever was happening and whatever she was feeling. If this was too much of a struggle, she'd find some way to distract herself. Working on crossword puzzles or listening to music really worked for Melia. Then, once she felt less overwhelmed by her urges, she would figure out what to do to cope with her feelings and the problems in her life.*

SUMMARY

❧ Urges are simply cravings or desires to do something—in this case, cravings or desires to harm yourself.

❧ Urges come and go, and although they can be very painful and uncomfortable, they don't last forever.

❧ Please see the following table for a list of some of the skills you can use to cope with urges to self-harm. Use this table to keep track of when you have used the skills and how they have worked for you. It might be useful for you to bring this summary with you in your wallet, pocket, or purse so that you have a reminder of what skills to use when you need them. For the skill of acceptance, in particular, see the exercise, "Learning How to Accept Your Urges to Self-Harm," earlier in the chapter.

Skills to Cope with Urges

Below, we've listed many of the skills we have gone through in this chapter to help you deal with urges to self-harm. You might find that filling out this form will help you to (1) remember the skills, (2) remember to practice or use them, and (3) figure out which ones seem to work best for you. Here are some instructions on how to use this form:

First, rate your ability to resist your urges to self-harm on a scale of 0 (can't resist for one more minute) to 10 (am confident I can continue to resist these urges and not self-harm) and put your rating in the Before column. Then, try out some of the skills listed in the table. After you use each skill, immediately rate your ability to resist urges again on a scale from 0 to 10 in the After column. After you've done this a few times, you might notice that some strategies work better than others in helping take the edge off your urges and increasing your ability to resist them.

Skill	Ability to Resist Urges Before (0–10)	Ability to Resist Urges After (0–10)
Distraction: Get Your Mind Busy		
Make your mind work.		
Think about something else.		
Use your imagination.		
Distraction: Create Strong Sensations		
Taste		
Touch		
Smell		
Sound		
Sight		
Distraction: Get Active		
Do some work.		
Do something you enjoy that keeps you busy.		
Watch a television show or movie that grabs your attention.		
Go out and do something.		
Mindfulness		
Practice urge surfing.		
Observe your urges.		

Physical Activities		
Do intense physical exercise.		
Do other intense physical activities.		
Do progressive muscle relaxation.		

Comments: Here, include any comments on what did or didn't work for you, what you tried, and what you might do the next time you have strong urges.

In this chapter, we taught you several different skills you can use to manage your urges to harm yourself and avoid acting on these urges in the moment. For many people, urges to engage in self-harm often occur in reaction to certain emotional states, such as anger, shame, or other emotions. In addition, you may have noticed that you use self-harm to feel better emotionally. If that's the case, then you'll definitely find chapter 12 helpful as well, because that chapter is all about different strategies that you can use to manage your emotions. And the more tools you have for coping with your emotions, the better able you will be to resist your urges to self-harm.

Chapter 12

Managing Emotions Related to Self-Harm

Trevor harmed himself whenever he felt really angry. With the help of his therapist, he learned ways to resist his urges to self-harm a lot of the time, and was often able to ride out these urges until they passed. He was also taking steps to improve his life in other ways, so that he wouldn't have as many urges. Yet, as much progress as he made, it felt almost impossible not to harm himself when he felt angry. Trevor's anger felt like a huge atomic fireball swelling up inside him. His anger was so intense and powerful that it scared him; he was afraid of what might happen if he ever expressed it to someone else. The only way he knew to release it without hurting someone else was to burn himself. It was as if harming himself served as a release valve, letting out all the steam inside of him until he could calm down and think more clearly.

So far, we've talked about ways to get motivated to stop self-harm and to resist urges to harm yourself. These skills will be incredibly important on your journey to recovery. In this chapter, we talk about another set of skills that may be just as important: skills for managing your emotions.

As we mentioned before, the most common reason people give for harming themselves is to feel better in some way. In fact, most people use self-harm to try to relieve, escape, or cope with painful, overwhelming emotions. If this is one of the reasons you self-harm, think about how much easier it would be to stop harming yourself if your emotions felt more manageable and less overwhelming. That's what this chapter is all about: teaching you skills to manage your emotions so that you don't need to rely on self-harm to feel better. You might even find that the more you learn to cope with your emotions in healthy ways, the less intense your urges to self-harm will become.

SKILLS FOR MANAGING YOUR EMOTIONS

Next we describe several different skills you can use to manage your emotions. Some of these skills may help make your emotions less overwhelming, and others will help you cope with your emotions when you have them.

Identifying Your Emotions

One of the first skills to learn is to identify how you are feeling (Linehan 1993b). Having *emotional clarity*, or knowing exactly what emotions you are having, can actually make your emotions seem more manageable. One reason for this might be that when we know how we feel, we're in a better position to figure out how to make ourselves feel better. You might have noticed that different coping strategies work better for different emotions. When you feel sad, you might find it comforting to curl up in a hot bath with some soothing music, or talk to your best friend. When you're angry, you might want to go for a long run or scrub your bathroom. The things that will "work" to make you feel better when you are upset actually depend a lot on exactly what emotion you're feeling at the time. That's why it's important to learn to identify how you feel and to label your emotions.

To learn how to identify your emotions, the first thing you need to know is that all emotions are made up of three different components:

cognitive (the thoughts that go along with the emotion), physiological (the way your body responds when you experience an emotion), and behavioral (the things you do or have urges to do when you experience an emotion). Let's take anger as an example: The cognitive component of anger may include thoughts such as, "This shouldn't be happening to me!" "What a jerk!" or "This is so unfair!" At a physiological level, feelings of anger are often accompanied by a racing heart, clenched fists, tight muscles, or a tight jaw. And the behavioral component of anger may include urges to scream, throw things, or punch something or someone.

Every emotion you have is made up of all three components. However, many people find that they aren't always aware of all compo nents of their emotions. For instance, you might not know how you feel until you find yourself wanting to do something, like cry or scream. Or, you might be aware of sad thoughts but feel completely out of touch with how sadness feels in your body. At other times, you might only be aware of your bodily sensations and have no clue what emotion you're having. Therefore, one of the first steps in learning to identify your feel-ings is to work on becoming more aware of all three components of your emotions when you are experiencing them. Indeed, the greater number of emotional components that you are aware of, the better chance you have of identifying exactly what you're feeling. And, knowing exactly how you feel will make it easier to figure out the best way to cope with those emotions. The following table provides some examples of the various components of a few basic emotions. See if they match your experience of these emotions.

So, how exactly do you learn to label and describe your emotions? Well, one place to start is to ask yourself the following questions when-ever you feel an emotion. By answering these questions each and every time you experience an emotion, you'll start to learn how different emotions feel in your body, how the thoughts that go along with one emotion differ from those of another, and how different emotions make you want to act in different ways.

IDENTIFYING THE THREE COMPONENTS OF AN EMOTION

Below, you can find different bodily sensations, thoughts, and actions (or action urges) that often go along with some basic human emotions.

Emotion	Bodily Sensations	Thoughts	Actions/Action Urges
Fear	Racing heart	"I'm in danger."	Freezing
	Sweating	"I'm not safe."	Running away
	"Tunnel vision"	"Something bad is about to happen."	Lashing out
	Trembling		
	Shortness of breath		
Sadness	Tightness behind the eyes	"Nobody loves me."	Isolating
	Sinking feeling in the pit of your stomach	"I'm all alone."	Crying
		"Things will never get better."	Seeking support
	Slowed heart rate		Wanting a hug
Anger	Racing heart	"Everyone's against me."	Picking a fight
	Shortness of breath	"This is unfair."	Raising your voice
	Muscle tension	"This isn't right."	Screaming
	Tightness in your jaw		Throwing something

The next time you feel one of these emotions, see if you can identify all of its components. And, feel free to add to this list so that it matches your experience of these emotions.

QUESTIONS TO HELP YOU IDENTIFY YOUR EMOTIONS

Ask yourself each of these questions whenever you are experiencing an emotion:

- ❧ What thoughts are associated with this emotion? What kinds of thoughts are running through my mind right now?

- ❧ What physical sensations are associated with this emotion? How does this emotion feel in my body?

- ❧ What does this emotion make me want to do or say? How does it make me want to act?

- ❧ What do I normally do in response to this emotion? How do I tend to act when I feel this way?

Based on these answers, what emotion am I feeling right now?

_____

The next time you are feeling an emotion, ask yourself the questions above and start to learn about how your emotions feel to you.

Once you know exactly what emotions you are feeling, you'll be in a better position to manage those emotions effectively. Below, we tell you about some skills for managing your emotions.

Expressing Your Emotions

As we mentioned in chapter 5, one way to cope with emotions is to express them in some way. Expressing or communicating emotional pain can help alleviate or lessen that pain. So, once you know what you're feeling, one way to cope with that feeling is to express it.

The good news about this skill is that there are many ways to express our feelings. Oftentimes, people think that expressing emotions means talking about them to someone else. And, this is one useful way of expressing emotions. However, there are many other ways to express emotions as well. Some of these involve expressing your feelings to others, and some involve expressing them to no one directly; some involve using words to express your feelings, and others involve expressing your feelings in other ways, such as through art or music. Because there are so many ways to express emotions, we're sure that you can find some ways that will work for you. See the following list for some of the different ways that you can express your emotions.

Ways of Expressing Your Emotions

- Talking to a friend or family member
- Writing about your feelings in a diary or journal
- Writing a poem about your feelings
- Painting a picture to depict your feelings; think about using different colors to represent different feelings
- Singing a song that reflects how you feel
- Crying
- Screaming into a pillow
- Working out
- Dancing
- Punching a punching bag
- Playing a musical instrument
- Making a collage or scrapbook of your feelings

Now that you've looked over this list, see if you can think of other ways you could express your emotions. Try to think of ways you could express a wide range of emotions, including anger, sadness, joy, loneliness, anxiety, and guilt.

Other ideas: _____

_____

Now, one thing to keep in mind is that not all of these strategies work all the time. What if the strategy you like best is talking about your feelings, but your best friend is out of town and can't be reached? Or, what if you like to express your anger by playing loud music on your guitar, but it's the middle of the night and doing that would wake up your family?

Because there's no single way to express your emotions that will always work, the best thing to do is to come up with as many ways for expressing your feelings as possible. The more options you have, the more likely you are to find something that will work in any situation. It's like trying to get the best toolbox possible. If you had only one tool in your toolbox, like a hammer, it might work really well some of the time, such as when you need to put a nail into the wall. But, how well do you think it's going to work if you need to saw some wood or fix a clogged drain? Not so well. That's why you need to make sure your toolbox is full of all different kinds of tools, like a hammer, screwdriver, saw, wrench, and even an electric sander! Only by owning a lot of different tools will you be able to fix a variety of problems in your home. And, the same principle applies when it comes to expressing your emotions. Only by knowing a variety of different ways to express your emotions will you be able to find a way that will work in any situation.

So, make sure to try out a bunch of different ways of expressing your emotions, and try to think about the times and situations when each might work best. The questions that follow will help you figure out when each strategy will work best for you.

When to Use Different Ways of Expressing Emotions

Write down all the different ways you have tried to express your emotions, focusing most on the ways that seem to work the best for you. Try to come up with as many different strategies as possible.

1.

2.

3.

4.

5.

6.

7.

8.

Next, for each of these strategies, write down the times and situations when it works best.

Strategy	Context (times, situations) when it works best
1.	1.
2.	2.
3.	3.
4.	4.
5.	5.
6.	6.
7.	7.
8.	8.

These answers should give you a much better idea of when each of these strategies will work the best for you. So, the next time you find yourself in one of these situations, try the strategy that fits best and see how it works.

Experiencing Your Emotions

This might surprise you, but one of the best ways to manage your emotions is simply to experience that emotion and let it run its course. One of the biggest myths out there is that the best way to manage your emotions is to try to control or suppress them in some way. In fact, trying to do just that will often make you even more upset and make your emotions feel even more overwhelming. Trying to control or suppress your emotions is a lot like trying to deal with a bear you run into while out on a hike. In this situation, you have a couple of options, but all of them have some pretty serious downsides. For example, one option you have would be to try to fight the bear. However, if you do this, you're probably going to lose. Most of us just don't stand a chance in a fight against a bear. Well, the same is true when you try to fight your emotions. When you fight your emotions, you will usually end up more upset than you were in the first place. Because our emotions are part of being human, fighting against them is a battle you simply cannot win.

Now, on the other hand, you could try to ignore the bear and just pretend that it's not there. This might work for a little while, but in the end, the bear is probably going to attack you anyhow (especially when it sees that your guard is down). And, this is also true of our emotions. If you pretend you're not having your emotions or try to ignore them, you'll often find yourself blindsided by your feelings, or doing things impulsively without thinking. Emotions play a very important role in our lives, and trying to ignore them means missing out on a lot of important information.

Finally, you could try to run away from the bear. The problem is that this really isn't a wise choice either. Believe it or not, bears are quite fast, and no matter what you do to try to escape (for example, jump into a ravine, climb a tree, and so on), the bear will eventually catch you. And, once again, this is also true of your emotions. Your emotions are an inseparable part of you, and trying to escape them is like trying to escape yourself. It's just not possible, and no matter what you do, eventually your emotions will catch up with you.

What this means is that the only choice you really have (and the choice that we believe will work the best for you in the long run) is to allow yourself to experience your emotions. Now, when we say "experience" your emotions, we don't mean that you are supposed to wallow in your emotions or try to make them last longer. We simply mean that you should experience whatever emotion you're having when you are having it, and then let it pass when it's ready. As crazy as this may sound, doing this will actually make your emotions last for a shorter amount of time than trying to fight them or get rid of them completely.

So, how do you go about allowing yourself to experience your emotions? Well, the first step is simply to stop the struggle to get rid of your emotions! Now, we realize this is easier said than done. It's natural to try to avoid or suppress uncomfortable feelings, and as a result, many people fall into this "escape mode" whenever they have an unpleasant emotion. It's kind of as if avoidance becomes a habit, just like biting your fingernails or cracking your knuckles. However, just as with any other habit, you can break this pattern of avoidance with practice.

The first step you can take is to notice just when you start to feel an emotion. Try to identify the very earliest signs of your emotion; for many people, this will come in the form of bodily sensations. Does you heart rate pick up speed? Do you feel butterflies in your stomach? The earlier you can identify an emotion, the easier it will be to prevent avoidance.

Then, when you notice an emotion coming on, work on staying in the present moment and focusing your attention on the emotion. Describe how the emotion feels in your body. Notice all the different components of the emotion. See if you can identify the thoughts, bodily sensations, and action urges that go along with the emotion (Linehan, 1993b). If you find it easier to focus on the bodily sensations that accompany the emotion, start by bringing your attention to how the emotion feels in your body, and describing all of the various physical sensations you are having. Then, bring your attention to the thoughts you're having and the action urges you're experiencing. If you find yourself getting caught up in your thoughts, gently turn your attention back to one of the other components of the emotion. And, remember to always be objective when describing your emotions; don't judge your emotions, label them as "good" or "bad," or beat yourself up for the thoughts that go along with these emotions. Instead, simply describe each component of the emotion objectively, almost as if you were taking inventory of what's in your kitchen. At first, it might be helpful to do this exercise in a quiet place where there are few distractions, and to practice with an emotion that's not too intense or distressing.

Next, as the emotion develops, notice how it changes, and whether it becomes stronger or weaker. Do your thoughts or bodily sensations change as the emotion develops? Pay attention to all these experiences. Try to ride the wave of your emotion. Think of yourself as a surfer riding the waves in the ocean—only this time, the wave is your current emotion. Notice how the wave crests and breaks. And, keep in mind that as uncomfortable as your emotions may be, they won't hurt you. They are just your body's way of trying to communicate with you. Remind yourself that most emotions peak fairly soon after you notice them and dissipate shortly afterward.

Finally, as your emotion begins to weaken, notice once again how your body feels. What thoughts are you having now? How quickly does the emotion decrease in intensity? How do you feel about the fact that you stayed present with your emotion and didn't try to avoid it? Try practicing this skill each time you feel an emotion, and you might be amazed by just how quickly your emotions will pass if you don't fight them.

Using Self-Soothing Techniques

Oftentimes, when people feel upset, a common desire is to be comforted in some way. Sometimes, we try to seek comfort in people close to us. Although this can be a great way to manage emotions, loved ones may not always be available to support you when you really need help. They may not live close by, or you might need help at a time when they're not available, such as the middle of the night. Therefore, it's important to develop ways to comfort yourself. These skills are sometimes called *self-soothing strategies* (Linehan, 1993b).

So, how do you come up with self-soothing strategies? Well, the first thing to do is to focus on your senses: touch, taste, smell, sight, and sound. The best self-soothing strategies are those that activate one or more of your five senses. When you are using these techniques, make sure to focus your attention completely on your sensations. Stay in the moment. If you find yourself getting distracted, notice that and then turn your attention back to your senses. There are many things you can do to soothe yourself using each of your senses, some of which are listed next. Many of these techniques come from the *Skills Training Manual for Treating Borderline Personality Disorder* (Linehan 1993b).

SELF-SOOTHING TECHNIQUES

Try using one of these techniques the next time you are very upset and in need of comfort.

Touch

- Take a warm bubble bath; sit in a hot tub or sauna.
- Get a massage.
- Play with your favorite pet.
- Relax in the sun.
- Hug a friend or loved one.
- Put on clothing that has a soft, soothing texture.

Taste

- Sip a cup of hot tea or cocoa (or some other hot drink).
- Drink something cold on a hot day, or eat a popsicle or an ice cream bar.
- Eat your favorite "comfort food."
- Eat dark chocolate (this also releases "feel-good" chemicals).
- Eat a piece of fresh fruit.

Smell

- Go to a flower shop (and pretend you're shopping even if you're not).
- Burn incense or light a scented candle.
- Inhale the aroma of lavender or vanilla.
- Breathe in fresh air.
- Bake cookies or fresh bread.
- Smell fresh coffee beans, or brew some fresh coffee.

Sight

- Look at pictures of loved ones or a favorite vacation spot.
- Go to the beach and watch the waves hit the sand.
- Watch a sunset.
- Watch the clouds in the sky.
- Watch your pet or children play or sleep.

Hearing

- Listen to relaxing music.
- Listen to birds singing.
- Listen to children playing.
- Take a walk through the woods and listen to the sounds of nature.
- Sit outside at dusk and listen to the crickets.
- Go to the beach and listen to the sound of waves crashing on the shore.

See if you can come up with some of your own self-soothing techniques. Anything you find comforting and nurturing might just do the trick!

Deep Breathing

Believe it or not, one of the best ways of coping with anxiety and anger is breathing. Sounds simple, right? Maybe, but most people don't breathe correctly. Breathing naturally uses your diaphragm, a big muscle below your stomach. How do you know if you're breathing naturally? Take a few minutes to breathe in and out slowly. When you breathed in, did your belly push out, and when you breathed out, did your belly go back in? Or, did you hunch your shoulders when you breathed in and drop them when you breathed out? If you noticed your belly expanding and falling, you're using your diaphragm to breathe. You are breathing properly. If you noticed your shoulders going up and down, you are not breathing properly, and you may actually be putting yourself at risk to experience anxiety.

Using your diaphragm to breathe will help you take deeper breaths, and taking deeper breaths means breathing slower. Deep, slow breathing is the body's natural way of combating anxiety and stress. In fact, breathing out slowly can actually slow down your heart rate and reduce muscle tension. When you use your chest and shoulders to breathe, you don't have enough room in your chest cavity for your lungs to expand. This results in short, shallow breaths, which can actually increase your heart rate and make you feel even more anxious or stressed out.

Therefore, one of the most basic (and important) strategies for managing your emotions is "relearning" how to breathe. Follow these steps to learn how.

"Relearning" How to Breathe

When you first practice this exercise, try to do it at a time when you already feel relaxed. It's easier to learn the basic techniques of deep breathing when you're not stressed out.

1. Find a comfortable and quiet place to practice your breathing. Sit up in a chair so that your back is straight and supported.

2. Close your eyes.

3. Put the palm of one of your hands on your stomach and the palm of your other hand on your chest across your breastbone.

4. Breathe in and out as you normally do. Which hand moves the most when you breathe, the one on your belly or the one on your chest? If the hand on your chest moves and the hand on your belly doesn't, this means that you're not breathing with your diaphragm.

5. Now, when you breathe in and out, deliberately push out your belly when you breathe in and let your belly fall when you breathe out. It may feel slightly unnatural at first. This is normal, and this feeling will go away very quickly with practice.

6. Continue to breathe in and out. Try to lengthen your breaths. Slowly count to five as you breathe in, and again when you breathe out. Also, try to breathe in through your nose and exhale through your mouth. This may help you take deeper breaths.

7. Practice this breathing exercise a couple of times a day. The more you practice, the more it will become a habit.

Once you've practiced this exercise a few times and are more familiar with deep breathing, try it out when you feel anxious, stressed, or angry. Even though it may seem simple, changing your breathing can have a profound effect on your emotions.

Distraction

Sometimes the best way to deal with your emotions when you're really upset is to pay attention to something else (Linehan, 1993b). As we mentioned in chapter 11, distraction is all about finding something else to pay attention to that gets your mind off whatever is troubling you. Now, before you start to practice distraction to cope with your emotions, it's important to keep in mind that you can overuse distraction. You might find that this works so well in the short term that you're always distracting yourself whenever you get upset. The problem is, constantly distracting yourself can turn into avoidance, and by now you probably remember the problems that go along with too much avoidance! So, we suggest that you use this skill in moderation, to make it through a difficult time. Then, when your emotions have lessened in intensity or it's safe to experience them, stop distracting yourself and turn your attention back toward your emotions. Using distraction skills in combination with some of the other skills we described previously is the best recipe for success.

Any of the distraction skills we described in chapter 11 can help distract you from emotional distress, just as they can distract you from urges to self-harm. A list of some of the strategies we described that may be of use is presented next. Now, you might notice that focusing on your five senses (taste, touch, smell, hearing, sight) is listed next as a distraction strategy and previously as a self-soothing technique. This isn't a mistake. Focusing on your senses can work either way. The difference is that when you use your senses to distract yourself, you want to use really strong, powerful sensations that get your mind off your emotions and worries. You'll notice that we recommend activities that produce strong sensations in chapter 11. When you use your senses to soothe yourself, you want to choose activities that are calming; the point of self-soothing is to create a "soft" experience that gently soothes you, whereas the point of distraction is to create a strong experience that grabs your attention.

HEALTHY DISTRACTION STRATEGIES TO COPE WITH EMOTIONS

Get Your Mind Busy

- ✺ Make your mind work.
- ✺ Think about something else.
- ✺ Use your imagination.

Create Strong Sensations

- ✺ Taste
- ✺ Touch
- ✺ Smell
- ✺ Hearing
- ✺ Sight

Get Active

- ✺ Do some work.
- ✺ Do something you enjoy that keeps you busy.
- ✺ Watch a television show or movie that grabs your attention.

SUMMARY

In this chapter, we focused on skills that can help you manage your emotions. Although these skills aren't about controlling self-harm directly, they can be used in conjunction with the skills from chapters 10 and 11. If you use self-harm to relieve emotional pain or make yourself feel better, the skills in this chapter should provide you with other ways of managing your emotions instead of self-harm. And, if you feel better, you may feel less of a need for self-harm. Below is a summary of the skills we discussed in this chapter.

- Try to identify exactly how you are feeling. Knowing what emotions you are experiencing can make your emotions seem less overwhelming and more manageable.

- Express your emotions in a healthy way.

- Allow yourself to experience your emotions. Don't fight them; just allow them to be.

- Try a self-soothing technique. Focus all of your attention on comforting or nurturing smells, tastes, sights, sounds, or touch.

- Remember to breathe! The slower and deeper, the better.

- Try focusing your attention on something else. Distraction can be a good way of managing overwhelming emotions. Just remember to turn your attention back to your emotions eventually. Distraction is only temporary!

Now that you are armed with accurate information and a growing toolbox of coping skills for managing self-harm urges and strong emotions, we hope you're well prepared for your journey on the road to recovery. No matter how prepared you are, though, the road to recovery is always bumpy. In the next (and final) chapter, we tell you how to avoid some common pitfalls and deal with some of the obstacles you're likely to face on your journey.

Chapter 13

Moving Forward: Living a Life Without Self-Harm

By the time you've made it to this chapter, you've probably gained a much better understanding of what self-harm is and isn't, the types of things that cause self-harm, the reasons why people self-harm, and (perhaps most importantly) what you get out of self-harm. You may have already begun to use some of the skills we taught you in previous chapters, and you may have noticed a positive change in your self-harm. We hope this book has helped you get started on the road to recovery and given you hope that you can eventually overcome your self-harm.

As confident as we are that people can and do recover from self-harm, we also know that this process is never easy. As we've mentioned before, self-harm can be a very difficult behavior to overcome. Any behavior that serves as many important purposes as self-harm and that works so well in the short term is hard to resist. Self-harm can be like a mythical siren, calling your name and luring you into the rocks along the shore. And, any behavior that's this powerful requires time and hard work to stop.

The good news is that just reading this book is a step in the right direction. Now that you are armed with accurate information and a better understanding of your self-harm, you're in a much better position to move forward on your journey to build a life without this behavior. And, the skills you learned in part III of this book will be important allies in your struggle to stop self-harm. However, even with all of this new information and these skills on your side, the road to recovery is a bumpy one. No matter how well armed you are, you're bound to encounter some obstacles along your journey. Some of these may be small, and others might be a bit bigger, but you can definitely expect that you will run into some.

AVOIDING COMMON PITFALLS ON THE ROAD TO RECOVERY

This chapter focuses on some of the most common obstacles people encounter, and teaches you ways to deal with these obstacles and continue moving forward in your journey toward recovery. We hope this information will help you make better use of the new skills you've learned here and the new understanding you have of your self-harm.

Don't Get Discouraged If the Path to Recovery Is Bumpy

Stopping self-harm is not an easy thing to do. If it were, there would have been no reason for us to write this book! On the contrary, overcoming self-harm is a process, and it's definitely not something that happens overnight. Any behavior that does something for you and that you rely on regularly is hard to eliminate from your life completely. For example, think of something that you do on a regular basis, such as brushing your teeth. Now, imagine that new research has come out saying that brushing your teeth is actually bad for you (and will make all of your teeth fall out!), so you have to stop brushing your teeth altogether. For most of us, this would be a very hard thing to do, because brushing our teeth has become a habit. You'd probably find yourself wanting to brush your teeth at certain times (like in the morning when your breath might not be so fresh), or looking for other behaviors that could take the place of brushing your teeth. You might also notice yourself thinking about brushing your teeth a lot more than you used to (before you tried to give it up). And, all of this would be normal. In fact, it would be your body's natural way of responding to the stopping of a habit.

The same thing could very well happen when you decide to stop self-harm. You may find yourself thinking even more about self-harm than you used to—especially at times when you used to rely on self-harm, such as when you experience very unpleasant emotions. You might also feel a little more on edge or irritable. It's important to remind yourself that this is all part of the normal process of trying to give up a behavior you used to rely on. And, remember that these feelings are temporary. They will pass.

When you feel this way, try to remind yourself of why you decided to stop harming yourself in the first place. Remind yourself of all the positive things that stopping self-harm will bring into your life. In fact, you may want to write down all of the positive consequences of stopping self-harm so that you don't have to come up with them on the fly. And, remember, even when times are tough, you have skills you can use to get yourself through the hard times. So, when things look bleak, take out this book and review the skills we covered in chapters 11 and 12. And don't be afraid to ask for support when you need it! You don't have to try to make it through this process on your own.

Avoiding the "Abstinence Violation Effect"

One thing that can make the road to recovery a bit bumpier than you may hope is called the *abstinence violation effect* (Marlatt and Gordon 1985). This is a pretty fancy phrase for something a lot of people experience when they try to stop an unhealthy habit. Basically, the abstinence violation effect refers to the tendency that we human beings have to set up hard and fast rules for ourselves. For example, when trying to stop an unhealthy behavior, many people set out with the goal of never doing it again. And, while we appreciate the desire to stay on target and give up unhealthy behaviors, the problem with a goal like this is that it doesn't take into account the fact that many people "slip" when trying to stop a behavior. In fact, many researchers think that "slipping" is actually an important part of the recovery process (Marlatt and Gordon 1985).

Think about it: If you don't allow yourself the possibility of having an occasional slip, then what will stop you from continuing to self-harm if you do have a slip (for example, if you begin to scratch yourself)? You would have already broken (or violated) your rule of abstinence (in this case, "I'll never self-harm again!"), so there wouldn't really be any difference between one small, minor slip and a big, major slip. A slip is a slip, so once you start harming yourself, you might as well run with it, right? Wrong! There's a big difference between a minor slip and a major slip. If you allow a minor slip to turn into a major one, it will be that much harder to get back on track and renew your commitment to living a life without self-harm. Thinking that any slip is a huge setback is a kind of black-and-white thinking, and can only get you into trouble.

So, if (or when) you do have a slip, it's important that you take the following steps:

1. "Catch" the slip as quickly as you can—even if you're in the middle of the behavior.

2. Recognize the slip as a slip. Try your best not to *catastrophize* (or think the worst). You did not just destroy your chance of living a life without self-harm. Don't beat yourself up. Remember, it's normal to slip from time to time, and this slip can provide you with important information on how to prevent future slips.

3. Identify what led to the slip. If it was an intense emotion, try to use some of the emotion regulation skills we talked about in chapter 12. If you had a hard time resisting your urges, use the skills in chapter 11, and if you just couldn't sustain your motivation to stay away from self-harm, use the strategies from chapter 10 the next time you have this problem.

4. See the slip as a learning experience. There's a saying: "In crisis, there is opportunity." Each slip is a chance to learn how to avoid future slips. So, put a positive spin on the slip and remember that it's a great opportunity to learn how to avoid slipping for the same reasons again.

5. Think about what you could do next time instead of self-harm. Come up with a concrete plan for preventing this kind of slip in the future.

And, most importantly, if a slip happens, be compassionate toward yourself. After a slip, many people feel guilty or ashamed. As we said before, overcoming self-harm is not an easy thing to do, and it's normal to encounter several bumps along the way. Recovery isn't

about experiencing the fewest bumps. Rather, it's abou
your bumps and finding a way to live a meaningful anc
without self-harm.

This category

Remember That You Will Probably Miss Self-Harm

In the previous chapter, we talked about a number of different emotion regulation strategies that you can use instead of self-harm. The idea is that if you learn other ways of managing your emotions, you might not need to rely on self-harm as much. In fact, we believe that your urges to harm yourself will start to lessen as you begin to feel better and learn other ways of managing your emotions. Although we've seen this work for many people, there are a couple of obstacles to keep an eye out for along the way.

One obstacle you may encounter is a feeling of loss or sadness when you give up your self-harm. For some people, giving up self-harm is like giving up a friend who was always there for them when they needed help. And, sadness and grief are normal reactions when you're moving away from or losing something that's important to you. If you notice that you are having these feelings, we suggest that you do the following:

- Remind yourself that this is completely normal. Many people experience sadness or a sense of loss when they give up self-harm.

- Notice your feeling of sadness (or whatever other emotion you have), and practice accepting it (use the skills for experiencing your emotions from chapter 12).

- Then, remind yourself of why you are moving away from self-harm. Look at the pros and cons form (Consequences of Self-Harm) that you filled out in chapter 10, and get back in touch with the downsides of self-harm and the reasons why your life will be better without it.

Another obstacle you may encounter is finding that the healthy emotion regulation strategies you've learned don't work quite as well as self-harm. The skills we taught you might not work as quickly as self-harm does to make you feel better, and they might not give you the same feeling of satisfaction that self-harm does. A lot of the people we've worked with have told us that they get something unique out of self-harm. For some people, the powerful, immediate relief is the biggest draw. For others, it might be the fact that they have a secret vice that nobody knows about, and for others, self-harm works as a self-punishment or makes them feel powerful or strong. You'll probably have a hard time duplicating these experiences with more healthy emotion regulation skills. And, this can sometimes make these skills seem like poor substitutes for self-harm, especially if you're in a lot of emotional pain.

So, we want to be clear: The skills we taught you for managing your emotions and controlling your urges to self-harm will never be quite as powerful or satisfying as self-harm in the short run. But (and here's the key!) they also don't come with all of the negative consequences and downsides in the long run. So, you need to ask yourself, "Even if these skills don't work quite as well initially, is it worth it to feel better in the long run and to move forward in my recovery?" And, remember, even if these skills don't give you quite as much immediate relief as self-harm does, they will help, and they will continue to work better and better the more you practice them. So, give them a try and you might be surprised to find how much better you start to feel after a while!

Your Beliefs About the Skills Matter as Much as the Skills Themselves

Another issue to keep an eye out for is your beliefs about what it means to use these coping skills. Some people resist using skills because they believe that skills are just temporary solutions. This is understandable, of course. If you harm yourself, you probably have life problems that need to be solved. You might also have emotional issues that you desperately want to come to terms with or resolve. Because the skills we described won't solve life's problems or get rid of emotional suffering, some people can be very hesitant to use them.

Stacey found that the skills in this book helped her tremendously in dealing with her urges and emotions, and avoiding self-harm—when she used them. The problem was that there were many times when she felt the urge to self-harm and thought to herself, "These skills are just a band-aid. They won't help me figure out my issues or fix my problems with my partner." As a result, she sometimes chose not to use the skills, even though she knew they would help. And at times, she ended up hurting herself.

Watch out for this type of thinking. We suggest that you ask yourself, "Would it be effective or helpful for me to use these skills right now?" If the answer is yes, then just do it! You can find a way to deal with your problems and address all of your struggles later, when your urges to harm yourself aren't as strong. Think of it as taking one step at a time. When you have done something to lessen your urges or manage your emotions, you'll have more energy to focus on solving your problems and coping in other ways. Before you do that, though, you need to make it through the moment without harming yourself. Remember, as we mentioned before, self-harm won't help you fix your life and will probably only add to your problems. The skills we taught you here, though, can take the edge off your urges and help you feel more capable of dealing with life in the here and now.

CONCLUSION

We set out to write a book that would help people who struggle with self-harm, as well as the people who care for them. In doing so, we have tried to present as much information as possible on the causes of self-harm, the types of problems that often go along with self-harm, the purposes this behavior serves, and the types of treatments that may be helpful. We also brought together what we think are some of the most important skills you need to help yourself stop self-harm. We sincerely hope that you see some of your own experiences within the pages of this book and find it helpful on your path to recovery.

Yet, no matter how much information we provide, we can never fully capture everyone's unique experience of self-harm. Every person is different, and no two people have the same experience with self-harm. So, it's possible (if not likely) that some of the chapters in this book may not have seemed to apply to you as much as some of the others. For example, maybe you can't relate to any of the causes of self-harm we described. Or, maybe you don't struggle with any of the problems we mentioned that often go along with self-harm. Instead, maybe you struggle with some other kinds of problems that we didn't talk about here.

We encourage you to take this book and make it as personal as possible. Tweak it and mold it until it fits your experiences with self-harm to a T. The information and skills discussed in this book will be most helpful if you find a way to tie them into your own life and your own experiences with self-harm. So, personalize this book. Make it your own. And remember, there's no one right way to overcome self-harm. Everyone has a different process to go through. So, find the path to recovery that works the best for you, and take it.

References

American Psychiatric Association. 1994. *Diagnostic and Statistical Manual of Mental Disorders* (DSM-IV). 4th ed. Washington, DC: American Psychiatric Association.

Andover, M. S., C. M. Pepper, K. A. Ryabchenko, E. G. Orrico, and B. E. Gibb. 2005. Self-mutilation and symptoms of depression, anxiety, and borderline personality disorder. *Suicide and Life-Threatening Behavior* 35 (5):581–91.

Arnold, L. M., D. F. Mutasim, M. M. Dwight, C. L. Lamerson, E. M. Morris, and S. L. McElroy. 1999. An open clinical trial of fluvoxamine treatment of psychogenic excoriation. *Journal of Clinical Psychopharmacology* 19 (1):15–18.

Bateman, A., and P. Fonagy. 1999. Effectiveness of partial hospitalization in the treatment of borderline personality disorder: A randomized controlled trial. *American Journal of Psychiatry* 156 (10):1563–69.

———. 2001. Treatment of borderline personality disorder with psychoanalytically oriented partial hospitalization: An 18-month follow-up. *American Journal of Psychiatry* 158 (11):36–42.

———. 2008. 8-year follow-up of patients treated for borderline personality disorder: Mentalization-based treatment versus treatment as usual. *American Journal of Psychiatry* 165 (5):631–38.

Beck, A. T., A. J. Rush, B. F. Shaw, and G. Emery. 1979. *Cognitive Therapy of Depression*. New York: The Guilford Press.

Bloch, M. R., M. Elliot, H. Thompson, and L. M. Koran. 2001. Fluoxetine in pathologic skin-picking: Open-label and double-blind results. *Psychosomatics* 42 (4):314–19.

Boudewyn, A. C., and J. H. Liem. 1995. Childhood sexual abuse as a precursor to depression and self-destructive behavior in adulthood. *Journal of Traumatic Stress* 8 (3):445–59.

Bradley, R., J. Greene, E. Russ, L. Dutra, and D. Westen. 2005. A multi-dimensional meta-analysis of psychotherapy for PTSD. *American Journal of Psychiatry* 162 (2):214–27.

Briere, J., and E. Gil. 1998. Self-mutilation in clinical and general population samples: Prevalence, correlates, and functions. *American Journal of Orthopsychiatry* 68 (4):609–20.

Brown, M. Z., K. A. Comtois, and M. M. Linehan. 2002. Reasons for suicide attempts and nonsuicidal self-injury in women with borderline personality disorder. *Journal of Abnormal Psychology* 111 (1):198–202.

Bulik, C. M., N. D. Berkman, K. A. Brownley, J. A. Sedway, and K. N. Lohr. 2007. Anorexia nervosa treatment: A systematic review of ran-domized controlled trials. *International Journal of Eating Disorders* 40 (4):310–20.

Chapman, A. L., and K. L. Dixon-Gordon. 2007. Emotional anteced-ents and consequences of deliberate self-harm and suicide attempts. *Suicide and Life Threatening Behavior* 37 (5):543–53.

Chapman, A. L., K. L. Gratz, and M. Z. Brown. 2006. Solving the puzzle of deliberate self-harm: The experiential avoidance model. *Behaviour Research and Therapy* 44 (3):371–94.

Chengappa, K. N., R., T. Ebeling, J. S. Kang, J. Levine, and H. Parepally. 1999. Clozapine reduces severe self-mutilation and aggression in psychotic patients with borderline personality disorder. *Journal of Clinical Psychiatry* 60 (7):477–84.

Clarkin, J. F., K. N. Levy, M. F. Lenzenweger, and O. F. Kernberg. 2007. Evaluating three treatments for borderline personality disorder: A multiwave study. *American Journal of Psychiatry* 164 (6):922–28.

Cloitre, M., K. C. Koenen, L. R. Cohen, and H. Han. 2002. Skills training in affective and interpersonal regulation followed by exposure: A phase-based treatment for PTSD related to childhood abuse. *Journal of Consulting and Clinical Psychology* 70 (5):1067–74.

Coccaro, E. F., R. J. Kavoussi, Y. I. Sheline, M. E. Berman, and J. G. Csernansky. 1997. Impulsive aggression in personality disorder correlates with platelet 5-HT$_{2A}$ receptor binding. *Neuropsychopharmacology* 16 (3):211–16.

Coid, J., B. Allolio, and L. H. Rees. 1983. Raised plasma metenkephalin in patients who habitually mutilate themselves. *Lancet* 2 (8349):545–46.

Dimidjian, S., S. D. Hollon, K. S. Dobson, K. B. Schmaling, R. J. Kohlenberg, M. E. Addis, R. Gallop, J. B. McGlinchey, D. K. Markley, J. K. Gollan, D. C. Atkins, D. L. Dunner, and N. S. Jacobson. 2006. Randomized trial of behavioral activation, cognitive therapy, and antidepressant medication in the acute treatment of adults with major depression. *Journal of Consulting and Clinical Psychology* 74 (4):658–70.

Dubo, E. D., M. C. Zanarini, R. E. Lewis, and A. A. Williams. 1997. Childhood antecedents of self-destructiveness in borderline personality disorder. *Canadian Journal of Psychiatry* 42 (1):63–69.

Eisler, I., C. Dare, M. Hodes, G. Russell, E. Dodge, and D. Le Grange. 2000. Family therapy for adolescent anorexia nervosa: The results of a controlled comparison of two family interventions. *Journal of Child Psychology and Psychiatry* 41 (6):727–36.

Evans, K., P. Tyrer, J. Catalan, U. Schmidt, K. Davidson, J. Dent, P. Tata, S. Thornton, J. Barber, and S. Thompson. 1999. Manual-assisted cognitive-behaviour therapy (MACT): A randomized controlled trial of a brief intervention with bibliotherapy in the treatment of recurrent self-harm. *Psychological Medicine* 29 (1):19–25.

Favazza, A. R. 1998. The coming of age of self-mutilation. *Journal of Nervous and Mental Disease* 186 (5):259–68.

Favazza, A. R., and K. Conterio. 1989. Female habitual self-mutilators. *Acta Psychiatrica Scandinavica* 79 (3):283–89.

Foa, E. B., T. M. Keene, and M. J. Friedman, eds. 2004. *Effective Treatments for PTSD: Practice Guidelines from the International*

Society for Traumatic Stress Studies. Paperback ed. New York: The Guilford Press.

Geist, R., M. Heinmaa, D. Stephens, R. Davis, and D. Katzman. 2000. Comparison of family therapy and family group psychoeducation in adolescents with anorexia nervosa. *Canadian Journal of Psychiatry* 45 (2):173–78.

Gratz, K. L. 2001. Measurement of deliberate self-harm: Preliminary data on the Deliberate Self-Harm Inventory. *Journal of Psychopathology and Behavioral Assessment* 23 (4):253–63.

————. 2006. Risk factors for deliberate self-harm among female college students: The role and interaction of childhood maltreatment, emotional inexpressivity, and affect intensity/reactivity. *American Journal of Orthopsychiatry* 76 (2):238–50.

Gratz, K. L, and A. L. Chapman. 2007. The role of emotional responding and childhood maltreatment in the development and maintenance of deliberate self-harm among male undergraduates. *Psychology of Men and Masculinity* 8 (1):1–14.

Gratz, K. L., S. D. Conrad, and L. Roemer. 2002. Risk factors for deliberate self-harm among college students. *American Journal of Orthopsychiatry* 72 (1):128–40.

Gratz, K. L., and J. G. Gunderson. 2006. Preliminary data on an acceptance-based emotion regulation group intervention for deliberate self-harm among women with borderline personality disorder. *Behavior Therapy* 37 (1):25–35.

Gunderson, J. G. 2001. *Borderline Personality Disorder: A Clinical Guide.* Washington, DC: American Psychiatric Publishing, Inc.

Gunderson, J. G., K. L. Gratz, E. C. Neuhaus, and G. W. Smith. 2005. Levels of care in treatment. In *The American Psychiatric Publishing Textbook of Personality Disorders*, 1st ed., ed. J. M. Oldham, A. E. Skodol, and D. S. Bender, 239–55. Washington, DC: American Psychiatric Publishing, Inc.

Hallahan, B., J. Hibbeln, J. Davis, and M. Garland. 2007. Omega-3 fatty acid supplementation in patients with recurrent self-harm: Single-centre double-blind randomised controlled trial. *British Journal of Psychiatry* 190:118–22.

Hayes, S. C., K. D. Strosahl, and K. G. Wilson. 1999. *Acceptance and Commitment Therapy: An Experiential Approach to Behavior Change.* New York: The Guilford Press.

Herpertz, S., H. Sass, and A. Favazza. 1997. Impulsivity in self-mutilative behavior: Psychometric and biological findings. *Journal of Psychiatric Research* 31 (4):451–65.

Herpertz, S., S. M. Steinmeyer, D. Marx, A. Oidtmann, and H. Sass. 1995. The significance of aggression and impulsivity for self-mutilative behavior. *Pharmacopsychiatry* 28 (Suppl. 2):64–72.

Houston, K., C. Haw, E. Townsend, and K. Hawton. 2003. General practitioner contacts with patients before and after deliberate self harm. *British Journal of General Practice* 53 (490):365–70.

Jacobson, N. S., K. S. Dobson, P. A. Truax, M. E. Addis, K. Koerner, J. K. Gollan, E. Gortner, and S. E. Prince. 1996. A component analysis of cognitive-behavioral treatment for depression. *Journal of Consulting and Clinical Psychology* 64 (2):295–304.

Joiner, T. E. 2002. The trajectory of suicidal behavior over time. *Suicide and Life-Threatening Behavior* 32 (1):33–41.

Kessler, R. C., P. Berglund, O. Demler, R. Jin, K. R. Merikangas, and E. E. Walters. 2005. Lifetime prevalence and age-of-onset distributions of *DSM-IV* disorders in the National Comorbidity Survey Replication. *Archives of General Psychiatry* 62:593–602.

Keuthen, N., M. Jameson, R. Loh, T. Deckersbach, S. Wilhelm, and D. D. Dougherty. 2007. Open-label escitalopram treatment for pathological skin picking. *International Clinical Psychopharmacology* 22 (5):268–74.

Kleindienst, N., M. Bohus, P. Ludäscher, M. F. Limberger, K. Kuenkele, U. W. Ebner-Priemer, A. L. Chapman, M. Reicherzer, R. D. Stieglitz, and C. Schmahl. 2008. Motives for nonsuicidal self-injury among women with borderline personality disorder. *Journal of Nervous and Mental Disease* 196 (3):230–36.

Klonsky, E. D., T. F. Oltmanns, and E. Turkheimer. 2003. Deliberate self-harm in a nonclinical population: Prevalence and psychological correlates. *American Journal of Psychiatry* 160 (8):1501–08.

Laye-Gindhu, A., and K. A. Schonert-Reichl. 2005. Nonsuicidal self-harm among community adolescents: Understanding the "whats" and "whys" of self-harm. *Journal of Youth and Adolescence* 34 (5):447–57.

Levine, D., E. Marziali, and J. Hood. 1997. Emotion processing in borderline personality disorders. *Journal of Nervous and Mental Disease* 185 (4):240–46.

Linehan, M. M. 1993a. *Cognitive Behavioral Treatment of Borderline Personality Disorder.* New York: The Guilford Press.

———. 1993b. *Skills Training Manual for Treating Borderline Personality Disorder.* New York: The Guilford Press.

Linehan, M. M., H. E. Armstrong, A. Suarez, D. Allmon, and H. L. Heard. 1991. Cognitive-behavioral treatment of chronically parasuicidal borderline patients. *Archives of General Psychiatry* 48 (12):1060–64.

Linehan, M. M., K. A. Comtois, A. M. Murray, M. Z. Brown, R. J. Gallop, H. L. Heard, K. E. Korslund, D. A. Tutek, S. K. Reynolds, and N. Lindenboim. 2006. Two-year randomized controlled trial and follow-up of dialectical behavior therapy vs. therapy by experts for suicidal behaviors and borderline personality disorder. *Archives of General Psychiatry* 63 (7):757–66.

Linehan, M. M., H. Schmidt III, L. A. Dimeff, J. C. Craft, J. Kanter, and K. A. Comtois. 1999. Dialectical behavior therapy for patients with borderline personality disorder and drug-dependence. *American Journal on Addictions* 8 (4):279–92.

Mack, J. E., ed. 1975. *Borderline States in Psychiatry.* New York: Grune and Stratton.

Marlatt, G. A., and J. R. Gordon, eds. 1985. *Relapse Prevention: Maintenance Strategies in Treatment of Addictive Behaviors.* New York: The Guilford Press.

Muehlenkamp, J. J., J. D. Swanson, and A. M. Brausch. 2005. Self-objectification, risk taking, and self-harm in college women. *Psychology of Women Quarterly* 29 (1):24–32.

Nada-Raja, S., K. Skegg, J. Langley, D. Morrison, and P. Sowerby. 2004. Self-harmful behaviors in a population-based sample of young adults. *Suicide and Life-Threatening Behavior* 34 (2):177–86.

Nock, M. K., and M. J. Prinstein. 2005. Contextual features and behavioral functions of self-mutilation among adolescents. *Journal of Abnormal Psychology* 114 (1):140–46.

O'Loughlin, S., and J. Sherwood. 2005. A 20-year review of trends in deliberate self-harm in a British town, 1981–2000. *Social Psychiatry and Psychiatric Epidemiology* 40 (6):446–53.

Paivio, S. C., and C. R. McCulloch. 2004. Alexithymia as a mediator between childhood trauma and self injurious behaviors. *Child Abuse and Neglect* 28 (3):339–54.

Parker, G., I. Parker, H. Brotchie, and S. Stuart. 2006. Interpersonal psychotherapy for depression? The need to define its ecological niche. *Journal of Affective Disorders* 95 (1–3):1–11.

Pattison, E. M., and J. Kahan. 1983. The deliberate self-harm syndrome. *American Journal of Psychiatry* 140 (7):867–72.

Rebok, G. W., M. C. Carlson, and J. B. S. Langbaum. 2007. Training and maintaining memory abilities in healthy older adults: Traditional and novel approaches. *Journals of Gerontology Series B: Psychological Sciences and Social Sciences* 62:53–61.

Rénéric, J., and M. Bouvard. 1998. Opioid receptor antagonists in psychiatry: Beyond drug addiction. *CNS Drugs* 10 (5):365–82.

Resick, P. A., and K. S. Calhoun. 2001. Posttraumatic stress disorder. In *Clinical handbook of psychological disorders: A step-by-step treatment manual*, 3rd ed., ed. D. H. Barlow, 60–113. New York: The Guilford Press.

Robin, A., P. Siegel, T. Koepke, A. Moye, and S. Tice. 1994. Family therapy versus individual therapy for adolescent females with anorexia nervosa. *Journal of Developmental and Behavioral Pediatrics* 15 (2):111–16.

Robin, A. L., P. T. Siegel, and A. Moye. 1995. Family versus individual therapy for anorexia: Impact on family conflict. *International Journal of Eating Disorders* 17 (4):313–22.

Robins, C. J., and A. L. Chapman. 2004. Dialectical behavior therapy: Current status, recent developments, and future directions. *Journal of Personality Disorders* 18 (1):73–79.

Rocca, P., L. Marchiaro, E. Cocuzza, and F. Bogetto. 2002. Treatment of borderline personality disorder with risperidone. *Journal of Clinical Psychiatry* 63 (3):241–44.

Rodham, K., K. Hawton, and E. Evans. 2004. Reasons for deliberate self-harm: Comparison of self-poisoners and self-cutters in a community sample of adolescents. *Journal of the American Academy of Child and Adolescent Psychiatry* 43 (1):80–87.

Roth, A. S., R. B. Ostroff, and R. E. Hoffman. 1996. Naltrexone as a treatment for repetitive self-injurious behavior: An open-label trial. *Journal of Clinical Psychiatry* 57 (6):233–37.

Ruedrich, S., T. Swales, C. Rossvanes, L. Diana, V. Arkadiev, and K. Lim. 2008. Atypical antipsychotic medication improves aggression, but not self-injurious behaviour, in adults with intellectual disabilities. *Journal of Intellectual Disability Research* 52 (2):132–40.

Russ, M. J. 1992. Self-injurious behavior in patients with borderline personality disorder: Biological perspectives. *Journal of Personality Disorders* 6 (1):64–81.

Safer, D. L., C. F. Telch, and W. S. Agras. 2001. Dialectical behavior therapy for bulimia nervosa. *American Journal of Psychiatry* 158 (4):632–34.

Schalling, D. 1978. Psychopathy-related personality variables and the psychophysiology of socialization. In *Psychopathic behavior: Approaches to research*, ed. R. D. Hare and D. Schalling, 85–105. New York: John Wiley & Sons.

Schmidt, U., and K. Davidson. 2003. *When Life Is Too Painful: Finding Options After Self-Harm*. London: Psychological Press.

Shapiro, F., and M. S. Forrest. 1997. *EMDR: The Breakthrough "Eye Movement" Therapy for Overcoming Anxiety, Stress, and Trauma*. New York: Basic Books.

Shaw, S. N. 2002. Shifting conversations on girls' and women's self injury: An analysis of the clinical literature in historical context. *Feminism and Psychology* 12 (2):191–219.

Simeon, D., B. Stanley, A. Frances, J. J. Mann, R. Winchel, and M. Stanley. 1992. Self-mutilation in personality disorders: Psychological and biological correlates. *American Journal of Psychiatry* 149 (2):221–26.

Simeon, D., D. J. Stein, S. Gross, N. Islam, J. Schmeidler, and E. Hollander. 1997. A double-blind trial of fluoxetine in pathologic skin picking. *Journal of Clinical Psychiatry* 58 (8):341–47.

Skegg, K. 2005. Self-harm. *Lancet* 366 (9495):1471–83.

Skodol, A. E., J. G. Gunderson, B. Pfohl, T. A. Widiger, W. J. Livesley, and L. J. Siever. 2002. The borderline diagnosis I: Psychopathology, comorbidity, and personality structure. *Biological Psychiatry* 51 (12):936–50.

Tangney, J. P., and R. L. Dearing. 2002. *Shame and Guilt.* New York: The Guilford Press.

Taylor, S., D. S. Thordarson, L. Maxfield, I. C. Federoff, K. Lovell, and J. Ogrodniczuk. 2003. Comparative efficacy, speed, and adverse effects of three PTSD treatments: Exposure therapy, EMDR, and relaxation training. *Journal of Consulting and Clinical Psychology* 71 (2):330–38.

Telch, C. F., W. S. Agras, and M. M. Linehan. 2001. Dialectical behavior therapy for binge eating disorder. *Journal of Consulting and Clinical Psychology* 69 (6):1061–65.

Tice, D. M., E. Bratslavsky, and R. F. Baumeister. 2001. Emotional distress regulation takes precedence over impulse control: If you feel bad, do it! *Journal of Personality and Social Psychology* 80 (1):53–67.

Tyrer, P., B. Tom, S. Byford, U. Schmidt, V. Jones, K. Davidson, M. Knapp, A. MacLeod, and J. Catalan. 2004. Differential effects of Manual Assisted Cognitive Behavior Therapy in the treatment of recurrent deliberate self-harm and personality disturbance: The POPMACT Study. *Journal of Personality Disorders* 18(1):102–116.

Van, H. L., R. A. Schoevers, and J. Dekker. 2008. Predicting the outcome of antidepressants and psychotherapy for depression: A qualitative, systematic review. *Harvard Review of Psychiatry* 16 (4):225–34.

Van Egmond, M., and R. F. W. Diekstra. 1989. The predictability of suicidal behavior: The results of a meta-analysis of published studies.

In *Suicide and its prevention: The role of attitude and imitation*, ed. R. F. W. Diekstra, R. Maris, S. Platt, A. Schmidtke, and G. Sonneck, 37–61. Leiden, the Netherlands: E. J. Brill.

Walsh, B. W. 2006. *Treating Self-Injury: A Practical Guide.* New York: The Guilford Press.

Weissman, M. M., J. C. Markowitz, and G. L. Klerman. 2000. *Comprehensive Guide to Interpersonal Psychotherapy.* New York: Basic Books.

Welch, S. S. 2001. A review of the literature on the epidemiology of parasuicide in the general population. *Psychiatric Services* 52 (3):368–75.

Wilson, G. T., C. M. Grilo, and K. M. Vitousek. 2007. Psychological treatment of eating disorders. *American Psychologist* 62 (3):199–216.

Winchel, R. M., and M. Stanley. 1991. Self-injurious behavior: A review of the behavior and biology of self-mutilation. *American Journal of Psychiatry* 148 (3):306–15.

Witkiewitz, K., G. A. Marlatt, and D. D. Walker. 2005. Mindfulness-based relapse prevention for alcohol use disorders: The meditative tortoise wins the race. *Journal of Cognitive Psychotherapy* 19 (3):221–28.

Young, J. E. 1994 *Cognitive Therapy for Personality Disorders: A Schema-Focused Approach.* Sarasota, FL: Professional Resource Press.

Zanarini, M. C., and F. R. Frankenburg. 2003. Omega-3 fatty acid treatment of women with borderline personality disorder: A double-blind, placebo-controlled pilot study. *American Journal of Psychiatry* 160 (1):167–69.

Zlotnick, C., J. I. Mattia, and M. Zimmerman. 1999. Clinical correlates of self-mutilation in a sample of general psychiatric patients. *Journal of Nervous and Mental Disease* 187 (5):296–301.

Zoroglu, S. S., U. Tuzun, V. Sar, H. Tutkun, H. A. Savas, M. Ozturk, B. Alyanak, and M. E. Kora. 2003. Suicide attempt and self-mutilation among Turkish high school students in relation with abuse, neglect, and dissociation. *Psychiatry and Clinical Neurosciences* 57 (1):119–26.

Kim L. Gratz, Ph.D., is an assistant professor in the department of psychiatry and human behavior at the University of Mississippi Medical Center, where she serves as director of personality disorders research. Gratz has written numerous journal articles and book chapters on borderline personality disorder, deliberate self-harm, and emotion regulation. Her research currently focuses on understanding the nature and consequences of emotion dysregulation and emotional avoidance among individuals who struggle with borderline personality disorder and self-harm. In addition, she has developed a brief emotion regulation group therapy for self-harm among women with borderline personality disorder. In 2005, Gratz received the Young Investigator's Award from the National Education Alliance for Borderline Personality Disorder. She is coauthor of *The Borderline Personality Disorder Survival Guide*.

Alexander L. Chapman, Ph.D., is an assistant professor and registered psychologist in the department of psychology at Simon Fraser University. He is director of the Personality and Emotion Research Laboratory, where he conducts research on self-harm, borderline personality disorder, emotion regulation, and impulsivity. Chapman has published numerous journal articles and book chapters and has given many national and international presentations on borderline personality disorder, dialectical behavior therapy, self-harming and suicidal behavior, and impulsive behavior. In 2007, he received the Young Investigator's Award from the National Education Alliance for Borderline Personality Disorder. In addition, he trains students and professionals to treat clients who self-harm or borderline personality disorder. Chapman is president of the Dialectical Behavior Therapy Centre of Vancouver, a center for the treatment of borderline personality disorder, self-harm, and related problems. He is coauthor of *The Borderline Personality Disorder Survival Guide*.

Foreword writer **Barent Walsh, Ph.D.,** is executive director of The Bridge, a nonprofit human service agency in Worcester, MA. He is an author, consultant, and trainer on the topic of self-injury.

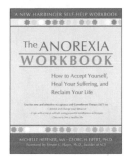

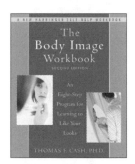
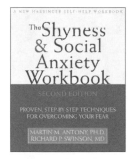